PISTOLS AND PETTICOATS

PISTOLS AND PETTICOATS

175 Years of Lady Detectives in Fact and Fiction

ERIKA JANIK

Beacon Press
Boston

BEACON PRESS
Boston, Massachusetts
www.beacon.org

Beacon Press books
are published under the auspices of
the Unitarian Universalist Association of Congregations.

19 18 17 16   8 7 6 5 4 3 2 1

This book is printed on acid-free paper that meets the uncoated paper
ANSI/NISO specifications for permanence as revised in 1992.

Text design and composition by Kim Arney

Library of Congress Cataloging-in-Publication Data

Names: Janik, Erika, author.
Title: Pistols and petticoats : 175 years of lady detectives in fact and
    fiction / Erika Janik.
Description: Boston : Beacon Press, 2016. | Includes bibliographical
    references and index.
Identifiers: LCCN 2015035609 |
    ISBN 978-0-8070-3938-0 (hardback) |
    ISBN 978-0-8070-3939-7 (ebook)
Subjects: LCSH: Policewomen—History. | Private investigators—Fiction. | Detective and
mystery stories. | BISAC: SOCIAL SCIENCE / Women's Studies. | LAW / Gender & the
Law. | POLITICAL SCIENCE / Political Freedom & Security / Law Enforcement.
Classification: LCC HV8023 .J36 2016 | DDC 363.25082—dc23

LC record available at http://lccn.loc.gov/2015035609

*For my Dad, who introduced me to detective stories,
and for all the women who have fought for their
place and their right to protect and defend
citizens for nearly two centuries.*

CONTENTS

Although "police officer" has been the gender-neutral term for members of a police department for several decades, "policewoman" was the common term used from the earliest years of women's efforts to break into careers in law enforcement. Indeed, "policewoman" originally designated a specific and different role from that of the policeman. That role has changed too, but "policewoman" is still widely used, despite varying degrees of acceptance by officers and varying interpretations of the term's traditional connotations. My use of "policewoman" is not meant as a political statement or to indicate a stance on women's role in policing but simply as a means of clarity and continuity.

PISTOLS AND PETTICOATS

CHAPTER ONE

Detecting Women

WITH HIGH HEELS CLICKING ACROSS THE HARDWOOD FLOORS, THE DIMIN-utive woman from Chicago strode into the headquarters of the New York City police. It was 1922. Few respectable women would enter such a place alone, let alone one wearing a fashionable Paris gown, a feathered hat atop her brown bob, glistening pearls, and lace stockings.[1]

But Alice Clement was no ordinary woman.

Unaware of—or simply not caring about—the commotion her presence caused, Clement walked straight into the office of Commissioner Carleton Simon and announced, "I've come to take Stella Myers back to Chicago."

The commissioner gasped, "She's desperate!"

Stella Myers was no ordinary crook. The dark-haired thief had outwitted policemen and eluded capture in several states.

Unfazed by Simon's shocked expression, the well-dressed woman withdrew a set of handcuffs, ankle bracelets, and a "wicked looking gun" from her handbag.

"I've come prepared."

Holding up her handcuffs, Clement stated calmly, "These go on her and we don't sleep until I've locked her up in Chicago." True to her word, Clement delivered Myers to her Chicago cell.

Alice Clement was hailed as Chicago's "female Sherlock Holmes," known for her skills in detection as well as for clearing the city of fortune-tellers, capturing shoplifters, foiling pickpockets, and rescuing girls from the clutches of prostitution. Her uncanny ability to remember faces and her flair for masquerade—"a different disguise every day"—allowed her to rack up one thousand arrests in a single year. She was bold and sassy, unafraid to take on any masher, con artist, or scalawag from the city's underworld.

Her headline-grabbing arrests and head-turning wardrobe made Clement seem like a character straight from Central Casting. But Alice Clement was not only real; she was also a detective sergeant first grade of the Chicago Police Department.

Clement entered the police force in 1913, riding the wave of media sensation that greeted the hiring of ten policewomen in Chicago. Born in Milwaukee to German immigrant parents in 1878, Clement was unafraid to stand up for herself. She advocated for women's rights and the repeal of Prohibition. She sued her first husband, Leonard Clement, for divorce on the grounds of desertion and intemperance at a time when women rarely initiated—or won—such dissolutions. Four years later, she married barber Albert L. Faubel in a secret ceremony performed by a female pastor.

It's not clear why the then thirty-five-year-old, five-foot-three Clement decided to join the force, but she relished the job. She made dramatic arrests—made all the more so by her flamboyant dress—and became the darling of reporters seeking sensational tales of corruption and vice for the morning papers. Dark-haired and attractive, Clement seemed to confound reporters, who couldn't believe she was old enough to have a daughter much less, a few years later, a granddaughter. "Grandmother Good Detective" read one headline.[2]

She burnished her reputation in a high-profile crusade to root out fortune-tellers preying on the naive. Donning a different disguise every day, Clement had her fortune told more than five hundred times as she gathered evidence to shut down the trade. "Hats are the most important," she explained, describing her method.[3] "Large and small, light and dark and of vivid hue, floppy brimmed and tailored, there is nothing that alters a woman's appearance more than a change in headgear."

Clement also had no truck with flirts. When a man attempted to seduce her at a movie theater, she threatened to arrest him. He thought she was joking and continued his flirtations, but hers was no idle threat. Clement pulled out her blackjack and clubbed him over the head before yanking him out of the theater and dragging him down the street to the station house. When he appeared in court a few days later, the man confessed that he had been cured of flirting. Not every case went Clement's way, though. The jury acquitted the man, winning the applause of the judge who was no great fan of Clement or her theatrics.

One person who did manage to outwit Clement was her own daughter, Ruth. Preventing hasty marriages fell under Clement's duties, and she tracked down lovelorn young couples before they could reach the minister. The *Chicago Daily Tribune* called her the "Nemesis of elopers" for her success and familiarity with everyone involved in the business of matrimony in Chicago.[4] None of this deterred twenty-year-old Ruth Clement, however, who hoped to marry Navy man Charles C. Marrow, even though her mother insisted they couldn't be married until Marrow finished his time in service in Florida. Ruth did not want to wait, and when Marrow came to visit, the two tied the knot at a minister's home without telling Clement. When Clement discovered a Mr. and Mrs. Charles C. Marrow registered at the Chicago hotel supposedly housing Marrow alone, she was furious and threatened to arrest her new son-in-law for flouting her wishes. Her anger cooled, however, and Clement soon welcomed the newlyweds into her home.

Between arrests and undercover operations, Clement wrote, produced, and starred in a movie called *Dregs of the City*, in 1920. She hoped her movie would "deliver a moral message to the world" and "warn young girls of the pitfalls of a great city."[5] In the film, Clement portrayed herself as a master detective charged with finding a young rural girl who, at the urging of a Chicago huckster, had fled the farm for the city lights and gotten lost in "one of the more unhallowed of the south side cabarets." The girl's father came to Clement and begged her to rescue his innocent daughter from the "dregs" of the film's title. Clement wasn't the only officer-turned-actor in the film. Chicago police chiefs James L. Mooney and John J. Garrity also had starring roles. Together, the threesome battered "down doors with axes and interrupt[ed] the cogitations of countless devotees of hashish, bhang and opium." The *Chicago Daily Tribune* praised Garrity's acting and his onscreen uniform for its "faultless cut."[6]

The film created a sensation, particularly after Chicago's movie censor board, which fell under the oversight of the police department, condemned the movie as immoral. "The picture shall never be shown in Chicago. It's not even interesting," read the ruling.[7] "Many of the actors are hams and it doesn't get anywhere." Despite several appeals, Clement was unable to convince the censors to allow *Dregs of the City* to be shown within city limits.[8] She remained undeterred by the decision. "They think they've given me a black eye, but they haven't. I'll show it anyway," she declared as she left the hearing, tossing the bouquet of roses she'd been given against the window.[9]

When the cruise ship *Eastland* rolled over in the Chicago River on July 24, 1915, Clement splashed into the water to assist in the rescue of the pleasure boaters, presumably, given her record, wearing heels and a designer gown. More than eight hundred people would die that day, the greatest maritime disaster in Great Lakes history. For her services in the *Eastland* disaster, Clement received a gold "coroner's star" from the Cook County coroner in a quiet ceremony in January of 1916.[10]

Clement's exploits and personality certainly drew attention, but any woman would: a female crime fighter made for good copy and eye-catching photos. Unaccustomed to seeing women wielding any kind of authority, the public found female officers an entertaining—and sometimes ridiculous—curiosity.

That certainly held true for Loveday Brooke. A professional detective with the Lynch Court agency in London, Brooke was smart, confident, and bold. She earned the complete confidence of her boss, Ebenezer Dyer. To those who questioned Brooke's detecting skills and fitness for the job, Dyer gruffly replied, "I don't care two pence-halfpenny whether she is or is not a lady. I only know she is the most sensible and practical woman I ever met."[11]

Brooke had a particular talent for disguise, but unlike Clement, she was not glamorous nor did she call attention to herself. She was relatively plain in appearance, being neither tall nor short, neither dark nor fair, and neither handsome nor ugly. But her ordinary looks allowed her to successfully camouflage herself as a nursery governess, a lodger, and a maid, the last of which role gave her a particularly privileged point of surveillance in upper-class homes.

Sent by Dyer to "hob-nob with the maids" for clues, Brooke entered Craigen Court, the residence of Sir George and Lady Cathrow, in pursuit of the thief who had made all the morning papers in 1890s London. Thirty thousand pounds' worth of jewelry had been stolen from a safe in Lady Cathrow's dressing room. Suspicion naturally fell on Lady Cathrow's maid, a young French girl named Stephanie Delcroix. Brooke, though, had her doubts.

Mrs. Williams, the housekeeper, who was in on Brooke's job, welcomed Brooke to the servant's hall. Dressed as a maid in the head-to-toe black of an upper-class servant, Brooke would pose as Williams's niece during her stay.

"When will it be convenient for me to see Lady Cathrow's dressing room?" she asked.

The housekeeper looked at her watch. "Now, at once." . . .

Loveday entered a large, luxuriously furnished room, and naturally made her way straight to its chief point of attraction—the iron safe fitted into the wall that separated the dressing-room from the bedroom.

It was a safe of the ordinary description, fitted with a strong iron door and Chubb lock. And across this door was written with chalk in characters that seemed defiant in their size and boldness, the words: "To be let, unfurnished."

Loveday spent about five minutes in front of this safe, all her attention concentrated upon the big, bold writing.

She took from her pocket-book a narrow strip of tracing-paper and compared the writing on it, letter by letter, with that on the safe door. This done she turned to Mrs. Williams and professed herself ready to follow her to the room below.

Mrs. Williams looked surprised. Her opinion of Miss Brooke's professional capabilities suffered considerable diminution.

"The gentlemen detectives," she said, "spent over an hour in this room; they paced the floor, they measured the candles, they—"

"Mrs. Williams," interrupted Loveday, "I am quite ready to look at the room below." . . .

Mrs. Williams led the way to the little room. . . .

Loveday wasted no time here. In fact, much to Mrs. Williams's surprise and disappointment, she merely walked across the room, in at one door and out at the opposite one, which opened into the large inner hall of the house. . . .

"I shall be glad if you will show me to my room now," said Loveday, a little abruptly. . . .

"Shall I send someone to help you unpack?" she asked, a little stiffly, at the door of Loveday's room.

"No, thank you; there will not be much unpacking to do. I must leave here by the first up-train tomorrow morning."

"To-morrow morning! Why, I have told everyone you will be here at least a fortnight!"[12]

Brooke was, indeed, on the train to another town the next morning. She sent another telegram asking Dyer to meet her for the apprehension of the true criminal, a former footman named Harry Emmett. She'd pinpointed him using her knowledge of penny novels, the vernacular of cab drivers, handwriting types, and her suspicion that some criminals have a sense of humor. Her speed and accuracy was no surprise to Ebenezer Dyer. They were a hallmark of Brooke's detecting.

One of the earliest professional female detectives in fiction, Loveday Brooke was the creation of Catherine Louisa Pirkis. Brooke appeared first in 1893 in a series of stories in the *Ludgate Monthly* that were collected, with an additional story, and published the following year as *The Experiences of Loveday Brooke, Lady Detective*.

Brooke was frequently summoned by Dyer to gather evidence after the police invariably proved inept in handling the case. She relied on logic and keen observation of rooms, people, text, and objects to solve cases. Important clues caused her eyelids to droop and her eyes to become slits as she pondered the information. Brooke drew different conclusions than the police and focused on their omissions to deduce solutions.

Brooke relished the work. Without obligations to family or home, she devoted all of her attention to her profession. It was one she chose for herself. She had an upper-class background but rather than work as a governess, the fate of the well-born unmarried nineteenth-century woman fallen on hard times, she "defied convention, and had chosen for herself a career that had cut her off sharply from her former associates and her position in society."[13] Brooke was so focused on her work that she couldn't even take a vacation. Her beach gear included newspapers, casebooks, and reference books.

Loveday Brooke was among the many women cracking cases and capturing criminals decades before Alice Clement took up the badge. It's true that most of these sleuthing women prowled between the covers of a book rather than between real shadows in dark city alleys, but a detecting woman was not wholly unknown.

Independent, courageous, and skilled at disguise, the nineteenth- and early-twentieth-century fictional female crime fighters excited legions of fans and set the stage for characters such as Nancy Drew, Jane Marple, and, later, Kinsey Millhone, Jane Tennison, Precious Ramotswe, Veronica Mars, V. I. Warshawski, and Kay Scarpetta. These paper detectives tended to solve more colorful and exciting cases—capturing jewel thieves and cracking murders—than early policewomen, who mostly shepherded young women home from dance halls and movie theaters. Women also wrote detective stories, some best sellers that made their authors, like Anna Katharine Green, household names. Of course, to most readers, the fictional detective must be male, despite the very early place of women in crime fiction and the very public crusade of women to enter American policing in the nineteenth century.

Stories of puzzles, mysteries, and crime had existed for centuries, but the detective story was a product of the modern age. The eighteenth century produced an immense body of literature about criminals and crime that fed the creation of the detective story. While the detective was a new figure in the mid-nineteenth century, the detective genre drew on existing strands of popular fiction in which women writers and female characters loomed large.

Detective stories had strong ties with Gothic novels of the late eighteenth century, a genre devoted to gruesome content, emotional trauma, and, most importantly for a culture obsessed with morality, virtue rewarded and vice punished. Gothic novels often featured an "almost detective," who would try but fail at investigation despite mental acuity and physical boldness. But solving a puzzle was rarely as interesting or as central to these stories as the plight of the principal character, whose innocence was frequently threatened by supernatural deviltry.

Ann Radcliffe's 1794 *The Mysteries of Udolpho* made her one of the most popular and influential English writers of her time. Her wild, bleak landscapes and threatening male characters shaped and popularized the Gothic style. The novel also made her famous, despite critics' generally low opinion of Gothic fiction, castigated as the "trash of the circulating libraries."[14] Radcliffe was seen as the exception. She excelled at arousing terror through events that appeared to have supernatural origins but turned out to have rational explanations. The strange, disembodied voices and noises heard at the Castle of Udolpho, for instance, are not those of ghosts but that of Monsieur Du Pont speaking from a secret passageway. Radcliffe's work balanced traditional moral values with strong political statements, particularly on the oppression of women. Her female characters were frequently abducted heroines, luckless wives, and repentant nuns who all suffered at the hands of men but also escaped through proto-detective methods to triumph in the end.

Despite Radcliffe's great influence on writers such as Mary Shelley, the Brontë sisters, Edgar Allan Poe, and Bram Stoker, among many others, little is known about the woman herself. Born in 1764 and raised in Bath, England, Radcliffe began writing to pass the time while her husband, editor of the *English Chronicle*, worked in the evenings. She published her first novella in 1789 and a two-volume romance in 1790, both anonymously. The three-volume Gothic novel *The Romance of the Forest* was the first book published under her own name, in 1791, earning her critical acclaim and a stage adaptation of the book at Covent Garden's Theatre Royale. But by 1800, with several novels to her name, Radcliffe began to retreat from literary and public life. The *Edinburgh Review* claimed, in 1823, that "she never appeared in public, nor mingled in private society, but kept herself apart, like the sweet bird that sings its solitary notes, shrouded and unseen."[15] Stories about her circulated nonetheless, most far more exciting than the likely truth. Some wondered if she had died, while others speculated that she'd driven herself insane from the horrors she conjured on the page. Radcliffe stopped publishing at the height of her success and died suddenly from an asthma attack in 1823.[16]

The sensation novels of the 1860s also informed the detective genre. These novels mixed many elements of the Gothic with realism to make its storylines seem at least somewhat possible, if not exactly probable. They pulled readers in with a gripping narrative that startled, gushed with emotion, or jangled nerves. Sensation novelists had a deliberate mission to excite. Many stories dealt with murder, family secrets, mistaken identity, or insanity inside the grand country homes of a middle- or upper-middle-class family. Sensation novelists' emphasis on uncovering things was a very nineteenth-century preoccupation. The era's great advances in science and technology opened up new areas of knowledge and ways of understanding the world. The idea that even the best, most respectable households might contain hideous secrets that scientific knowledge could help reveal was a scandalously appealing thought to a generation of readers.[17]

Mary Elizabeth Braddon was one of the founders and leading exponents of the sensation novel form. Her life was nearly as sensational as the fiction that made her famous. She began her career as an actress at age seventeen, performing under the stage name "Mary Seyton." It was a defiant career choice for a middle-class woman at a time when actresses were seen as little better than prostitutes. Braddon began writing on the side, first producing "penny dreadfuls," cheap serial stories filled with violence, poisoning, crime, and murder. She then turned to writing full-time, crafting novels that featured far-from-virtuous female characters. In *Lady Audley's Secret* (1862), the seeming angelic title character is revealed to be a villain willing to commit heinous crimes to maintain her luxurious life. When the young Lucy Graham marries widower Sir Michael Audley and becomes Lady Audley, little is known of her past other than her time as a governess for a Mrs. Vincent. But when George Talboys's wife, Helen, is reported dead and then Talboys himself disappears, Sir Michael's nephew Robert Audley—a friend of the Talboyses—begins to look into his new step-aunt's past and her possible connection to Talboys. Robert uncovers the truth in a detective-like manner, collecting evidence and comparing the handwriting in letters supposedly from Helen with the writing of Lady Audley. He realizes that Lucy was, in fact, Helen Talboys and had faked her own death and created a new identity as Lucy Graham. Lady Audley knows Robert is on to her, and, determined to maintain her position, she sets fire to the inn where he is staying before he can reveal her secret. Robert survives, however, and confronts her. Lady Audley claims she lost her mind. A doctor confirms her insanity and Robert has her imprisoned in an insane asylum in Belgium for the rest of her life.

The heroine of Braddon's next book, *Aurora Floyd* (1862), was another unconventional woman, though one less violent than Lady Audley. Aurora Floyd is a beautiful, dark-haired young woman raised by her rich and adoring banker father after her mother's untimely death. As a child, she becomes fascinated with racehorses and dogs, interests that many see as unfeminine. When she foolishly elopes with the handsome but dishonest groom Conyers, she breaks her father's heart. Floyd returns to her father one year later and, wishing to put the whole incident behind her, marries the devoted John Mellish, even though she's still married to Conyers. Floyd and her father are determined to hide her bigamy. They almost succeed until Conyers reappears and threatens to expose her secret unless she pays him off. When Conyers ends up dead, Floyd becomes a prime suspect. She's innocent, though her unwomanly behavior, most memorably when she takes a horsewhip to a stable hand mistreating her dog, seems to prove her violent capacities. Floyd makes no apologies for her mistakes, even as she recognizes her part in trapping herself and her father in a life of deception and bribery. This is a mystery, but with no detective and a very flawed heroine.

Braddon became enormously successful, even as contemporaries vilified the morals and actions of many of her characters. She likely felt more kindly toward them because of a scandal in her own life. Braddon became first the assistant and then the common-law wife to publisher John Maxwell, who was separated from but unable to divorce his mentally unstable wife. Braddon acted as stepmother to his five children and eventually had five children of her own with Maxwell, causing critics to disparage her relationship with a bigamist.[18] Novelist Margaret Oliphant, in criticizing Braddon's sensation novels and their violently passionate women, suggested that the author knew too much about bigamy for her own good.[19] From her own experiences, Braddon likely understood what circumstances and a desire for a new life could drive people like Lady Audley and Aurora Floyd to do.

Despite her controversial past, Braddon had become a respected literary figure by the 1880s. She married Maxwell in 1874, after the death of his wife, and the two became prominent figures in their communities. Braddon eventually wrote some ninety novels, essays, and several plays, none as transgressive as *Lady Audley* and *Aurora Floyd*, though still rich in death and betrayal. She also edited the magazine *Belgravia*, which serialized many of her novels. Despite her commercial success, Braddon never achieved the critical recognition she desired because of the low reputation of sensation novels and her emphasis on crime. "A book without a murder, a divorce, a seduction, or a bigamy, is not apparently considered worth either writing or reading, and a mystery and a secret are the chief qualifications of the modern novel," complained a reviewer in *Fraser's Magazine* in 1863.[20] That most of the crimes in sensation novels happened not to the poor and working class, as was previously common, but to the educated middle class jarred many critics and signaled a major literary shift. The fiendish Lady Audley, who committed arson and attempted murder in shocking contrast to her social standing and feminine appearance, scandalized and thrilled readers.

Sensation novelists such as Braddon were particularly adept at creating women who stepped outside the bounds of normal female behavior. In Wilkie Collins's *The Woman in White* (1860), the spinster Marian Holcombe sets out to investigate her beloved sister Laura's suitor, Sir Percival Glyde, and to discover the identity of the woman in white, Anne Catherick.[21] Catherick bears a striking resemblance to Laura and seems to know a lot about Glyde. Even though she's only a sidekick to her friend and art teacher Walter Hartright, Holcombe is daring, intelligent, and confident. "This is a matter of curiosity; and you have got a woman for your ally," she asserts. "Under such conditions success is certain, sooner or later." In the course of the novel, Holcombe manages to identify the two villains, Glyde and his friend Count Fosco, and is captured, falls ill, recovers, and discovers that Glyde is an illegitimate child and not considered entitled to his position in society. The never-married Holcombe's masculine appearance keeps her from being the romantic hero, while also giving her the latitude and freedom to act that few conventional women possessed. She's a daring spinster in the mode of those who would become common in the detective genre by the early twentieth century.

Braddon, too, created sleuthing women besides her murderous heroines. In *Eleanor's Victory* (1863), fifteen-year-old Eleanor Vane investigates the circumstances of her father's death, a case that centers on the interpretation of an incomplete fragment of a letter he left behind. She's an incompetent detective, though, losing evidence and botching clues as she makes deductions based largely on her imagination. Braddon introduced another female sleuth in Margaret Wilmot, who tracks down a murderer in *Henry Dunbar* (1864), only to discover that he is her father. The engaging complexity of these characters, along with the thrills of the plot, ensured that sensation novels drew devoted female readers. That these novels also addressed subjects that many middle-class Americans considered inappropriate, and did so in a melodramatic style, made them all the more scandalous and appealing.[22]

Sensation novels went hand-in-hand with the sensational journalism of the period, which capitalized on the culture's obsession with death. Many writers were influenced by the explicit crime reporting in the nation's newspapers, magazines, and tabloids, which seemed to suggest that murders and conspiracies lurked in every shadow, a situation not unlike the current media landscape with its roster of TV shows like the *CSI* series and *True Detective*. Few magazines were as popular as the *National Police Gazette*, founded in New York City in 1845.[23] Early issues featured extremely detailed crime narratives, which its publishers claimed helped police bring criminals to justice. Each issue printed the names of alleged offenders, their aliases, physical descriptions, and sometimes even their home addresses. The introduction of full-page woodcuts illustrating the titillating and often gruesome content helped expand readership to the less than literate and propelled the magazine to national popularity. Crime also drove the sale of cheap broadsheets, which claimed to tell true stories from the streets, prisons, and gallows. Reported in real time, starting with the discovery of a body, followed by an inquest, investigation, and, finally, the discovery of a culprit, true-crime stories accustomed readers to the temporal dislocations that characterized detective stories. Purchased for a pittance, these publications allowed Americans to lap up all the lurid crime they desired.

Biographies of murderers were among the best sellers of the nineteenth century. The supposedly authentic memoirs of English household servant Maria Manning, the so-called "Lady Macbeth of Bermondsey," who in 1849, along with her husband, killed her lover and buried him beneath her kitchen floor, became a publishing sensation. Its creator, Robert Huish, had written two previous penny dreadfuls. He published his semi-fictionalized story of the Mannings in twenty-four parts before releasing it in book form, a novel that clocked in at more than eight hundred pages.[24] Newspapers covered the Mannings' case from every angle. Even the *Times* of London, most certainly not a sensational tabloid, ran at least seventy-two different stories about the crime and trial. Among the thousands (amply provided with good seating, food, and drink) to attend the Mannings' execution was Charles Dickens, who wrote to the *Times* expressing his horror at the "wickedness and levity of the immense crowd" screeching and laughing and taking "indecent delight" in the deaths.[25] His shock did not, apparently, prevent him from using Manning as a model for his murderess in *Bleak House*. Dickens incorporated Maria Manning's traits into his characterization of the French maid Hortense, who kills the lawyer investigating the scandalous past of her employer, Lady Dedlock.

True crime became a regular reference point in fiction. Wilkie Collins based some of the details of his detective-ish sensation novel *The Moonstone* on two crimes reported with breathless detail in the newspapers of the day: the 1860 murder of four-year-old Francis Kent, to which the victim's half-sister Constance later confessed, and the 1861 Northumberland Street Affair, in which a blood-covered man appeared in the window of a house in London after battering his alleged assailant to death. Collins's Sergeant Cuff was based on the real inspector who investigated the Kent murder. The hostility of the upper-class Kent family to the lower-class police is also reflected in the novel, and Collins placed the house where the murder victim is lured on Northumberland Street, a reference to the bloody man that contemporary readers would have known.[26] Not everyone liked the gory intersection of journalism and fiction. Oxford professor Henry Longueville Mansel complained about what he called "the criminal variety of the Newspaper Novel," where writers only needed to "keep an eye on the criminal reports of the daily newspapers" to find a story that would virtually write itself.[27]

That violence, horror, madness, and murder formed such a large part of people's reading seems at odds with our buttoned-up and prim image of nineteenth-century culture. But the repressed attitude of the era is far overstated. Anxieties about the body, including the celebrated myth that Victorians thought piano legs immodest and covered them with special sleeves, are a construct of the twentieth century, not a reality of the nineteenth. Religious revivalism, as well as scientific and technological advances, fostered a generation eager to explore the meaning and experience of death. This fascination extended, naturally enough, to crime. The pleasure taken in the vicarious experience of violence, whether through graphic video games or brutal novels, transcends generations, taking on different forms depending on the particulars of the age. In the nineteenth century, the rise of literacy and cheap printing allowed sensation and vice to flourish in new ways and in new literary forms.[28]

With readers hungrily consuming true-crime stories, more and more writers made murder the central plot point of popular fiction. The creation of a new profession—the detective—marked a major social innovation that heralded a new approach to crime and a new character ripe for fictionalization.

Fictional detectives and police officers appeared on the page at the same time that police forces organized in growing American cities. Police departments evolved out of the old system of night watch.[29] In colonial America, responsibility for law enforcement fell to the individual community and its appointed constables. Many towns implemented volunteer watch groups, which guarded against prowlers and thieves, mostly by shouting and chasing them away, to assist the constable. These volunteers also lit street lamps, recovered lost children, and captured runaway livestock. Constables had similar tasks but also brought suspects and witnesses to court. Boston's Night Watch formed in

1636, and in 1651, the aptly named Shout and Rattle Watch organized in New York City. Members of city watches operated primarily for crime prevention, potentially deterring would-be criminals by
their presence alone; few took part in any actual crime busting. Critics
claimed that night watchmen slept on the job (most had day jobs),
solicited prostitutes, and ran from real danger. The *New York Gazette*
described the watch as a "Parcel of idle, drunken, vigilant Snorers, who
never quelled any nocturnal Tumult in their lives; but would, perhaps,
be [as] ready to join in a Burglary as any Thief in Christendom."[30]
That was a familiar refrain. The uselessness of the watchman had been
remarked upon since at least Shakespeare's time.[31] In *Much Ado About
Nothing*, for instance, the local watch, headed by the citizen constable
Dogberry, is comically inept. In more sparsely populated rural areas of
colonial America, crime busting was left to sheriffs, who caught criminals, worked with the courts, and collected taxes. Law enforcement
was a low priority for sheriffs, however. In many areas, the sheriff's
salary was tied to the amount of taxes collected, so they earned more
money collecting taxes than collecting criminals.[32]

Volunteers worked reasonably well as long as an area remained
somewhat agrarian, but as cities grew, so, too, did the scale and number of problems. The system was pushed to its limits. A network of
neighbors could not adequately deal with the more serious crimes of
a larger and more diverse population. The influx of immigrants and
economic depressions of the nineteenth century stoked violence and
discord. Although the sources of tension varied, few cities escaped
serious rioting and mob violence. Investors attacked failing banks.
Workmen protested long hours and poor pay by destroying their
workplaces. Crowds attacked medical schools that secretly harvested
cadavers for experimentation from graveyards. Sheriffs and untrained
volunteers were ill prepared to deal with sometimes violent crowds.
To keep order in urban areas, more formalized means of social control began to take shape.[33]

American police departments began forming in the mid-nineteenth
century, following the model established by the English home secretary, Robert Peel, who organized London's Metropolitan Police in
1829. Peel used his military experience to craft a national organization in Britain that fell somewhere between a military and a civil force.
The officers' nickname "bobby" comes from his name.[34] Americans
borrowed selectively from the British model. Political factions argued
over the type of police force to create, fearful of what their opponents

would do in control of an armed body of men. But slowly, local resistance and political struggles gave way to the formation of municipal departments: New York City, in 1845; St. Louis, in 1846; and
Chicago, in 1854. In some cities, several agencies vied with the police
department for law enforcement duties, creating inevitable confusion
and bitter partisan fights for power that lasted for decades.[35]

Early policing was heavily entrenched in politics. Politicians rewarded their supporters with positions on the police force, and as
thanks for employment, police officers helped politicians stay in office
by encouraging citizens to vote and deterring voters from opposing
parties. The political nature of the work meant that there were virtually no standards for hiring or training officers and made job security almost nonexistent. The relationship was so intertwined between
police and politicians that the entire police department often would
change personnel along with a political administration. This revolving
door of police and politicians would also profoundly influence wom-
en's ability to join and remain on a city police force.[36]

Among the British innovations that did not come over to America
were uniforms. Peel's officers wore blue from the very beginning to
distinguish themselves from the red coats of the army. In the United
States, on the other hand, freedom of dress apparently fell high on the
list of American values. Uniforms smacked of British pretension and
elitism. The only people who wore them were soldiers and servants,
both symbols of values that democratic Americans generally opposed: standing armies and wealthy elites.[37] Demonstrating in front
of the home of the New York City chief of police in 1854, city officers
claimed that uniforms "conflicted with their notions of independence
and self-respect."[38] Others decried the great expense of public money
to outfit what amounted to a local army. In Philadelphia, city coun-
cilmen denounced the uniforms as a "badge of servitude" after fifteen
officers resigned in protest, refusing to wear even a uniform hat.[39] City
administrators and police officials argued that uniforms made police
officers visible to the public for assistance. Sartorial winds in Northern states shifted with the Civil War, elevating the status of uniforms,
so that after the war, the blue coat became fairly standard American
police attire. The question of dress was far from settled, though. Police fashion would again rear its head when women joined the force,
and it remained an issue for decades.

Besides crime, city police took on an expansive list of municipal services. Along with arresting offenders, police departments

distributed food and clothing to the poor, cleaned streets, inspected boilers, conducted censuses, rounded up livestock, and attempted to contain vice. A significant portion of the policing budget went to providing shelter, and station houses often contained dorm-style rooms to house needy people overnight. All of these activities fell under the jurisdiction of a police force charged with keeping public order. The number of nightly lodgers made it incredibly difficult to keep station houses clean, creating dreadful conditions for officers to live, work, and sleep in. Housing reforms in the late nineteenth century that moved indigents out of station houses also improved the public image of police by giving them cleaner places to live and work. Not until the late nineteenth and early twentieth centuries did police abandon all of these services to focus on crime.[40]

Even with all these public services, most Americans expected little from police departments. Limited technology made it hard for officers to respond to the immediate needs of their constituents. Citizens generally accepted brawls, domestic disputes, and drunkenness as a normal, if not wholly comfortable, part of modern city life.[41]

Regardless of their effectiveness, though, the creation of police forces symbolized a modern "civilizing" force that recast violence in popular culture as an amusing hobby and generated an appetite for a new kind of literature: one where a horrible crime disturbs the social order, but not irreparably. The idea of murder as entertainment was an idea that would blossom into one of the greatest mass-market interests in history.[42]

CHAPTER TWO

Sleuths in Skirts

O N AUGUST 22, 1856, PRIVATE DETECTIVE ALLAN PINKERTON LOOKED UP TO see a woman standing at the door of his Chicago office. She introduced herself as Kate Warne and proclaimed herself in need of a job. She was not, however, looking to be a secretary, as Pinkerton first thought. No, she wanted to be a detective.[1]

Even though no woman sleuthed, Pinkerton agreed to hear her out. Warne said she was a widow in need of a livelihood. She appeared to Pinkerton to be about twenty-three years old. Warne reportedly told the hesitant Pinkerton that she "could go and worm out secrets in many places to which it is impossible for male detectives to gain access." He described her as slender with brown hair, "graceful in her movements and self-possessed" with "a broad, honest face" that invited trust. She impressed him with her street smarts and intellect, so he decided to take a chance.[2] He never regretted his decision. Warne offered something Pinkerton's male agents did not: the ability to gain the confidence of other women. Under Pinkerton, she became America's first-known female private eye and one of his finest sleuths.[3]

Little is known of Warne, except that she joined the Pinkerton National Detective Agency at a critical time. Just a few years into his business, Allan Pinkerton would enflame Americans' enthusiasm for detection with his high-profile cases and fantastical detective novels. He saturated audiences with tales of his escapades, tapping public interest in adventure, mystery, and rational problem solving. Unlike most crime writers, Pinkerton was a real detective with actual life experience. He worked hard to build an image of his agency and of detection as a serious profession, and made himself and his operatives, like Warne, the country's foremost private eyes.[4]

Though many books took crime as their subject, the detective story placed at its core the singular figure of the detective, as well as the investigation and resolution of a crime, usually murder. Detectives solved cases for many reasons, but personal satisfaction in exercising their logical minds and their professional expertise figured boldly in ways not seen in earlier crime fiction. The characters that detected in Gothic, sensation, and other crime stories had a personal motive for their involvement. Their sleuthing also tended to be a one-time outing. In a nation fascinated with the possibilities of phrenology, psychology, and physiognomy, the professional detective's use of scientific reasoning to arrive at answers marked him—and the detective was usually a "him"—as a new and utterly compelling figure.

Edgar Allan Poe wrote what is generally considered the first modern English-language detective story. His 1841 story "The Murders in the Rue Morgue" introduced French detective C. Auguste Dupin, who solves the mystery of a corpse found in what appears to be an impenetrable locked room. An eccentric and nocturnal gentleman of leisure, Dupin helps the police solve crimes for his own amusement. As such, he's less interested in everyday robberies and petty crimes than in the bizarre and difficult cases that allow him to showcase his superior intellectual skill and powers of logical reasoning. As would become common with most fictional detectives, Dupin solves crimes with his brain rather than brawn.

Poe's second Dupin story, "The Mystery of Marie Roget," was based on a real unsolved murder, that of Mary Cecilia Rogers, in New York. Poe, offering his story for publication to the editor of the *Boston Notion*, wrote that he drafted a story "in a manner altogether *novel* in literature. I have imagined a series of nearly exact *coincidences* [to the Rogers case but] occurring in Paris."[5] Rather than hit the streets in search of clues, Dupin analyzes newspaper stories from the comfort of his home. He then puts forward a solution to the crime, in what became the first case of armchair detection.

The final Dupin story, "The Purloined Letter," often considered the best of Poe's three Dupin stories for its reliance on pure reason, concerns the theft of a letter containing compromising information from the room of an unnamed woman. The culprit is known from the start of this case, the unscrupulous Minister D—, so the action centers on finding the letter in his room, something the police have been unable to accomplish. Dupin, of course, finds the letter, and the solution to the case demonstrates that the most unlikely solution is often the right one.[6]

Although the stories are considered a literary milestone today, Poe's Dupin stories drew scant attention at the time. Some reviewers questioned Dupin's skill in presenting the solution to a fictional crime devised by the writer. Poe understood the limitations of the form. This is why, for his second Dupin outing, he was drawn to the real-life story of Mary Rogers's murder. Poe didn't consider himself a writer of detective fiction. "Detective" was itself both a new word and a new concept, so it's not surprising that Poe concerned himself more with the storyline of romantic terror, perfected half a century earlier by Ann Radcliffe.[7]

Though Poe is considered the creator of the first fictional detective, Dupin did not inspire a rash of imitators. It was Sherlock Holmes, appearing nearly a half century after Dupin, who became the iconic detective.[8]

Dupin was not the only detective to debut in 1841. A sleuthing woman appeared in Catherine Crowe's *Adventures of Susan Hopley; or, Circumstantial Evidence*, a book that drew far more attention than Poe's Dupin stories.[9] *Susan Hopley* was Crowe's first novel, though it was first published anonymously and only later acknowledged as the creation of a woman.

The intricately plotted story concerns the attempt by Susan, a maid, to solve both the mysterious disappearance of her brother, Andrew, and the murder of her guardian, Mr. Wentworth. It's widely believed that Andrew murdered Wentworth for his money, but Susan turns sleuth to find and redeem her brother: "The most earnest desire Susan had . . . was to go over to the house that had been the scene of the catastrophe, and inspect every part of it herself."[10] Susan has a foreboding dream that appears to reveal what happened to both men, and she spends the rest of the book gathering evidence to validate that dream. She's lucky early on, finding clues on the ground beneath Andrew's window. After her employer fires her for her connection to the murder suspect, she continues to gather evidence as she moves from job to job. Other would-be detectives are in pursuit of the killer, too, including a clerk from Wentworth's firm and the family lawyer.

In the end, Andrew is found murdered and Susan is vindicated when the real villains are revealed.

Susan Hopley became a best seller and was immediately adapted for the stage by George Dibdin Pitt. The play debuted in London in May 1841 to great acclaim. It then toured with the Henry Nye Chart theatrical company, which counted future sensation writer Mary Braddon as a member. One wonders if Braddon may even have played Hopley herself.

Although Crowe was far ahead of her time as an author, her heroine became largely forgotten. Crowe's literary reputation diminished with the 1848 publication of *The Night Side of Nature*, a two-volume collection of ghost stories mixed with spiritualism, phrenology, and other speculative or supernatural subjects. Those weren't new interests for Crowe, who moved through Edinburgh literary and intellectual circles and was known for her wide interests and eccentricity. At an 1847 dinner for visiting writer Hans Christian Andersen, hosted by Dr. James Young Simpson, who would later discover chloroform, Crowe and another guest drank ether. Andersen recorded in his journal of the evening, "I had a feeling of being with two mad people, they laughed with open, dead, eyes."[11] Crowe's involvement in the ghostly and spiritual culminated in a bizarre incident in Edinburgh a few years later. Many thought she had gone mad, including Charles Dickens, who reported her much gossiped about mental breakdown to a friend in 1854: "Mrs Crowe has gone stark mad—and stark naked—on the spirit-rapping imposition. She was found t'other day in the street, clothed only in her chastity, a pocket-handkerchief and a visiting card. She had been informed, it appeared, by the spirits, that if she went out in that trim she would be invisible. She is in a mad-house and, I fear, hopelessly insane."[12] Crowe recovered from her illness but wrote little afterward. Her trailblazing female detective was forgotten.[13]

The person who brought the concept of detection to the masses was not a fictional detective but a real-life one: private eye Allan Pinkerton, who had hired the first female investigator. Born in Scotland in 1819, Pinkerton worked as a cooper, or barrel maker, until his political activism forced him to flee to North America, in 1842.[14] He opened his own cooperage outside Chicago, but fell into detective work after helping the local sheriff capture a band of counterfeiters hiding near where he harvested wood for his barrels. Pinkerton's aptitude for detection led to his recruitment by the Chicago Police

Department as its first full-time detective. In most police departments, patrolmen performed some detective duties, but the work was not a specialized function and required no special training. It did come laden with all the same political pressures that all police departments faced, however. Pinkerton soon realized he could earn more money and be free of political tides on his own, so in 1850 he quit the police department to open the Pinkerton National Detective Agency.

In the nineteenth century, private agencies filled gaps left by rudimentary city police forces. Most police departments struggled to provide adequate services within city limits, leaving parts of the city and rural areas entirely unsupervised. As police had replaced night watchmen in most cities by the 1860s, many businesses contracted with private agencies for night-watch services. Private detectives also found work handling interstate crime and complex investigations as politics and jurisdictional limitations made it hard for city forces to be truly effective. These weaknesses created a thriving market for private detectives like Pinkerton.[15]

Pinkerton's work consisted largely of protecting railroad and express companies from fraud, scams often perpetrated by the company's own employees. His agents blurred the line between spying and detection as they trailed suspects and went undercover to gather information. In 1856, he made history by hiring Kate Warne, the first in what eventually became a whole bureau of female operatives under her supervision.

Warne took to undercover work easily, eliciting information from wives of suspected criminals in embezzlement and security cases, just as she'd promised when seeking a job. Early in her career, Warne was brought on board to help with the case of the Adams Express Company, a railroad company that had suffered the loss of forty thousand dollars, a huge sum in those days. Pinkerton believed that the manager of the company's Montgomery, Alabama, office, a man named Nathan Maroney, had stolen the money. Warne befriended Maroney's wife, who eventually led Warne to the money, buried in a boardinghouse cellar. Warne's work led to Maroney's conviction. Pinkerton later wrote of Warne's involvement in the case, "She had the proud satisfaction of knowing that to a woman belonged the honors of the day."[16]

Not everyone was so thrilled with Warne. Critics and family members of both Warne and Pinkerton accused them of carrying on an affair. The two did frequently pose undercover as husband and wife. In later years, Pinkerton's son Robert tried to prevent the agency from hiring additional women. Pinkerton refused to yield, insisting on his aim "to use females for the detection of crime where it has been useful and necessary."[17]

In 1861, Warne took part in foiling an assassination attempt on President Abraham Lincoln. Pinkerton had received a tip on a plot to assassinate the new president as he passed through Baltimore on his way to Washington, DC, to take office. Warne, dressed as a Southern lady, infiltrated Confederate social circles in Baltimore to gather details on the whispered plan. Her work confirmed suspicions, and Warne helped devise and carry out a scheme to get Lincoln safely to Washington. On a night train out of Philadelphia, Lincoln was disguised as Warne's invalid brother. He arrived unharmed in the capital.[18]

The Civil War provided tremendous opportunities for detective work. Wartime needs not only stimulated industry but also cases of fraud, embezzlement, and corruption. Hundred-dollar enlistment bonuses encouraged bounty jumpers to join the military, collect the money, desert, and then reenlist elsewhere. Around military camps, drinking, gambling, theft, and prostitution became major problems. All created opportunities for entrepreneurial detectives like Pinkerton.

During the war, Pinkerton provided intelligence for the Army of the Potomac under General George McClellan. Pinkerton investigated suspected spies, gathered information behind Confederate lines, and uncovered firms swindling the federal government. Warne also served during the war as a Pinkerton field agent. She helped break up a spy ring in Washington, DC, run by Confederate sympathizer Rose O'Neal Greenhow, rewriting Greenhow's ciphered dispatches to Southern leaders with useless or false information. Warne may have been the "female detective" Greenhow describes in her memoir as searching her body and clothes.[19] "I blush that the name and character of woman should be so prostituted. But she was certainly not above her honourable calling," wrote Greenhow of the female detective sent to her room. "As is usual with females employed in this way, she was decently arrayed, as if to impress me with her respectability."

Pinkerton's wartime record was spotty, however, and he lost his position when McClellan was relieved of duty. But his participation still generated significant publicity for his agency and for detection as a profession.[20]

After the war, the Pinkerton Agency grabbed national headlines in pursuing the Dalton Gang, Frank and Jesse James, and Butch Cassidy and his Wild Bunch. His agency also created the Rogues' Gallery, the first comprehensive database of criminals in America, filled with newspaper clippings and mug shots.

Warne continued working with the agency, but fell ill in 1867. Pinkerton stayed by her side until she died the following year. She was only thirty-five years old. Fueling gossip over the nature of their relationship, Warne was buried in the Pinkerton family plot in Chicago's Graceland Cemetery, directly beside the spot reserved for Pinkerton himself.

Women remained active in Pinkerton's agency until his death in 1884, when his sons finally succeeded in eliminating female operatives from the agency for several years.[21]

Pinkerton's own failing health and concern about improving the public image of detecting led him to turn to writing—or at least supervising the writing of—embellished tales of his remarkable life of crime busting. Pinkerton was a talented storyteller and a savvy businessman, and he surely recognized the opportunity to profit from the growing public interest in crime stories. Between 1874 and the end of his life, Pinkerton published sixteen books. His agency's methods and style of advertising had become so ingrained in popular culture that by the 1870s his name, he proclaimed, had "grown to be a sort of synonym for detective."[22] His first book, *The Expressman and the Detective*, combined realistic details from actual cases with sensational drama and characters.[23] It became an immediate success, selling fifteen thousand copies in its first sixty days. Pinkerton dictated the outline of most of his stories to stenographers, who in turn handed their notes over to professional ghostwriters, a system not unlike that behind the creation of the Nancy Drew and Hardy Boys series in the twentieth century.

Pinkerton wanted to make money, but he also hoped his stories would enhance the prestige of detection. "My profession, which had been dragged down by unprincipled adventurers until the term 'detective' was synonymous with rogue, was, when properly attended to and honestly conducted, one of the most useful and indispensable adjuncts to the preservation of the lives and property of the people," he wrote.[24] Detection, Pinkerton maintained, was a business with standards and codes of conduct. Of his own agents, he valued honesty and morality above any particular experience or skills, so his agents came from a variety of backgrounds. Some agents worked for Pinkerton as preparation for a career in policing, while others became agents temporarily, before pursuing other jobs. One of those temporary agents was the twentieth-century hard-boiled writer Dashiell Hammett.

Although he claimed to hate detective fiction because, he said, its writers cheapened the profession "with their emphasis on theatrics and mysterious exploits," Pinkerton's high profile and widely publicized (by himself and others) cases obviously influenced the work of detective novelists.[25] Pinkerton lacked the literary talent of Braddon or Poe, but that suited his audience just fine. Many readers found the writing of those authors too cerebral for the escapist reading they sought. Pinkerton grounded his adventurous tales in common sense and sought to demystify detection by revealing the legwork actually required to solve cases. His stories assured his place as America's foremost detective.[26]

The popularity of Pinkerton's books and of all fiction, detective or otherwise, were helped by rising literacy, the spread of cheap novels and magazines, and the growth of a middle class with leisure time to spare. In the early nineteenth century, novels cost too much for few outside the upper classes to enjoy. But by the 1830s, the introduction of the steam rotary press created abundant and inexpensive reading material that could be distributed farther and faster through a growing network of railways. Most detective and mystery stories were first serialized in popular magazines and newspapers. Added to this expansion of literary material was the era's obsession with self-improvement, which helped give reading an enriching sheen.[27]

Popular interest in criminal stories also lay with the social tensions surrounding policing. Encounters between the lower-class police and the upper class, particularly respectable ladies, posed problems of etiquette in fiction and in life. How would the officer address a lady? What questions were acceptable during an interrogation? Many middle-class Americans did not like the idea of the police intruding into the privacy of their home. The home was supposed to be a safe haven from the corrupting influences of the outside world, which certainly included the uniformed police. Americans wanted suspects apprehended and crimes solved, but they also wanted to protect the sanctity of the domestic space from the very public intrusion a police officer symbolized. The ethics of listening at doors, snooping through drawers, and trailing suspects came up again and again in nineteenth-century crime novels. Detectives justified their actions as a means to a greater end of protecting citizens from harm.

Though criminals from the upper classes could often count on their societal status to shield them from the law early in the century, this became less and less the case as the decades passed and law enforcement became more structured. The potential for criminality lurking in reputable homes, and its inhabitants' concern for respectability and appearances, would become a major storyline in nineteenth- and twentieth-century novels.[28]

Around 1864, Metta Fuller Victor, writing under the pen name Seeley Register, a first name meaning happy or fortunate, published *The Dead Letter: An American Romance*. Written by a woman, it was perhaps the first true detective novel, a full-length work with a clear detective figure rather than a character who undertakes detective-like activities, in the English language. Published serially in *Beadle's Monthly*, the book did not feature a female detective but it did lay the foundational plot for domestic detective fiction: a brutal crime occurs in the household of a prosperous family, and someone emotionally involved with the family becomes an amateur investigator to either aid the police or show that they are on the wrong track.[29]

In *The Dead Letter*, narrator Richard Redfield is a lawyer-in-training for wealthy attorney Mr. Argyll. Redfield hopes to become both Argyll's law partner and son-in-law by marrying Argyll's daughter, Eleanor. But Eleanor is already engaged to a handsome young banker named Henry Moorland—at least she is until Moorland ends up murdered on the road near the family home. Redfield is among those implicated in the murder, and as such, loses his position. He goes to work as a clerk in a dead-letter office. As in many domestic novels, untangling the love triangles and professional rivalries of the household holds the key to the murder.

A New York detective named Burton arrives to investigate, but he has little luck until Redfield finds an undelivered letter from the murderer to his employer. Redfield delivers the letter to Burton, who determines the author is a discredited pharmacist named George Thorley. The two track him down. Burton's detecting method mixes the analytical with pseudoscience. At one point, he consults his clairvoyant daughter for information leading to the whereabouts of a suspect. Such a plot device is a fitting choice, given the popularity in the 1860s of mesmerism for tapping into the unconscious mind and mediums for channeling the departed. In the end, Burton, in a now familiar scene, gathers the family members and suspects to reveal the true killer: George Thorley, who was hired by Mr. Argyll's nephew

James to murder Moorland so he could marry into the family and gain their fortune.[30]

Victor set her detective story in the home, where everyone in the family has a personal interest and stake in the crime, making it difficult for the reader to solve. The domestic setting of her novels and solutions cast in terms of how they affected family relationships made Victor's early foray into detective writing less controversial than it might have otherwise been for a woman writer. A style that later became known as "cozy," stories like Victor's were devoid of graphic violence: victims are always discovered and murderers captured in an atmosphere of comfort and decorum within a restricted environment. It was a model that Agatha Christie would adopt in the twentieth century, though she did not confine herself exclusively to the home, choosing other contained spaces such as trains, airplanes, ships, and islands.[31]

The Dead Letter sold well. Published in hardcover, with a then high price tag of fifty cents, the book's publishers clearly felt that there was an audience affluent enough to afford something more than a dime novel. Although Victor's work is little known now, an 1869 advertisement for The Dead Letter boasted that more than eighty thousand copies had sold.[32]

Mysteries were only one of the many types of books Victor wrote; she adapted to fit the changing tastes of nineteenth-century readers. She had a successful career as a writer of poetry, romances, short stories, social issue novels, humor, cookbooks, and more than twenty-five dime novels for publisher Beadle and Adams. In other words, Victor wrote what sold. She began writing early, publishing her first book, Last Days of Tul, a Romance of the Lost Cities of Yucatan, at age fifteen. She wrote many of her books behind a series of pen names, some male, some female, and some of an ambiguous gender. She also wrote, under her own name, novels that opposed slavery, alcohol, and polygamy. Victor became best known for her abolitionist dime novel Maum Guinea and Her Plantation "Children" (1861). The use of her own name for reform-oriented books and pseudonyms for less reputable genres may have been her solution to the limitations women faced in the literary marketplace. And she did all this while raising nine children and despite tremendous social pressure for married women to focus on their family alone.[33]

Harriet Prescott Spofford may have published a pseudo-detective story even earlier than Victor. She was a prolific writer who began her career contributing anonymously to story papers in Boston to support her family before writing, among other things, several crime stories. Her first, "In a Cellar," published in the *Atlantic Monthly* in 1859, brought her literary fame. The story is set in Paris where a large diamond is stolen from the Marquis of G—. An unnamed retired English diplomat arrives to detect in an amateur role. Through chance and coincidence, he manages to recover the diamond but fails to real-ize the true identity of the thief, his valet. Spofford created a more fully formed detective in her 1865 story, the eponymous "Mr. Furbush." In his first appearance, Furbush is called in response to "an extraordinary murder that occurred at one of our fashionable hotels."[34] The victim, Agatha More, has been "strangled in her own handkerchief." Furbush solves the crime using the new technology of photography. In the third and final Furbush story, "In the Maguerriwock," from 1868, Fur-bush is a private detective investigating the disappearance of a peddler on the frontier. The exact reasons for the crimes committed in these stories are never fully explained, and the focus is often on characters other than the detective, but Spofford's emphasis on cracking cases certainly qualifies her as a detective writer.[35]

Writing at the same time as Spofford was Louisa May Alcott. Although best known for *Little Women* (1868), Alcott also wrote sensational thrillers that incorporated crime, violence, murder, insan-ity, drug use, and unconventional women. Her first detective story, written under the pen name A. M. Barnard, featured a character who was no Jo March. V.V., or Virginie Varens, is a malevolent, socially ambitious beauty with "the nerves of a man" and the "quick wit of a woman."[36] Her boldness is physically marked by the tattoo on her wrist that she conceals beneath a wide gold band. In "V.V.: or, Plots and Counterplots" (1865), Varens is rescued from penury by her cousin Victor, who expects to marry her in return for his generosity. She has other plans and flees, secretly marrying Scottish nobleman Allan Douglas for his title and money. Victor, knowing nothing of the marriage, discovers them and thinking him her lover, stabs Allan. When Varens reveals the marriage, Victor threatens her into silence and the two flee to Spain, where Varens gives birth to the son con-ceived on her wedding night with Douglas. Varens can't leave well enough alone and craves acknowledgement of her son by the Douglas family (and their money), and so she escapes back to England. She manipulates the Douglas family and drives the fiancée of the current Douglas heir, Earl Douglas, to suicide. Earl Douglas, in turn, calls in a French private detective named M. Antoine Dupres (clearly modeled after Poe's Dupin) to investigate the murder of his cousin, Allan. Dupres is an ambiguous figure, being neither a professional police detective nor really much of an amateur, declaring that he "should make a superb detective."[37] Dupres, unlike the detectives who would follow him in literary history, proves fallible and it is, instead, Earl Douglas who drives the ending of the story. But even partly formed, a detecting figure like Dupres shows Alcott's interest and familiarity with crime narratives as she, along with Victor and Spofford, pioneered the genre for women.[38]

Among those to benefit from these early women writers was Anna Katherine Green, whose detective stories would make her one of the most successful authors of the nineteenth century.[39] Born in New York City in 1846, Green was raised by her sixteen-year-old sister and father after her mother died when she was three. Her father eventually remarried, and his new wife, Grace, encouraged Green's writing and her education. In 1863, Green enrolled at Ripley Female College in Vermont, becoming one of few women of her generation to earn a college degree. She returned home after graduation. As a single woman, she had few other options. But Green kept writing, seeking to make a name for herself as a professional author.

In 1878, the thirty-two-year-old Green went to publisher G. P. Putnam's Sons in New York City clutching the manuscript she'd worked on for six years. It was a detective story called *The Leavenworth Case: A Lawyer's Story*. Green had filled the backs of envelopes, stationery, notebooks, and torn-out ledger pages with her draft, writing in secret to avoid the disapproval of her father, who had little regard for fiction. He certainly wouldn't approve of a detective story. Graceful and quiet, Green was an unlikely crime writer. She, in fact, considered herself a writer of verse, not whodunits, but she struggled to find a publisher for her poetry. Green hoped that this story would launch her career.

Even with the success of Victor and Braddon, detective fiction was an unusual choice to establish a writing career. It had not yet achieved the mass popularity it would enjoy in the twentieth century. Green could have followed better-trod paths as a novice writer. Books written by and for women flooded the market and became huge sellers. Newspaper columnist Fanny Fern's *Fern Leaves*, a collection of her columns, for instance, sold seventy thousand copies in 1853. But Green did not want to be a women's writer. Though her work contained elements common to women's literature, including a plot set in the home, Green wrote for the mass market. Detective fiction combined the two most popular news topics of the day: society gossip and front-page crime.[40]

Green's *The Leavenworth Case* begins with the murder of Manhattan millionaire Horatio Leavenworth.[41] When he is found dead in the locked study of his Manhattan home, the immediate suspects are members of the household who had access to the room. Chief among these are Leavenworth's nieces, Mary, heir to his fortune, and Eleanore, who has been largely shut out from her uncle's will in favor of Mary. The story has its share of glamour and intrigue but also realistic details of the crime and evidence modeled on actual scientific and legal procedures. Green even provided a diagram of the murder scene for readers to match wits with the detective. The narrative followed the conventional steps of the emerging form: an inquest into the cause of death, an examination of evidence, an interview of witnesses by the detective, and, finally, a confrontation of the likely murderer.[42]

Called in to investigate is Inspector Ebenezer Gryce, a deliberate man in his mid-fifties who did not, apparently, look the part of detective. "Mr. Gryce, the detective, was not the thin, wiry individual with the piercing eye you are doubtless expecting to see," the novel's narrator tells readers. "On the contrary, Mr. Gryce was a portly, comfortable personage with an eye that never pierced, that did not even rest on you."[43] It seems an odd observation to make at a time when the detective had hardly become a stock figure. Arthur Conan Doyle was himself still a medical student when Green's novel was published, several years away from his first detective story and the launch of his iconic hero. But Green was prescient in creating a character like Gryce. The person no one thinks much of as a detective is often the most wily and able character of all.

Gryce's upright manner and self-effacing charm appealed to a broad swathe of American and European readers. Green likely based him on policemen she had met through her father, James Wilson Green, a Manhattan lawyer. Unlike his European peers and Poe's French detective Dupin, Gryce is neither eccentric nor snobby but an ordinary American possessed of inordinate rationality. His lack of eye contact while speaking is his most notable physical trait. Gryce examines medical evidence, fabrics, and typefaces to draw conclusions. He also relies on paid operatives, including a master interrogator named "Q," short for "Query." Q, a male, excels at disguise, effectively donning the garb of a female beggar at one point. In the end, Gryce breaks the case by pretending to accuse Mary of the crime, setting up a trap into which the real killer, Mr. Leavenworth's secretary, Trueman Harwell, falls. After *The Leavenworth Case*, Gryce would appear in eleven other novels and one short story, becoming the world's first full-fledged serial detective.[44]

Green's novel was the first significant American heir to the detective stories of Edgar Allan Poe. Like Poe's first Dupin story, *The Leavenworth Case* was a locked-room murder. But while she knew Poe's work, Green modeled her story on works of the French novelist Emile Gaboriau, who published his first novel in France, in 1863. Gaboriau transformed his experiences as a court reporter into fiction, weaving technical data with family scandal and murder. As a lawyer's daughter, Green had her own firsthand knowledge to draw on, having grown up surrounded by talk of law, courts, and police. She developed a keen understanding of the legal system, and the accuracy of her descriptions of legal proceedings drew the critical scrutiny of a state legislator in Pennsylvania, who argued that the book could not possibly have been written by a woman.[45]

Green introduced several new elements into detective writing. *The Leavenworth Case* includes expert testimony, scientific analysis of clues, ballistics, medical reports, crime-scene schematics, reconstructed letters, and the first suspicious butler (in this case, he didn't do it). Much of what Green did can feel clichéd now, but *The Leavenworth Case* established the storylines, plot devices, and situations that later became commonplace in detective fiction. Green also gave detection a distinctly American flavor with her portrayal of a society demarcated by wealth rather than birth, scenes set in gritty urban neighborhoods, and courtrooms bound by American legal rules.[46]

As a novice author, Green was totally unknown, and yet *The Leavenworth Case* became a national sensation, selling a million copies over a decade, far more than any detective novel to date, and catapulting her to fame. Wilkie Collins was among the first to recognize Green's talent. "Her powers of invention are so remarkable—she has so much imagination and so much belief (a most important qualification for our art) in what she says," he remarked.[47] "Dozens of times in reading [*The Leavenworth Case*] I have stopped to admire the fertility of invention, the delicate treatment of incident—and the fine perception of event on the personages of the story." The publication of *The Leavenworth Case* in book form rather than as a serial, and by a reputable publisher (G. P. Putnam's Sons), also helped boost the standing of detective stories, which had largely been the province of dime novels and mass-market magazines. Setting her story in an aristocratic New York home captured the imagination and attention of Americans eager to read about the dark secrets of elite society.

The success of *The Leavenworth Case* marked the first of many professional and personal accomplishments for Green. Living at home upon finishing college, Green was financially independent. In 1884, at age thirty-eight, she married struggling actor and furniture designer Charles Rohlfs. It was a surprise for someone considered old enough to be a spinster, nor was the marriage a typical one for someone like Green. Rohlfs was eight years her junior and from a working-class German immigrant family. He was also tall and dynamic in contrast to the unassuming and quiet Green. The newlyweds moved upstate, to Buffalo, and had three children. But motherhood did not stop her working. Her husband even designed a writing chair for her, with a wide contoured right arm to better accommodate her notebooks. Though none of Green's subsequent novels ever equaled the success of *The Leavenworth Case*, she continued to write daily, her words providing her family's primary income for forty-five years. In 1891, Rohlfs even starred as the villain in a successful stage version of *The Leavenworth Case*.

Green won a wide and loyal readership among both women and men. Among her fans was Agatha Christie, who recalled her sister, Madge, reading *The Leavenworth Case* to her.[48] Fellow novelist Mary Roberts Rinehart and Presidents Theodore Roosevelt and Woodrow Wilson counted themselves admirers.[49]

By the end of her career, Green had mastered the art of sending her readers on a false path, eliciting surprise at the end with a convincing solution that readers had not considered. She wrote more than three dozen books, all crime, aside from one collection of poems and a play, this at a time when writers tended to explore a variety of genres. Her influence and reputation became so great that Arthur Conan Doyle wrote her a fan letter asking to visit her during his 1894 tour of the United States. Doyle was a relative newcomer to the literary world, compared to Green's well-established place in it.

Green created detectives with heroic morals rather than physical power: none carries a weapon or raises a fist against a suspect. But all have their quirks and foibles that made them relatable. The *New York Times* claimed that Green had turned the clue puzzle—a style with a clearly defined structure, using rational problem solving, and featuring upper-class victims and killers—"into a fine art" and transmitted it to a new century, where it became the characteristic form in detective novels of the 1920s and in those of Agatha Christie in particular.[50] By the end of the nineteenth century, Green would be known as the "Mother of Detective Fiction."[51]

Women not only wrote detective fiction but also figured as fictional detectives in their own right, and not by playing second fiddle to an eccentric in a deerstalker and cape.[52] Fictional female detectives first appeared on the page in the 1860s, decades before women joined municipal police departments. The advent of the female detective depended on social and economic changes that allowed people to conceive of a woman in this role, even if respectable society still deemed it improper for a woman to have an actual profession beyond that of governess, teacher, or nurse. Detection resembled other jobs that were emerging for women in the second half of the nineteenth century, particularly that of the reformer and social worker. Both roles focused attention on social issues outside of the home, particularly those related to women and children that threatened the civil and moral order. Reformers and social investigators hoped they could improve conditions in the home, even if the home in question was not their own, by raising awareness and prompting action.[53]

Fictional "lady detectives," as they were commonly known, were independent, confident women who used their knowledge of human behavior and domestic life and "female intuition" to solve crimes. Their capacity to go unnoticed or, more likely, to be underestimated, gave women a leg up in detection. At least twenty fictional female sleuths arose from the pens of nineteenth-century male and female authors. The bulk came initially from England, as the lady detective was slower to catch on in the United States.

Even in fiction, female characters couldn't just become detectives because they wanted to, though; they had to have a plausible reason.[54] Early female detectives turned to sleuthing out of financial necessity or to clear the name of a father, brother, husband, or other beloved male. To compensate for taking on a manly profession, female characters were often overendowed by their authors with womanly charms.

Younger female detectives tended to cease detecting once they solved their case or married. In many stories, the two often happened simultaneously with the sleuth marrying her nemesis, partner, or even the villain. Older spinsters or widows usually had longer detecting careers.

The same year that Metta Victor published her detective novel *The Dead Letter*, British writer Andrew Forrester introduced the first fictional female detective, Mrs. Gladden. *The Female Detective*, released in May of 1864, was ostensibly Gladden's casebook, a crime narrative of seven cases that Forrester claimed only to have edited, using "Gladden" as a pseudonym to protect the real detective's privacy. But the book is certainly fiction, and "Forrester" himself was a pseudonym for the novelist James Redding Ware. Gladden works as an operative for a detective branch of the London Metropolitan Police, though no woman would work for the real London force until 1883. Few believed that Gladden was a detective, though, even when she demanded to review evidence from other investigators. "His mind," she observes of a bumbling constable, "could not grasp the idea of a police officer in petticoats."[55] Gladden uses this to her advantage and tries to disguise her official position as much as possible to catch criminals. This spares her from having her abilities challenged on the basis of her gender, and it also gives her access to people and places she might not otherwise have, because, as a woman, and one past her marital prime, she's easy to overlook.[56]

Gladden organizes her cases logically. In her quest for evidence, she notices everything and misses no one, not even dim servants, and she uses her previous detecting experience as a guide to finding clues. Gladden admits that luck plays some part in solving cases, but she achieves nothing without careful preparation. Unlike Sherlock Holmes, she does not follow one strand of evidence to its conclusion but deliberates among several possibilities.

Forrester's stories put forth a strong argument for women's ability to serve as professional detectives at a time when male writers rarely bestowed any female characters with common sense, mental capacity, or physical agility. At the same time, Forrester provides Gladden little background or identifying characteristics to mark her behavior or appearance as distinctly female. It's a deliberate choice, so the focus is on her professional skills as a detective rather than her gender. "Who am I? It can matter little who I am," declares Gladden on the first page.[57] Her colleagues refer to her simply as "G." She is not married, though she declines to say whether she's a widow working to support a family or a spinster responsible only for herself. She justifies her work as an economic necessity but also a calling: "I had no other means of making a living; or it may be that for the work of detection I had a longing which I could not overcome."[58] Seeing herself as a detective first and foremost, Gladden believes she occupies a unique position to make a difference, particularly in the lives of women and children.[59] "Criminals are both masculine and feminine—indeed, my experience tells me that when a woman becomes a criminal she is far worse than the average of her male companions," she claims, "and therefore it follows that the necessary detectives should be of both sexes." It was a prescient point that proponents of women working as prison matrons and police officers would also argue.[60]

Gladden was not the only woman solving crimes for long. Only six months after the publication of *The Female Detective*, W. Stephens Hayward introduced Mrs. Paschal, "one of the much dreaded, but little-known people called Female Detectives," in *Revelations of a Lady Detective*, later reissued as *The Experiences of a Lady Detective*.[61] Like Gladden, Paschal also works for the London police, though it's made clear that, as a widow, she took the job for income. She claims to be one of several women employed in detective work in the department, solving cases of theft, murder, kidnapping, and forgery. She also rescues a young man from being fleeced by his beautiful mistress. She prides herself on observing and collecting clues that others have missed, in one case using forensic evidence, including bruised wrists and torn clothing, to conclude that a young woman in a morgue was the victim of murder rather than a suicide, as the police believed. In every case, Paschal requests information from the police, organizes the investigation, and receives a reward for its successful completion. Paschal's boss, Colonel Warner, the chief of the London Police Detectives, seems to trust her judgment and skill fully and without hesitation. After assigning her a serious case, Warner asserts, "I do not know a woman more fitted for the task than yourself."[62]

Few of Paschal's cases are as interesting as she is, though. A confident and smart woman in a man's world, she works hard at her craft. She learns to use a silver Colt revolver and becomes so comfortable handling it that she's reluctant to be without it. (Policewomen would not regularly carry arms until several decades into the twentieth century.) Paschal asserts her authority, unhesitatingly ordering around the plainclothes policemen she sometimes brings with her to bust a joint. She practices tailing suspects and moving unobserved through large homes. She's determined to succeed and considers herself unusually quick-witted and hardened for a woman. "I was usually fertile in expedients, and I thought I should be able to find my way out of the dilemma in some way," Paschal explains. "I was not a woman of one idea, and if one dart did not hit the mark I always had another feathered shaft ready for action in my well stocked quiver."[63] At one point in her first case, "The Mysterious Countess," she must drop through a hatch in pursuit of a villain (another woman), but her stiff crinoline won't fit. Rather than find a new route, Paschal abandons the "obnoxious garment" and continues to give chase. In another, she enters a convent disguised as a novitiate seeking spiritual advice from a nun suspected of misdeeds. When a young client compliments Paschal for her skill, her response demonstrates how seriously she is taking her job and her responsibility: "If I were not, I should be unfit for the position I hold and unworthy the confidence that Colonel Warner places in me."[64]

In "Which Is the Heir?" Paschal is sent to investigate the claims of a "gypsy" woman to the title and estate of young Lord Northend. The woman declares that she switched the late Lord Northend's baby with another more than twenty years earlier and raised the real Northend baby, known as Lambrook, as her own. The man now calling himself Lord Northend, she asserts, is an imposter, and she's hired a lawyer, Mr. Jacob Jarvis, to push her claim to the Northend fortune. Paschal, on learning of the case, declares it "as clear a case of extortion as I ever met with," but she knows she needs more than just a hunch to solve the case.[65] She first investigates Jarvis and discovers that his name has been struck from the list of qualified lawyers for some unknown breach of conduct. Paschal then follows the gypsy woman and her son, first onto the train where she pretends to be asleep while eavesdropping on their conversation, and then to a fair, where she discovers Lambrook performing a horrifying act with three live rats. Through her sleuthing, Paschal determines that Jarvis makes his living in connection with the various fairs and had convinced Lambrook and his mother to go along with his scheme against Lord Northend. When Paschal confronts Jarvis about Lord Northend at his office, he rebuffs her, asking her why this is any of her business. "Perhaps," Paschal replies in her typical offhand and careless manner, "I take an interest in enterprising people, or I may be in some way connected with the police." At the word "police," Jarvis nearly screams. "Do they employ women?" he asks, horrified. Paschal, ever cool, answers, "Sometimes, when they think it necessary to do so." Confident and unflappable was Paschal's way.[66]

Though divorce was becoming a possibility for middle-class couples in Britain at the time, igniting heated public debate about married women's lack of legal power and vulnerability to their husbands who controlled their property, including custody of any children, the lives of most women in 1864 certainly did not suggest the creation of characters like Gladden and Paschal: fictional detectives unburdened with domestic responsibilities and given somewhat free reign in a male profession. Neither Forrester nor Hayward explores on the page the ramifications of their characters' untraditional behavior and career choice, nor did they comment publicly on their decision to create such a character. Paschal occasionally acknowledges that stereotyped expectations of women give her an advantage in solving cases, but she's uninterested in dwelling on her personal life. The thrill of crime busting is her chief passion in life. Despite some characters' surprise at encountering a lady detective, on the whole, both books make little reference to sex inhibiting either their investigation or the capture of criminals. Even without comment from the authors, though, both Paschal and Gladden signaled something new: the woman who makes a profession of cracking cases that confound men.[67]

Hayward and Forrester may have been trying to grab readers with a new and exciting angle on crime. Hayward's book was originally published with a racy cover: a well-dressed woman smoking and lifting up her skirts to show her ankles. It was an image of Paschal far more salacious than the detective described in its pages, and one clearly intended to tempt readers. Paschal's story may not have been about sex, but it did present a woman living far outside the norm.

Conditions were changing for women. The formative years of detective writing coincided with the development of the women's suffrage movement and women's advancement into public life. Elizabeth Blackwell became the first female doctor shortly after Poe invented the modern detective form. In 1869, three years after Victor's *The Dead Letter* was published, Arabella Mansfield began practicing law in Iowa. Anna Katherine Green published *The Leavenworth Case* in 1878, the same year that a national woman's suffrage amendment was introduced to Congress. And just as Americans read their first Sher-lock Holmes stories in the newspaper in 1887, the women's rights movement gained new momentum as activism, reform work, and volunteerism soared among middle-class white women.[68] By the late nineteenth century, female sleuths of varying types had become, if not common, then more numerous, but only on the page.

CHAPTER THREE

Sisterhood Behind Bars

OLD SAL WAS A HANDFUL. ARRESTED THREE OR FOUR TIMES A YEAR, SHE usually required several policemen to wrestle her into a cell. Few escaped the challenge without suffering bruises and scratches.

Prison reformer Susan Barney had seen women like Sal before. In her travels across the country as the national superintendent of Prison, Jail, Police, and Almshouse Work for the Woman's Christian Temperance Union, Barney had seen female inmates starving, filthy, racked with illness, and packed into small rooms with a single bed. She and her fellow WCTU members thought that the appointment of police matrons and prison matrons could go a long way toward improving the situation for all female prisoners. After all, a woman's caring, empathetic disposition made her the natural caretaker of her sisters. "A pure woman there could have an influence which would mean vastly more than men realize," Barney said before the 1888 meeting of the International Council of Women.[1]

Barney made this same argument to the policemen holding Old Sal in Rhode Island. The officers were not convinced but agreed to let her prove her point on a particularly tough case—transporting the screaming and scratching woman from her cell to court—if only to humiliate Barney.

"We have got her here this morning, and we would like to see you bring her in," one officer said. "If you can do that we will not oppose you any more."

The police chief offered Barney the assistance of two men—it had taken four to wrestle Sal into the cell—but she refused. She strode past the officers to the cellblock holding the woman known as Old Sal. Barney knocked before opening the door. There, in the long dark cell, she found a woman crouched against the wall, "looking more like a wild beast than a human being." Old Sal, expecting the usual policemen, was surprised at the sight of Barney.

"Who are you?" she asked.

"I am your friend," replied Barney.

"No, you are not; I haven't got any friends," Old Sal said with bitterness in her voice. "I thought it was queer when somebody rapped at the door. I never had that done in all the times I have been here before."

Peering at Barney, she asked, "Who are you anyway; a policeman?"

"No," replied Barney. "I am a policewoman."

Old Sal's surprise at her answer was evident. Policing was itself a new profession and city forces only a few decades old. None had female officers on staff.

Barney reminded Old Sal of her court appearance but proclaimed her "not fit to go" in her current state of dishevelment. Barney brushed Old Sal's hair with her fingers and straightened her wrinkled clothing. The two women talked all the while.

Barney learned that Old Sal had first been arrested when she was not even sixteen. She was at least sixty years old now and had spent her life in and out of police stations across the city.

Old Sal recalled her first time in jail. "Ah, I was almost scared to death. I cried all night."

"If I had been there then and had wiped the tears off your face, if I had put your hair up and put my hand on your shoulders as I have now, what would it have meant to you?" asked Barney.

"Oh, I would never have got back again, but nobody ever cared," Old Sal said miserably.

The two continued to talk, about Old Sal's family, the death of her mother, and religion. Walking out of the cell, Barney took Old Sal's arm and the two walked quietly to the courtroom. The policemen "said they would have cheered us if it had been proper," Barney recounted later.

Few men, though, cheered the intrusion of women into law enforcement. Prisons, thought to be filled with the worst of humanity, were no place for respectable ladies. But reformers like Barney believed prisons and police stations were exactly where women like her needed to be. Reformers blamed men for seducing innocent women, and for the discrimination and abuse imprisoned women faced in the male-dominated prison system. Seeking to help their erring sisters, prison reformers argued that fallen women were not only worthy of rehabilitation but that women would prove superior to men in dealing with imprisoned women and preventing women's crime. This work in prisons became the springboard for women's move into policing and detection.

For decades, women had been investigating and reporting on the poor treatment of women in prison. Quaker Elizabeth Gurney Fry first visited the women locked in London's Newgate Prison in 1813 at the urging of Quaker missionary and family friend Stephen Grellet. He'd told her of the appalling disorder inside the city's prisons and asked for her help. Conditions inside Newgate shocked Fry. Only a few decades old, Newgate had replaced its six-hundred-year-old predecessor, which had burned down in 1780. The new prison was already overcrowded and dirty. Three hundred women packed two small wards. They slept on the floor without nightclothes or bedding. They washed, cooked, and slept in the same space. Many of the women were starved and half-dressed. The prison housed many children, too, who had nowhere else to go with their mothers imprisoned. The smell inside Newgate nearly overwhelmed Fry. She left horrified but also charged with a mission to alleviate the female inmates' miserable conditions.

This wasn't Fry's first visit to a prison. Born in 1780 to a wealthy Quaker family in Norwich, England, Fry began working to improve the welfare of the sick, poor, and imprisoned as a teenager after hearing the preaching of American Quaker William Savery. She collected clothes for the poor, visited the sick, and set up a Sunday school to teach children from local factories to read. As a teenager, Fry begged her father to take her to see the women locked in the town's House of Correction. "If this is the world, where is God?" Fry wrote after the visit, contrasting her own privileged life with that of others in her own community.[2]

At age twenty, she married Joseph Fry, a Quaker from a wealthy banking family. She kept working through marriage and motherhood, and by 1811, had become a Quaker minister, traveling long distances to speak. Despite these good works, though, Fry found that the demands of her family—she and her husband would eventually have eleven children—occupied more and more of her time. She worried that she had abandoned her duty to help the poor in favor of tending to her own growing family. Her visit to Newgate changed her.

Personal difficulties, including the birth of two more children and the death of a daughter, kept Fry away from Newgate for a few years, but she returned in 1816 ready to work. She enlisted the help of friends to form the Ladies Association for the Reformation of the Female Prisoners in Newgate. The group organized a school for the children of female inmates, offered Bible classes, and provided materials for the prisoners to sew and knit. She also set out rules that all the prisoners agreed to follow and help enforce, including the regular washing of their hands and faces before beginning work for the day. Crucially, Fry also appointed a matron to tend to the female inmates. News of what Fry had achieved at Newgate led to the formation of other organizations that visited female inmates in prisons around the country, and in 1818, she testified before a committee in the House of Commons on London prison conditions, the first woman ever to do so. Three years later, a national women's organization formed to improve Britain's prisons.[3] "When Elizabeth Fry . . . rapped at the prison doors in England, she not only summoned the turnkey, but sounded a call to women in other lands to enter upon a most Christlike mission," declared Susan Barney.[4]

Fry laid out her methods in an 1827 book that became a touchstone for American prison reformers. *Observations in Visiting, Superintendence, and Government of Female Prisoners* made the then unorthodox argument that fallen women could be reformed and described the principles for doing so. "My Quaker belief is that there is something of God in everyone, and that includes criminals. So the aim when we put someone in prison should be to try to reform them, not just to punish them," Fry wrote.[5] She supported the hiring of female officers and guards who would protect women from male sexual abuse, provide a sympathetic ear, and, most important of all, set an example of respectable womanhood. She called for women inmates to have clean water, sufficient food, and windows for both daylight and fresh air. Women had an obligation, argued Fry, to come to the aid of their fellow sisters in need. The call to sisterhood would prove a powerful motivation to female reformers on both sides of the Atlantic.[6]

Following in Fry's footsteps, Quaker and other white middle- and upper-class evangelical women began investigating American prisons in the 1820s and 1830s. Spurred by religious revivalism, which had popularized the idea of salvation through good works, women took to benevolence work to fulfill their task of moral guardianship beyond the home. Many reformers had grown up in families with progressive views and had attended all-female schools that shaped their sense of women's role as virtuous protectors of social values. The women drawn to prison reform resembled those drawn to abolition, temperance, and women's rights; indeed, some women participated in several reform movements. This sense of sisterhood and salvation reinforced by religion and education drove reformers to come to the aid of widowed, orphaned, homeless, or otherwise destitute women.[7]

Female prisoners in the United States tended to be young, between twenty and thirty at the time of first conviction. They also tended to be working class, immigrants, or black. Black female felons were overrepresented in the Northern prison population, despite being a proportionally smaller population than that of whites. This pattern did not take hold in the South until after the Civil War because slave owners rather than police meted out punishment.[8] Women's offenses tended to be petty street crimes, drunkenness, or prostitution, rarely those involving violence or murder. For activists, penal reform increasingly meant both improving conditions inside the prisons and using prisons to reform people rather than simply detain them. Aiding released women in their transition back to respectable society and discouraging recidivism became their primary goal.[9]

Women who stepped into public life came into conflict with a culture that defined them exclusively in relation to the home. The ideal nineteenth-century woman was to be pious, pure, submissive, and, most of all, domestic. A prison was considered far too dangerous and rough for a proper woman to visit, much less focus on working in one as a profession. But ideology and real life often clashed in a nineteenth-century culture that also valued social mobility, individual development, and hard work. A higher standard of living made possible by industrialization and increased educational opportunities left many educated middle- and upper-class women with increased leisure time to devote to charitable and reform work, particularly as anxiety about the urban poor became a national concern. By the late nineteenth century, efforts that had begun as volunteer work often transformed into more professional and paid social-service positions. Believing, like men, in the redeeming power of work, these reforming women pioneered new occupations and public roles for themselves that transformed their domestic role into one of service to the larger community.[10]

Nineteenth-century ideals of female purity and morality also condemned more women to prison. New categories of crime emerged, including sexual offenses that dealt with chastity or decency, which applied almost exclusively to women. Criminal women now faced the double condemnation of breaking both the law and their contract with cultural womanhood. As inherently moral beings, women who violated the supposed natural order fell beyond the reach of respectable society. "A Woman, when she commits a crime, acts more in contradiction to her whole moral organization, i.e., must be more depraved, must have sunk already deeper than a man," wrote philosopher and legal scholar Francis Lieber in 1833.[11] Impure women now threatened society and, worse, potentially encouraged men's criminality. Immorality required containment to be stopped. Where once a prostitute might have repented, accepted her punishment, and returned to society, now women received the label "fallen" and a social stigma that often prevented them from finding work and husbands. So with no other options, many went back to prostitution and entered an endless loop of incarceration.[12]

Another woman who answered Fry's call to arms was Dorothea Dix. In 1841, Dix volunteered to teach Sunday school classes to female convicts in the East Cambridge Jail, near Boston. There she found inmates shivering in an unheated, filthy room. A number of these women had committed only one crime: suffering from mental illness. When she asked administrators why the women had no stove to keep warm, Dix was told that lunatics could not feel cold and even if they could, the inmates would only set the building on fire. Aghast, Dix found her cause. Dix suffered frequent bouts of illness herself, including what some believe may have been severe depression, so she may have felt some affinity for people with limited means who are diagnosed as mentally ill but left to fend for themselves.[13] She surveyed every prison and jail in Massachusetts, and then expanded her survey outward, publishing her findings and conclusions in *Remarks on Prisons and Prison Discipline in the United States* (1845). Dix argued for the creation of separate women's prisons, especially in those institutions that employed no women to oversee female inmates, which was the case in more than half of the institutions she toured.[14]

In 1839, New York's Mount Pleasant Female Prison became the first of its kind in the United States. Located on a hill behind Sing Sing, the male penitentiary, and overlooking the Hudson River in Ossining,

Mount Pleasant had three tiers with twenty-four cells on each tier, all surrounded by a high wall. It was established for practical rather than progressive or compassionate reasons: the state had run out of room to hold its female inmates. Officials in the prison ward at New York City's Bellevue Hospital were so eager to relieve overcrowding that they transferred their female inmates to Sing Sing, where they were held in the men's cellblock until Mount Pleasant opened.

Discipline soon became a major problem at Mount Pleasant, due largely to overcrowding. During one riot, in 1843, it took several days to subdue knife-wielding inmates. A matron ran daily activities, but overall authority for Mount Pleasant lay with Sing Sing's all-male Board of Inspectors, who had little understanding or sympathy for female criminals. Mount Pleasant's matrons hoped to eliminate the exploitation of women within prison but the inmates continued to experience high levels of abuse from male guards.[15] Punishments were often severe and included straitjackets, extended bread-and-water diets, solitary confinement, and a "shower bath" that bombarded prisoners with water until they were close to drowning.[16]

While most of Mount Pleasant's matrons kept order through strict daily routines, matron Eliza Farnham took a different and bold path far ahead of her time. Hired in 1844, Farnham, along with her aide Georgina Bruce, believed she could rehabilitate rather than simply punish her charges by strengthening their moral character. Conditions at the prison had been tough before Farnham's arrival, particularly after several prisoners refused to follow the rules or perform their duties and began terrorizing their fellow prisoners. The previous matron, "a respectable, but incompetent person, had finally been attacked and the clothes torn from her body. The Board, on making a visit to the prison, had been met by shouts of derision and insolent defiance, and they had to make a hasty exit to escape the kids [wooden food tubs] flung at them by the rioters."[17] Anything the twenty-eight-year-old Farnham could do to reestablish control was likely welcomed.

A dedicated phrenologist, Farnham understood that criminal tendencies could be overcome. Phrenology posited that the brain consisted of multiple organs that each corresponded to various character traits, good and bad. By building up the more positive, moral character traits in the brains of her charges, Farnham believed phrenology could reform her charges. To this end, she introduced an educational program and personally instructed the women each morning. She stocked a library of improving literature that inmates could bring back to their cells and redecorated to counteract the grimness of the environment. She also invited musicians to perform, including the Hutchinson Family Singers, the most popular entertainers of the 1840s. "The exquisite beauty of the words with the touching character of the music, and more than all, the deep feeling manifest in the half-tremulous tones of the singers, seemed to conjure before each unfortunate creature a picture of domestic peace, holiness, and virtue," wrote Farnham after one such visit.[18] Farnham preferred kindness over punishment, but she could be a strict disciplinarian, including meting long periods of solitary confinement, cropping women's hair, and gagging inmates.[19]

Farnham's reforms proved too radical for her male managers, though. She had improved conditions so much that Mount Pleasant had become a much nicer place to be than Sing Sing, which created problems with the male prisoners.[20] Sing Sing's chaplain accused Farnham of excluding the Bible from the prison and of stocking her library with immoral and irreligious novels. Others argued that educating prisoners took time away from the work of making and washing clothes for male guards and inmates, which contributed to the prison's profits. Farnham fought back, calling the accusations against her "false" and "puerile," and she maintained that the "Bible is now and has been, during my connexion with the prison, a part of the furniture of every cell." Of the novels in the library, Farnham asserted that they had been circulated "with the sanction of the chaplain." The profits at Mount Pleasant were low, she retorted, because women earned less than men no matter what they did and where they worked, in prison or otherwise.[21] Farnham ultimately lost her battle, and she resigned in 1847. Her departure marked a return to the patterns of work, neglect, and severe discipline more typical of women's units. Conditions inside continued to deteriorate. By the 1870s, overcrowding forced authorities to close Mount Pleasant and transfer its inmates to a county penitentiary. Farnham's innovations, though shocking to her contemporaries, would become widely endorsed by penal reformers toward the end of the nineteenth century.[22]

Prison reform took on additional urgency when men in the newly formed Prison Association of New York raised alarms about female criminals. Visiting the city's penal institutions, these male reformers questioned whether anything could redeem women who broke society's moral boundaries—the prostitute, murderess, and thief. An 1845 report went so far as to suggest that female inmates be committed to a brothel to curb the "contamination of evil communication" between male and female inmates.[23] Even though male reformers were just as concerned about sexual abuse in prisons as women, their suggestion to send a fallen woman to a brothel, no matter how serious they were about the idea, reflected the popular belief that an immoral woman had no hope of redemption.[24]

Women reformers' experiences inside city prisons, as well as their faith in moral uplift, led them to a different conclusion. All the evidence they'd collected pointed to men as the culprits and women the victims. These reformers not only questioned living conditions inside prisons but also the underlying attitudes that forever condemned fallen women and created permanent obstacles to their reform. Criminal women, they insisted, were victims of a male-dominated system that contributed to their degradation by creating circumstances outside of women's control: poverty, poor heredity, or cruel men. "Our experience," declared New York City members of the Women's Prison Association, "has shown us conclusively that in nine cases out of ten, no choice was ever made for none was offered."[25] Society, they asserted, owed the fallen a better chance. Many reforming women had themselves chafed against the limitations placed on them by virtue of gender, so they were keenly alert to injustices against other women. "Every woman in misfortune or disgrace is the proper object of care to the happier and safer part of her sex," wrote reformer Caroline Kirkland. "Not to stretch forth to her the helping hand—not to labor for her restoration to respectability—not to defend her against wrong and shield her from temptation—is to consent to her degradation and, in some sense, be party to her ruin."[26] For reformers, a crime against a female prisoner had become a crime against all womankind.[27]

Novelists brought this more sympathetic view of criminal women to the wider public beginning in the 1860s. Stories by Elizabeth Stuart Phelps, Harriet Beecher Stowe, and Rebecca Harding Davis suggested that urban life drove women to crime. Some authors went so far as to blame men outright for women's lot. Davis's novel *Life in the Iron Mills*, for instance, countered the positive image, promulgated by factory owners, of healthy girls working in a mill with scenes that revealed the dehumanizing effects of industrialization and the sexual division of labor. Phelps's 1870 novel *Hedged In* explored the constraints on an unwed adolescent mother named Nixy Trent. Trent manages to overcome her past to become a teacher and an upstanding member of her community, demonstrating to readers that a fallen girl could not only recover but contribute positively to society. In many similar novels, women came to the rescue of their fictional fallen sisters, leading them to God and an honest living. It was a theme that played out in the era's crime fiction as well, with seemingly immoral women led astray by forces outside their control. By the 1890s, novelists of all kinds had fully embraced the theme that immoral women could achieve total uplift and redemption.[28]

Both male and female prison reformers called for facilities to be separated by sex, but female reformers took it even further in wanting to put women in charge of female prisoners. The appointment of prison matrons—usually funded by private organizations initially until cities could be convinced to include matrons in their budgets—became the major focus of the reformers' work, particularly in the second half of the nineteenth century.[29]

Women already worked in some prisons. In 1845, the American Female Society successfully petitioned for the appointment of six matrons in the New York City prison system, the first matrons in the United States. But reformers also wanted matrons in police stations, the first point of contact between prisoners and the justice system. The American Female Society had tried to extend the use of matrons to police work, but their efforts met with ridicule and fierce opposition from the police hierarchy. It was a story that would repeat throughout the century.[30]

The Woman's Christian Temperance Union spearheaded demands for matrons, as did the Federation of Women's Clubs, the National League of Women Voters, and other local women's clubs and associations. The most powerful women's group of the era, the WCTU was founded in 1874 to protest the negative effects of alcohol on families and communities. Behind the WCTU's temperance agenda was the idea of protecting the sanctity of the home. Recognizing the interconnectedness of social problems, WCTU president Frances Willard used the idea of women helping women, an increasingly popular reform message, to involve the organization in everything from suffrage to establishing kindergartens. But prison reform was the first non-temperance issue the WCTU took on. The group argued that men's intemperate drinking and related sexual indulgence led to the exploitation of women, whether in the home, brothel, or jail. Many WCTU members had personal contact with inmates through their charitable work, so they were well aware of the sometimes horrifying lives of female convicts and their struggles for justice.[31]

The WCTU's Susan Barney laid out the organization's strategy for securing matrons in the manner of a detective laying out a case: "Ascertain facts; number of women arrested during the previous years; accommodations provided, care furnished. Make a few unannounced visits to cells in Police Station and Police Court."[32] She urged public meetings with presentations by both men and women on the necessity of matrons to educate the public and garner newspaper coverage. "Last but not least," she continued, "start for success and continue until it is assured."

Women's groups around the country followed Barney's lead. The WCTU first wanted day matrons to see that detainees dressed properly for court, on the assumption that a well-dressed woman had a much better chance of appearing respectable and thus redeemable in the eyes of a judge. They later changed to advocating for twenty-four-hour-a-day matrons to care for female inmates in station houses. WCTU members in cities across the country visited female prisoners and attended court sessions. They pushed for matrons in every city facility and vowed to fight until they had achieved their goal.[33]

Portland, Maine, hired its first police matron in 1878. The city's local WCTU chapter funded a part-time prison visitor in 1877 after a female physician reported witnessing appalling conditions while tending sick inmates; the matron became a fully paid Portland employee the following year. In many cities during the early years of this practice, private organizations provided salaries for matrons. Providence, Rhode Island, followed Portland and became the first to institute twenty-four-hour-a-day matrons in that city's prisons and police stations.[34] In the 1880s, matrons were appointed in Jersey City, Chicago, Boston, Baltimore, St. Louis, Detroit, Denver, San Francisco, and Philadelphia. Most were hired over the objections of male police and prison officers. By 1890, WCTU efforts had resulted in the hiring of matrons in thirty-six cities.[35]

The ideal matron, according to Susan Barney, was a "middle-aged woman, scrupulously clean in person and dress, with a face to commend her and a manner to compel respect; quiet, calm, observant, with faith in God and hope for humanity."[36] Barney spent more than two decades advocating for matrons in cities such as New York, where in 1881 alone, twenty thousand women were detained in station jails, nearly a quarter for drunk and disorderly conduct, and all searched by male officers.[37] Reformers called for the appointment of matrons in each of the city's thirty-one precincts. Even after an 1888 law passed allowing for the appointment of two matrons to each station, the initiative remained unimplemented and unfunded. The *New York Times* noted that women suffered "real abuses" housed in cells opposite men and forced to give birth without other women present. The paper favored the appointment of matrons but not for the protection of women as reformers insisted. Instead, they feared for the men, harkening back to the still common view of the irredeemable woman. "The effect upon comparatively innocent men and boys is not to be ignored, and these are often exposed to [the] corrupting manners" of the women in their midst.[38]

Although the job varied, the core duty of matrons was to shelter and protect endangered or law-breaking women and children in custody. Most matrons searched female suspects; processed, escorted, and supervised women in detention facilities; and cared for lost children. One New Hampshire matron called her courtroom visits "one of the most humiliating things connected with the work," but she believed her presence was essential for women to receive a fair trial.[39] Another reformer reported that a judge urged her to leave the courtroom when she went to observe a young girl's trial. She refused, and after the hearing, the judge admitted that he had been more careful on account of her presence. "Didn't you ask all the questions that were necessary?" she asked. "Yes," said the judge, "but if you had not been here, we might have got a little fun of the lady." That "fun" usually meant humiliating a woman alone in a courtroom of men. Reformers feared just this behavior and sought to protect the dignity of women in police and judicial hands.

Matrons did other work as well. Anytime a police department had a job they thought needed a woman, matrons were enlisted; if one wasn't available, policemen often asked their wives or girlfriends to step in. Some matrons took on detective functions, gathering evidence against fortune-tellers or going undercover disguised as a female domestic.

In 1881, the WCTU received permission to hire a matron for Chicago's Harrison Street police station. Sarah J. Littell worked under the authority of the Chicago police, but her job was organized and paid for by the WCTU. The following year the city council voted to appoint four additional matrons, paid for out of the police budget, to watch over female inmates. By 1895, under the supervision of a Miss Waller, a "gentlewoman of marked executive ability, with a deep sympathy for unfortunate humanity," the number of matrons had risen to thirty. The qualifications for matrons grew more rigorous as their numbers and law-enforcement responsibilities expanded. A physical exam required matrons to be in "excellent health and very muscular," the latter quality likely hard to find in a culture that discouraged women from physical activity. A widowed or older married woman with "irreproachable character" and in possession of "more than ordinary mental traits" was preferred. She must have a full experience of the world, "without having become hardened by her contacts with it." Littell spent nearly twenty-five years as a matron, overseeing many notable prisoners, including anarchist Emma Goldman, famous shoplifter Lena Kleinschmidt, and murderer Mollie Mott.[40]

Mott was a particularly notorious member of the bunch, her life resembling a plotline usually found in dime novels. The leader of several gangs of outlaws, Mott had been tried for innumerable crimes and served two terms in prison. She made a lasting name for herself during an 1887 street duel with the Chicago police at Twenty-Second and Wentworth, where she loaded revolvers while her accomplice, Dyer Scanlan, fired at the police attempting an arrest.[41] Mott had also trained other female criminals, including Kittie Adams, who became an expert pickpocket and shoplifter. Mott married at least six times, and her husbands often died while committing a crime or in battle with the police. She was undeterred by her continued arrests, the *Chicago Tribune* asserting, "Her picture is said to be in every rogues' gallery in the country." Mott was likely a familiar face to the Chicago matrons.[42]

In 1904, when New York City police planned to raid a poolroom frequented by women that fronted illegal gambling, Sergeant Fitzpatrick enlisted the help of Mary Quinn, a matron at the West Sixty-Eighth Street Station.[43] The male detectives hid in doorways adjacent to the poolroom as Quinn waited for another woman to follow her into the place. One of the men grew impatient and called out, "How about it? Aren't you going in?" Quinn snapped back, "If I'm running this raid, I'll run it my own way, so don't you butt in!" She finally made her way inside, following on the heels of a woman who seemed familiar with the place. There, Quinn found eight or nine women clapping their hands nervously while one cried, "They're off! They're off!" When Quinn inquired what was "off," one woman answered, "Why, you must be awful green. The horses are off!" That was all the confession Quinn needed, and she declared them all under arrest.

In 1910, New York City's deputy police commissioner recruited matrons Maude Leslie and Isabella Morrison to collect evidence on thirty suspected palm readers and fortune-tellers.[44] This wasn't Leslie and Morrison's first investigation. Their undercover work had helped convict several fortune-tellers two years earlier, while driving others out of business. But fraudulent fortune-tellers didn't stay away for long, and as some started creeping back into the city, the matrons were sent back out on the case. During investigations, Leslie and Morrison usually pretended to be clerks running errands for jewelers. One palmist "madame" protested her arrest not on the grounds of unfairness but for the time of day it occurred. "You might have called later for that," she cried. "It is an outrage to disturb me at this ungodly hour. I have an engagement at a Broadway restaurant for dinner and I simply won't let you interfere with it." The female sleuths pressed the case, and the charlatan finally consented to follow them to night court instead of the dinner table. Leslie and Morrison's detecting resulted in sixteen additional arrests.

In another case, in 1915, Brooklyn police matron Marin Young disguised herself as a high school girl to catch a thief within Curtis High School on Staten Island.[45] Students had been reporting the loss of clothing and money for nearly a year. Suspicion had fallen on the janitor, a scrubwoman, as well as on some of the teachers, but there were no leads or solid evidence to crack the case—until Young arrived at the school. Young planted a bag with two marked one-dollar bills in the girls' locker room. Then she took her seat in the back of the classroom where she could see all the students. When student Bessie Armstrong got up and left the room, Young followed her into the locker room and caught her stealing the bag. The male detectives on hand arrested Armstrong; Young brought some of her classmates to Armstrong's home. There they found a "mass of clothing and school materials." Several sweaters were stuffed up the chimney in the parlor, while "among the other articles were twenty-eight pairs of gloves, fifteen fountain pens, and an assortment of hats, raincoats, jackets, winter coats, bloomers, books, and countless other things." Quinn's and Young's successes helped bolster the case for women's employment in law enforcement.

Even without contending with professional criminals like Mott and the others, matrons had incredibly difficult jobs. They lived within the prison walls and worked long hours for low wages. In New York City, matrons worked in ten-hour day shifts or fourteen-hour night shifts. They also had to climb stairs dozens of times a day. Matrons rarely had their own support staff, depending instead on the services of the chaplain and physician, who also served the male inmates and were sometimes reluctant to visit the women, often housed in another building or room. Most matrons did not object openly, knowing that complaints about the difficulty of the work would only confirm what many men already believed: the job was unsuitable for women.[46]

Resistance to matrons and separate women's prisons was fierce. Men questioned whether women could manage their own institutions and exercise complete control over inmates. Women were generally seen as incapable of controlling anyone, let alone unruly or vicious criminals. The work was also considered unfeminine and its practitioners subject to moral degradation through their exposure to debased women.[47] Less explicitly expressed, women's institutions and female law enforcers threatened masculinity and male dominance in society. Burnham Wardwell of the Massachusetts Prison Commission argued that a prison without male officers was like a home without a husband. Public attitudes toward and understanding of gender contended that women who transgressed into masculine domains forced men into more feminine positions.[48] It was as though law enforcement—and society, by extension—had some unspoken balance between masculinity and femininity that women's presence in the stationhouse threw off.

Those cities that appointed matrons generally considered the experiment a success.[49] The rare failure was chalked up to appointment of the wrong woman to the post, often for political reasons. To ensure success, women's organizations often suggested worthy candidates to mayors. In 1888, Massachusetts passed a law requiring the appointment of matrons in cities with populations of more than twenty thousand. The state legislature included a clause that put the hiring decision in the hands of a committee of women.[50]

By the late nineteenth century, police departments had begun to shed many of their general-purpose activities, like housing the homeless and returning runaway animals, to focus primarily on crime. Women's success advocating for matrons in prisons and police stations convinced many reformers that women had a larger and more vital role to play in law enforcement: as policewomen investigating and even preventing crimes against women.[51]

CHAPTER FOUR

Spinster Sleuth

"**I** AM NOT AN INQUISITIVE WOMAN," AMELIA BUTTERWORTH DECLARES IN *That Affair Next Door*.[1] But when she hears a carriage pull up outside at midnight, she rushes from her bed to have a look. Outside, she sees a man and woman enter the neighboring Van Burnam mansion, laughing. Butterworth goes back to bed, but the sound of the door opening rouses her to the window once more. Although she has "to rush for it," she catches a glimpse of the man leaving. The woman is nowhere to be seen. Not being inquisitive, Butterworth claims that she "misses much that would be both interesting and profitable to know." But it's clear early in her story that she does not miss much.

Curious about the fate of the woman, Butterworth summons a policeman early the next morning. He's reluctant to listen to her story but finally accedes to her request to look in the house. He and Butterworth, along with the family's scrubwoman, discover the body of Louise Van Burnam, crushed beneath a cabinet. The sight of the dead woman upsets Butterworth, but she determines that she can't lose her wits "in the presence of a man who had none too many of his own." She remains steadfast, knowing she must maintain her composure to command respect as a woman.

Anna Katharine Green's Amelia Butterworth was no ordinary woman. Fiftyish, upper middle class, and respectable, she's "anxious . . . to be of help where help is needed." She asks question after question, and is "destined to prove a thorn in the sides of everyone connected" with the murder. The arrival of Inspector Ebenezer Gryce, the detective first introduced in Green's best-selling *The Leavenworth Case*, brings out Butterworth's competitive spirit. She's not deterred by the "half-admiring, half-sarcastic" tone he takes in addressing her. What strikes her most about the "portly and easy-going" detective is his age, "75 if he was a day," she remarks. Feeling as capable as he, Butterworth charmingly asserts, "Though I have had no adventures, I feel capable of them." It's not hard to believe her.

Inspector Gryce humors Butterworth at first, but her perseverance and refusal to be excluded from the murder investigation takes him aback: "This aged detective is used to women, I have no doubt, but he is not used *to me*," she thinks. He's even more appalled at her suggestion that the two collaborate: "What to me seemed but the natural proposition of an energetic woman with a special genius for his particular calling, evidently struck him as audacity of the grossest kind."

Butterworth recognizes the male sense of pride her presence threatens. When she shares her observations about the victim's hat and clothing, Gryce is not unimpressed, hailing her "women's eyes for women's matters." He does not, however, think she may be helpful for anything other than clothing and family. Even as she recognizes male ego, Butterworth can't help but be incensed by it. After failing to receive credit for her contributions to the investigation at the inquest, she reflects, "Men are so jealous of any interference in their affairs." She considers abandoning the trail, but when the police arrest the younger son, Howard Van Burnam, for murder, Butterworth decides she cannot sit by and let a man she's sure is innocent stand accused. She explains her reasoning to Gryce, who disregards her logic even though their methods are not that different. Both use deductive and inductive reasoning and act on intuition. They differ more in experience than in method. Butterworth has more knowledge of women and the wealthy, while the working-class Gryce, despite his experience with people of all classes, remains ill at ease with the elite. Rather than be discouraged, Butterworth takes his dismissive attitude as a challenge and declares that she will take on the investigation not as his "coadjutator, but as your rival."

Butterworth exercises all her cunning in dealing with the police and in locating evidence she believes they have overlooked. Rather than relying on others for clues or to supply missing information, Butterworth takes direct action, and proves her mettle in dealing with women, in particular. She matches women to the clothing they likely wore. She finds and befriends Ruth Oliver, a second woman seen at the house prior to the murder, and she chats up the scrubwoman she feels has withheld important insights. With her maid, Lena, Butterworth retraces the path she believes the murderer took at midnight, a course of action few respectable women would attempt. All of Butterworth's actions underscore her declaration that she is "spare in figure and much more active in my movements than one would suppose from my age and dignified deportment."

Butterworth is adamant that she can solve the case without relying on men. "The work upon which I was engaged could not be shared by one of the male sex without lessening my triumph over Gryce," she asserts. Butterworth expects to arrive at a solution before Gryce and is confident that her success will force him to admit her talents. For a while, both Butterworth and Gryce believe that Howard Van Burnam is innocent but have identified different murderers: Butterworth believes it is Ruth Oliver and Gryce, Howard's brother, Franklin Van Burnam. Their efforts stall when they compare notes. Although Butterworth's theory proves as incorrect as Gryce's, her sleuthing still manages to show him up by bringing attention to Oliver's role in the case. "I admired him and I was sorry for him," Butterworth admits, "but I never enjoyed myself so much in my whole life." It's only when the two put their heads together and set a trap that they make the deductions that clear the brothers Van Burnam and lead to Oliver's reveal. Louise Van Burnam was the victim of mistaken identity on the part of Oliver's husband, John Randolph, who had intended to kill Oliver so he could marry another woman.[2]

In her second outing, *Lost Man's Lane* (1898), Butterworth encounters a psychopathic murderer in a setting straight from a Gothic novel of an earlier century. She also discovers rattling doors, footsteps in empty rooms, screams in the night, and a phantom coach. This time Gryce stays in the background, ensuring Butterworth's safety but letting her lead the investigation.[3]

In Green's final story, *The Circular Study*, published in 1900, Gryce and Butterworth form a true partnership, with their shared efforts bringing about the solution to the puzzle. Even with her relatively short career, Green's sleuth broke stereotypical boundaries for women and created the model for the intelligent spinster detective, still active to this day.

Butterworth was hardly the only spinster around, on or off the page. The generations of women born between 1865 and 1895 had the highest proportion of single women in Western history. More than six hundred thousand young men died in the Civil War, America's bloodiest conflict.[4] The abundance of spinsters in the late nineteenth century challenged conventional beliefs about women's matrimonial trajectory. Society generally approved of women beyond marriageable age having careers, a necessary accommodation to their need to earn money. Unmarried women were not considered spinsters until they reached the age that they would likely remain unmarried. The exact age at which women crossed from hopeful to hopeless remained free floating, varying by person and community, however.[5]

Spinsterhood didn't always have such a negative connotation. The word was originally an honorable term, meant for any woman who spun yarn: a woman was not considered ready for marriage until she had spun a complete set of linens. But by the seventeenth century, the word had narrowed to mean any unmarried woman, and picked up a parcel of negative associations on its way to the nineteenth-century idealization of marriage and motherhood. Spinning cloth became work pushed off on single women as a way to earn their keep rather than a skill proving their fitness for matrimony. Marriage organized society and women's lives in particular, dominating all other forms of commitment and all other relationships. Since women had no place outside the home, single women threatened men and their place in society. They became "redundant," having failed in the main business of women's life. A woman who rejected marriage, voluntarily or otherwise, was marked as an outlier, flawed in some way that repelled suitors, harmed the social order, and left her without a social identity.[6]

There were good reasons—if not socially acceptable ones—for women not to marry. Legal rights greatly favored the unmarried woman, as women subsumed their rights to their husbands at the altar. Married women could not own or inherit property. They often couldn't run a business in their own home. And they certainly couldn't easily sue for divorce. And, of course, for some women the choice was driven by their own sexual preferences and rejection of the idea of being tied to a man. The emotional and psychological pressure to marry exerted on women likely reflected a cultural anxiety that women would recognize their raw deal and choose not to marry.[7]

And some women did make that choice. In the late nineteenth century, some single women with respectable ways of earning money came to regard marriage as unnecessary for self-respect or financial stability. They didn't oppose marriage as an institution, as some more radical reformers did, but set certain standards for suitors to meet to gain their hand. They called themselves "bachelor maids." "A great many bachelor maids are not living alone because they so choose, but have been unable to find a suitable companion," declared Helen Gould, a self-proclaimed bachelor maid.[8] Women like Gould formed bachelor maids' clubs, first in New York and Washington, DC, and then in other cities and towns around the country. Sixty women, "banded together by an 'all-for-one-and-one-for-all' compact that would make the Musketeers themselves pale with envy," formed the inaugural membership of the New York Bachelor Girls' Club.[9] The women first considered calling themselves "The Old Maids' Club," but the bad feelings associated with spinsters—defined by "corkscrew curls and a tabby cat," proclaimed one member—led them to embrace the concept of bachelorhood instead.[10] The growing number of these young single women led the *Washington Herald* to publish a popular advice column in 1907 called "Bachelor Girl Chat"; similar columns soon found homes in the women's pages of newspapers across the country.[11]

It wasn't just young women who embraced bachelorhood. In the late nineteenth and early twentieth centuries, some of the most visible and influential women in the United States were unmarried: Susan B. Anthony, leader of the suffrage movement; Frances Willard, president of the WCTU; and Jane Addams of Chicago's Hull House. Reformers and progressives often cast these independent women as the vanguard of women's struggle for equality, but not everyone thought that way.[12]

Spinsterhood preoccupied cultural critics throughout the second half of the nineteenth century, becoming a dire economic and moral peril in the 1890s. The topic resurfaced again in the 1920s with the demographic imbalance created by World War I, particularly in Europe. Speculation on the future prospects of all these superfluous women became a national pastime among politicians, cultural commentators, and novelists.

Although the increasing number of unmarried women elicited alarm, the spinster was nonetheless a familiar cultural figure, from the Old Maid of the Victorian card game to Jane Austen's Miss Bates in *Emma* and the embittered Miss Havisham of Charles Dickens's *Great Expectations*. While unmarried women certainly had existed in literature before the nineteenth century, the growing numbers of them during this period burnished popular perceptions of spinsters as socially flawed. In the United States and Britain, the never-married woman was a stock character hauling all manner of negative baggage. Spinsters were narrow-minded gossips and busybodies, or amusing, pathetic, even evil. The scrubwoman at the Van Burnam house mutters that Amelia Butterworth is a "meddlesome old maid" when she forces her way into the house with the police officer to investigate the fate of the woman she saw the night before. Even if single women mustered all the cheerfulness they could, they occupied a difficult position—unmarried and childless in a society that expected all women to be fully engaged in marriage and motherhood. Deemed physically repulsive, spinsters drew revulsion from men, mirth from women, and fear from children if they drew any reaction at all. They certainly were not anyone's idea of a heroine.[13]

And yet it was these same traits that made them good detectives, at least in fiction. A grandmotherly woman cut such an unassuming and nonthreatening figure that she could move through society relatively unnoticed; that she also tended to favor old-fashioned clothing also contributed to her invisibility. Crime writers created spinsters who solved cases by observing details and human reactions, mostly sedentary activities suitable for an elderly woman. The woman people barely notice can get away with detecting unnoticed. And many fictional elderly spinsters use preconceptions about older women to their advantage, coaxing valuable information from witnesses and suspects behind a masquerade of feeblemindedness.[14]

The character of Amelia Butterworth is well aware of the perceptions of her type, noting that "much is forgiven of a woman of my stamp." Her reasons for detecting are mixed. She believes in justice and in protecting the innocent, particularly other women mistreated by men. She also believes she's a better detective than Ebenezer Gryce, Green's series detective called in to investigate the murder of Louise Van Burnam in *That Affair Next Door*. But Butterworth is no feminist (and not just because that term was far from common in her day). She's proudly old fashioned and dignified, and finds most young women shallow and uninteresting.

Spinster characters also freed their creators from having to develop the love interest that dominated most stories with young female protagonists. A spinster's life is uncluttered by domestic relationships and the suspicion of a romantic motivation for her investigative work.

Butterworth mentions that her duties at home press on her but not so much that she feels any need to abandon the investigation. "I was astonished to find how much I was enjoying myself, notwithstanding the thousand and one duties awaiting me," she thinks. In this way, spinsters appeared similar to many of the great male detectives who tended toward the asexual, such as Sherlock Holmes. The spinster detective's achievements, like many male detectives, were based not on romantic success but on mental acuity.[15]

The relationship between Gryce and Butterworth was not uncommon in detective fiction of the day. The spinster's counterpart was often an eccentric but wise middle-aged or elderly male detective. This was, in part, because the most successful fictional female detectives were amateurs. Detection as a hobby appeared less threatening and irreconcilable with contemporary views of femininity. So, many spinsters had some kind of male policeman in the wings to push their cases forward: Stuart Palmer's Hildegarde Withers has Inspector Oscar Piper, Patricia Wentworth's Miss Maud Silver has Detective Frank Abbott, and Agatha Christie's Miss Marple has chief constable Colonel Melchett, among others. This relationship often begins badly, as the male officer is usually unconvinced that this middle-aged or elderly woman can be anything more than a hindrance to his pursuit of justice. But, eventually, he is persuaded by her razor-sharp intuition and observations.[16]

Butterworth's self-confidence stems from her father's faith in her intelligence and ability. Where society placed its hopes in its sons, Butterworth's father evidently believed his daughter would live up to her mark. Solving the mystery next door makes Butterworth realize that he was right, as she notes that the case "had aroused in me a fever of investigation which no reasoning could allay." Butterworth begins jotting down notes concerning the case on the back of a grocery bill. The headings for her evidence—"Accident," "Suicide," and "Murder"—demonstrate her shrewd reasoning powers as she evaluates evidence to determine the most likely cause of death.[17] Butterworth also believes that her decision to change her name at a young age from "Araminta" to "Amelia," announced early in the novel, confirms her status as a "sensible woman and not the piece of antiquated sentimentality" that her given name suggests. Changing her name also shows Butterworth's determination to forge her own identity.

The emergence of the fictional spinster-sleuth suggested one use for the large number of so-called redundant women. The image of the spinster as lonely, frustrated, and unneeded is exposed and undone on the page in sleuths like Butterworth and the range of fictional women that proliferated after her in the early twentieth century. Detection gave women mobility and provided an acceptable outlet for probing into people's lives. Through sleuthing, the spinster turned gossip into an art and snooping into a useful science.[18]

Traces of Amelia Butterworth can be found in the stories of the spunky spinster and curious old lady characters that became common between the world wars, in the so-called Golden Age when detective fiction flourished and readers sought to forget the horrors of World War I through immersion in the reliable world of detection where good always prevails. The Golden Age writers, scarred by the war themselves, wrote not to stir things up but to heal with the cerebral satisfaction of an elegant solution to a puzzle. Theirs were the stories often referred to as "cozy" for their familiar domestic settings and comforting storylines that always restored the social order. Perhaps the most distinctive feature of the period, though, is that some of its most celebrated and longest-lasting authors were women.[19]

The most famous was Agatha Christie. Her spinster sleuth, Miss Jane Marple, shared the same insatiable curiosity that animated Butterworth. Christie recalled reading Green's stories as a young woman and even included a tribute to her in the novel *The Clocks*, featuring her professional sleuth, Hercule Poirot. Green and Christie shared more than just elderly women characters. Both often set their mysteries in a domestic or other enclosed space, revealing the secrets of the home and its occupants through clue puzzles.[20]

Miss Marple appeared in several short stories before her arrival in 1930 in the full-length novel *The Murder at the Vicarage* in which she solved the mystery behind the death of Colonel Protheroe.[21] A resident of the English village of St. Mary Mead, Miss Marple has all the hobbies one would expect of a woman of her ilk—she knits, gardens, and bird-watches. The first glimpse of her comes when the vicar's wife tells her husband that she's invited that "terrible Miss Marple" for tea with some other ladies from town. "She's the worst cat in the village," she explains to her husband. "She always knows every single thing that happens—and draws the worst inferences from it." Although the vicar's wife soon comes to appreciate Miss Marple, everything she says about her is true. Miss Marple knows everything about everyone and collects new information and observations as she bird-watches or works in her garden. She has no rival in the art of seeing without being seen. By sketching the stereotypical old maid, Christie created an unexpected detective who deceives everyone, even the criminals, by her stereotypically innocent appearance.

Like Butterworth, Miss Marple is also intelligent and inquisitive, paying attention to details of human behavior, what others might call gossip, that allow her to solve crimes. She defends her snooping as a product of living alone in a small town. "One has to have a hobby," explains Marple. "There is, of course, woolwork, and Guides, and Welfare, and sketching, but my hobby is—and always has been—Human Nature. So varied—and so fascinating. And, of course, in a small village, with nothing to distract one, one has such ample opportunity for becoming what I might call proficient in one's study." The vicar himself remarks that there "is no detective in England equal to a spinster lady of uncertain age with plenty of time on her hands." Unlike Butterworth, though, Marple is not fully economically independent, relying on her nephew, Raymond, for extras. Modeled on Christie's grandmother, Marple appeared in novels and stories into the 1970s.[22]

Christie was born September 15, 1890, in Torquay, in southwest England. She had little formal education and mostly taught herself out of books. After her father's death, when she was eleven, Christie's mother struggled to support the family. In 1912, she met Archie Christie, a member of the Royal Flying Corps, and the two married in 1914. Christie had never given much thought to a career and began writing detective stories during World War I, partly to relieve the monotony of working in a makeshift hospital dispensary in Torquay. Her expertise in poisons, gained from her wartime job, was put to good use in her novels. Her first detective novel, *The Mysterious Affair at Styles*, published in 1920, featured a murder by strychnine.

Christie began to churn out books and win good reviews, but her personal life took a turn in the 1920s. The death of her mother plunged her into sorrow and strained her relationship with Archie. The marriage broke down when Archie fell in love with another woman. Christie tried to convince him to change his mind, and one day, in December 1926, she got in her car and drove away from Archie and their daughter, Rosalind.

When her car was found abandoned the next day, the press speculated wildly on her whereabouts. Christie was found ten days later at the Harrogate Spa Hotel listed under the name Theresa Neale

(Archie's mistress was Nancy Neale). Archie identified Agatha as his wife, but she claimed not to recognize him. An extremely shy and private person, Christie never spoke of this time in her life, nor did she include an accounting of it in her autobiography. Christie and Archie divorced in 1928. By then, she was already a popular writer, but her mysterious disappearance, bearing hallmarks of detective fiction, made her a celebrity.

Christie continued to write detective novels, averaging one a year. She also remarried. One year after her divorce, she met archaeologist Max Mallowan on a trip to the Middle East. Christie and Mallowan made annual trips to his digs in Iraq and Syria, where she tended to write in the mornings and help on site in the afternoons. Her experiences in the Middle East informed many of her stories, including *Appointment with Death, Death on the Nile*, and *Murder in Mesopotamia*. Miss Marple was originally planned as the detective for *Death on the Nile*, according to Christie's notes, but the resulting case became Poirot's to solve. Marple did enjoy long-distance travel, like Christie herself, in *A Caribbean Mystery*.[23]

Unmarried older women appear in almost all of Christie's books in one guise or another. There is nothing pathetic or scorned about her spinsters. Most are clever and show themselves to be individuals with worthy lives and life experiences. Miss Marple, for instance, solves murder "by virtue of the arcane knowledge only ladies of her age and station still have."[24] Christie's other women share similar traits with Marple. Lavinia Fullerton, the spinster in *Easy to Kill* (titled *Murder Is Easy* in the United Kingdom), has identified a murderer on the loose in her village and goes to Scotland Yard to share her evidence, utterly convinced, like Marple, that she knows more than the local police. Caroline Sheppard, the doctor's sister in *The Murder of Roger Ackroyd*, is nosy but lovable and funny. Hercule Poirot's friend and occasional sidekick Ariadne Oliver is a feisty and successful detective writer who Christie admitted had a "strong dash" of herself in her.[25] She's called "Mrs. Oliver," but a "Mr. Oliver" doesn't seem to exist, and she gives every indication of living alone. She calls Poirot for help whenever she becomes involved in a crime, proposing dozens of possible solutions with her vigorous imagination. While she never has a rational cause for her suspicions, her comments and observations often lead Poirot to the answer. Her frustration with the limitations placed on strong women like herself lead to her repeated complaint, "Now if a *woman* were Head of Scotland Yard . . ."[26]

Not all old women in Christie are good, though. Lavinia Fullerton's friend Honoria Waynflete in *Easy to Kill* appears similar to Miss Marple but commits seven murders before she's finally apprehended. The stereotypes surrounding spinsters shield Waynflete from suspicion. She's so good that the only person who suspects her of murder is another older woman.[27]

Spinsters detect in the novels of Dorothy Sayers as well. Miss Katherine Climpson runs a typing agency known as the "Cattery," set up by Sayers's primary detective, Lord Peter Wimsey. "All the employees were women—mostly elderly . . . and of the class unkindly known as 'superfluous,'" writes Sayers in *Strong Poison* (1930).[28] Wimsey laments that the energy of elderly women goes so often to waste. "Thousands of useful maids, simply bursting with useful energy, forced by our stupid social system into hydros and hotels and communities and posts as companions, where their magnificent gossip powers and units of inquisitiveness are allowed to dissipate themselves or even become harmful to the community," he explains to Detective-Inspector Parker.[29] Climpson oversees "widows without family" and "women deserted by peripatetic husbands and living on restricted alimony"; in other words, women without domestic responsibilities.[30] The agency is merely a cover, though, for the elderly spinster to investigate suspicious characters, particularly women, for Wimsey. Climpson is quick-witted and is distinguished by her "clear head and retentive memory," as well as her talent for disguise. She's able to "ask questions which a young man could not put without a blush." Wimsey lauds her reasoning powers rather than the more patronizing "women's intuition." She's not completely free of gendered stereotypes, however. Climpson's skilled at reading people and social situations, a skill that Wimsey claims is more common in women, who have learned to negotiate the minefield of personal relationships. When she arrives at the scene of a crime, Wimsey asserts, "Of course she asks questions—everyone expects it. Nobody is surprised. Nobody is alarmed."[31] It's work that Climpson enjoys and is good at.

So good that in *Strong Poison* Climpson helps save another woman, a young detective writer named Harriet Vane, from an accusation of murdering Vane's former lover, Philip Boyes. Vane lives with a man she isn't married to and supports herself through her writing, both far from ordinary occupations for young women of 1930. Boyes convinces Vane that he is philosophically opposed to marriage, and she accepts this, but when he later proposes, Vane leaves him, furious at his hypocrisy. Later, when Boyes's death is linked to arsenic poisoning, suspicion falls on Vane because it was one of the murderous methods she had been researching for her new book. Serving as a juror in Vane's trial, Climpson holds out and forces a hung jury, which gives Wimsey, convinced of Vane's innocence, time to investigate and solve the case. Wimsey discovers that Boyes was unknowingly in line to inherit his aged great-aunt's substantial estate. Boyes's cousin, a solicitor named Norman Urquhart, had been embezzling the majority of the great-aunt's holdings but lost them in the stock market. Urquhart knew that he would be exposed when the aunt died, so he killed Boyes with an arsenic-laced omelet to inherit the estate and conceal his fraud. Urquhart covered his tracks well. The two men shared the meal, even the omelet, but Urquhart had built up immunity to the poison by having ingested small doses over a long period. The spinster coming to the rescue of a wayward woman was a common fictional motif, not unlike the role played by real-life policewomen with prostitutes and other troubled young women. But in this case, the woman in trouble was not a prostitute or thief but a detective writer herself, surely the first time a detective saved one of her own.[32]

Green's Amelia Butterworth also takes on the protection of younger, though not fallen, women.[33] She invites the Van Burnam daughters to stay with her, even though she resents their calling her a "dear old soul" and a "wonderful old thing," inwardly huffing, "I may be wonderful but I am not old, and it is time they knew it." But Butterworth still feels protective of them and of the young woman she first believes to be a murderess, Olive Randolph.

Surely the busiest of all spinsters was Patricia Wentworth's Miss Maud Silver, a spinster private investigator in London who specializes in thefts and art forgeries. Nearly all her cases have a romantic couple at the center, an interesting choice for a spinster story. Introduced in the novel *Grey Mask*, in 1928, Silver goes on to work on more than thirty cases. Prim, polite, and often dressed in old-fashioned dresses and dowdy hats, Silver is a retired governess turned private detective to the elite. Her harmless appearance allows her to infiltrate upper-class homes, where she collects evidence as a social caller rather than as a professional investigator. Like Miss Marple, she's a prodigious knitter, often putting suspects at ease with the clacking of her needles, but she's much less hard-nosed than Marple, preferring poetry to gossip. Silver also tends to work with her protagonists to solve the mystery rather than alone like Marple. Her relationship with the police, however, is uneasy. She undertakes cases and collects clues in places where police might be unwelcome, much to the chagrin of Scotland Yard's Chief Inspector Lamb. Silver wins the respect of another officer, Inspector Frank Abbott, and they frequently rely on each other for assistance in solving cases.[34]

In the early twentieth century, schoolteacher Hildegarde Withers was the only American spinster detective of note after Green's Butterworth.[35] Withers solves crimes with the assistance of her male foil, Inspector Oscar Piper of the New York Police Department. The two have a typically combative relationship. When they first meet, Piper asks her several questions since she's a witnessed a crime. "Okay then. Your full name?" "Hildegarde Martha Withers." "Occupation?" "At present, answering foolish questions. Young man, I told you I was a teacher." Angular of frame, carrying an umbrella, and bedecked in elaborate hats, Withers was the creation of Stuart Palmer, who modeled her on his high school English teacher Fern Hackett in Baraboo, Wisconsin. Palmer claimed that Hackett made his life miserable for two years but that she also encouraged his writing. In the novel *The Penguin Pool Murder* (1931), where Withers makes her debut on a school field trip to the New York Aquarium, she discovers a body floating in the penguin tank. This leads her to Piper of the city's homicide division, where she declares, "It is the ambition of my life to play detective." Withers proves herself more than equal to the task of ferreting out clues and, eventually, the identity of the murderer.

The dead man is stockbroker Gerald Lester. Piper and Withers start looking into who might have wanted to kill him. There are several possibilities. The stock market crash of 1929 (the novel was published two years later, in 1931) wiped out many of Lester's clients, who may have wanted revenge. Lester has also been unfaithful to his wife, Gwen, though she also has a lover, attorney Philip Seymour. Coincidentally, Gwen and Seymour had planned to meet at the aquarium on the day of Lester's murder. Add to this list of possible suspects, the pickpocket "Chicago" Lew, who attempts to steal Withers's purse at the aquarium. The evidence mounts against both Gwen and Seymour, and they are arrested and bound for trial. It's at Gwen's murder trial during a cross-examination of Withers by Gwen's attorney, Barry Costello, that Withers realizes who the true murderer is: Costello himself.

Withers and her apricot poodle, Talleyrand, appeared in fourteen novels and more than two dozen short stories between 1931 and 1969, solving cases that take her from New York to Los Angeles, Mexico City, and England. She has a sharp eye, and Piper calls her "God's gift horse to all dumb cops." Unlike many other female sleuths, she does not use disguise, relying instead on diligent questioning, and she has an unwillingness to settle for the most convenient answer. She's also proactive, thriving on the hunt for clues rather than processing information through her own experiences as Marple does. Withers also appeared in several films, the most famous of which starred Edna May Oliver. Although other film adaptations followed, Oliver's portrayal of Withers proved indelible.

Not every spinster defied expectations with wit and cunning. Amanda and Lutie Beagle inherit the family business—a private detective agency—from their brother without ever having asked him what that business was. Marjorie Torrey, who, as Torrey Chanslor, wrote the two novels featuring the Beagles, in 1940 and 1941, was primarily known as an illustrator of children's books.[36] The Beagle stories were her only books written for adults. Prim women in their sixties, the Beagle sisters gave up their life of knitting, baking, and gardening in upstate New York (their hometown the appropriately named East Biddicut) to become investigators for the Beagle Detective Agency, in Manhattan. The sisters have very different reasons for undertaking their new profession. For the efficient and common-sense-minded Amanda, it is a family duty and responsibility, and she runs the agency with a firm hand. For the bubbly and foolish Lutie, it's an adventure, a chance to try out the skills learned by reading scores of mysteries borrowed from the town library. Their younger niece, Marthy Meecham, narrates the stories and joins in the investigations along with a cat named Tabby and Rabelais, a bawdy parrot with the mouth of a sailor. Lutie does most of the detecting, going to clubs and magic shows to look for evidence, while Marthy dutifully follows along, mostly to keep Lutie out of trouble. While the Beagles manage to solve their cases, detection is hardly the point of the stories. It is instead an opportunity to showcase the amusing exploits of foolish old women trying to solve serious crimes.[37]

Women like Butterworth, Marple, and Silver challenged notions of the superfluous woman, but did so without threatening patriarchal authority. At least not too much. Butterworth's successes shake up Gryce, who, she hears, after her first case, "has never quite been the same man since the clearing up of this mystery," his "confidence in his own powers . . . shaken."[38] Most successes unmasked dysfunction in the homes of respectable families rather than taking on crimes that challenged the social order, but they did so with skills peculiar to their marginal place. Spinster sleuths turned their solitude into power and their social redundancy into freedom. Although other types of women would take up detecting, particularly as the number of spinsters in actual fact declined in the 1920s, the spinster remained an influential detecting force, walking a fine cultural line between power and fear throughout the twentieth century.[39]

CHAPTER FIVE

The First Policewomen

O N SEPTEMBER 10, 1910, ALICE STEBBINS WELLS TOOK THE OATH TO JOIN the 350-member, all-male Los Angeles Police Department. Wells stood a little over five feet tall. She wore no uniform, carried no weapon, and usually kept her badge stuffed in her pocketbook. Wells had lobbied hard for her position. "It was a man's world," she later recalled of the day. "There were no women employed in the department as telephone girls, record bureau clerks or secretaries. Male clerks, stenographers or officers performed the limited amount of duties."[1]

Born in Manhattan, Kansas, in 1873, Wells earned degrees from Oberlin College and Hartford Theological Seminary, and ran a small church in Oklahoma before settling with her husband and two children in Los Angeles.[2] There, Wells continued her preaching, but she became convinced that policing offered an opportunity to reduce crime and cure social ills through "applied Christianity." Protective work for women and children, she argued, would yield better results in the hands of public officials endowed with police powers than with moral reformers, because the police department operated at "the strategic point at which virtue can meet vice, strength can meet weakness, and guide them into preventative and redemptive channels."[3] And of course, the people best suited to work with women and children were those naturally attuned to the needs of both: female police officers.[4]

Backed by more than one hundred influential citizens, Wells petitioned the mayor and police commissioner for the appointment. "I don't want to make arrests," she said, making her case. "I want to keep people from needing to be arrested, especially young people." It took three months of politicking by Wells before the city council passed an ordinance, in August 1910. One month later, Wells received her badge (it read "Policewoman #1"), patrol box key, a rulebook, and a first-aid book. She did not receive a gun.[5]

Women had functioned as police before Wells, even if they didn't have the title "policewoman." Marie Owens began work first as an investigator for the Chicago health department, then enforcing child-labor laws, and then as a detective sergeant for the Chicago Police Department.[6] The daughter of Irish immigrants, Owens and her husband, Thomas, moved to Chicago in the early 1880s. He worked as a gas fitter while she tended to their five young children. When typhoid fever killed Thomas, in 1888, Owens went to work as a factory and tenement inspector. She discovered children as young as seven running assembly lines and operating heavy machinery: the legal working age was fourteen. Owens transferred to the police department in 1891 as public outrage over child exploitation increased political pressure on city leaders to enforce child-labor laws with real authority. Tough and independent, she was given the power of arrest, a police badge, and the title of detective sergeant, though she was only listed on the books as a "patrolman."

Enforcing child-labor laws was not easy, but having police power helped. "Manufacturers in some cases were not inclined to admit me to their workshops, but armed with the strong arm of the law and the will to do good I soon found that in most cases the merchants met me half way and rendered me some great assistance," Owens wrote in a 1901 op-ed in the *Chicago Tribune*.[7] Owens convinced some department stores to close earlier in the evening to reduce the working hours for women and children. She pushed for workplace schools, so young employees could get an education as well as make a living. She also visited courts and assisted detectives in cases involving women and children. Her captain raved about her skill and work ethic: "Give me men like she is a woman and we will have the model detective bureau of the whole world."[8] Owens was sympathetic to the plight of the women and children she encountered in the course of her rounds. She often allowed children to keep working when they were the primary breadwinners in their family. "I see so much unhappiness and misery that could be relieved by a few dollars," she told a reporter. "If I were only able to supply those dollars how happy I should be!" Owens retired in 1923 after a thirty-two-year career with the department.[9]

Much of the misery Owens encountered in her job grew out of the tremendous and largely unstructured growth of American cities in the nineteenth century. Middle- and upper-class white Americans enjoyed a higher standard of living that gave women more leisure time to devote to community service, social reform, recreation, and shopping. Industrialization increased demand for labor and brought immigrants looking for opportunities and the promise of a better life. Many of these new immigrants had different lifestyles, religions, and sexual mores than the white Protestant Yankees who had long defined respectable behavior in the United States. This stoked conflicts over church, family, work, and leisure. The economic shift from home to factory also brought young women from rural areas with few job opportunities to cities where they worked in retail, clerical, or factory positions. For the first time in history, young single women in large numbers lived apart from their families, often in workhouses or boarding homes. In their free time, young people began visiting a growing number of dance halls, skating rinks, and theaters that catered to working-class urban Americans. Workplace experience had taught these women to expect recreation as a reward for hard work, as employment had long allowed young men. Some young women adopted bolder styles of dress and dance, and challenged the idea that a woman's only place was in the home. All of these changes brought women of various classes into the public life and space of the city. Modern urban society broke down, on at least one level, the divisions between race, class, and gender, which had long governed social relations and interactions. Before, the only women walking alone on city streets tended to be prostitutes or alcoholics, and they were treated with all the disrespect male police officers believed such fallen women deserved. But now respectable women traveled together in groups or even individually to shop, visit charities, or to participate in demonstrations. Yet they were often met with abuse from police officers. Women on suffragist picket lines were often horrified to be touched by a male officer called to move them along, even if nothing inappropriate happened. Occasionally, solitary law-abiding women alone on city streets were mistaken for prostitutes or vagrants, particularly if their charity work brought them into neighborhoods of ill repute. Women detained at police stations felt they suffered further indignities to their gender and class, as many of the police officers were working-class immigrants, who had no training for how to deal with the status and expected niceties of their female detainees. The experience of encountering police in a confrontational way had a profound effect on middle-class and upper-class women.[10]

Concern for the treatment of women and children in public, as well as distress about the urban poor, fueled women's entry into the workforce and the drive for social-service careers in the second half of the nineteenth century. One such profession was social work, which came to be intimately tied to women's policing. Social work as a field and academic subject grew out of the church and secular organizations that had worked to address the consequences of poverty and urbanization earlier in the century. Using concepts derived from business and science, social services professionalized in the late nineteenth century, adopting a methods-based investigative strategy to solve society's problems, one that bore much in common with the ratiocination of detection. Matrons first brought this social-service approach to incarcerated women and children in jails and prisons. Reformers saw policewomen as the next step: preventing crime committed by women and children through social-service intervention.[11]

Many reformers believed that policewomen could avert crime, rather than react to it, as policemen often did. Chicago activist and civic leader Louise de Koven Bowen argued that cities needed a *moral* police force to protect young people from the temptations of commercial amusement facilities.[12] Policewomen, she contended, would protect naïve young women from accepting the invitations of men with bad reputations at movie theaters, dance halls, and city parks. Theirs was a job that matched investigation with maternal protection. "In fact, we need women police to 'mother' the girls in all public places," wrote Bowen, "where the danger to young people is great." As it did with promoting police and prison matrons, the Woman's Christian Temperance Union (WCTU) now spearheaded efforts to create positions for policewomen in cities around the nation. The group's sponsorship of speakers on the issue, and local lobbying by its chapters, provided publicity and political strength for the policewomen movement.

Public hysteria around prostitution and so-called white slavery, or enforced prostitution of often very young women, beginning in the 1890s, spurred the policewomen cause. Novels, plays, and news articles about innocent white girls overwhelmed by the temptations of the city and forced into prostitution by "white slavers" bombarded the public. Ministers, social workers, doctors, journalists, and other Americans joined to form an unusually massive assault on urban vice. Reformers were particularly worried about the young immigrant woman newly arrived and looking for home and work, and being preyed upon by thieves and rapists and lured into prostitution. Whether prostitution had actually increased during this period is debatable, but anxiety about the issue reflected a changed attitude toward fallen women, one that reformers and some women's novelists had argued for decades. Prostitutes were no longer seen as irredeemable and depraved, worthy of the terrible neglect they suffered in prisons, but rather as victims of unscrupulous sex traffickers and poor community support. Few reformers focused on the social conditions that often led women into prostitution: low wages, discrimination, political disenfranchisement. Focusing on the concept of "white slavers" was far easier. For many Americans, the exposure of thriving commercial prostitution in major cities in the media became the basis of a blanket indictment of urban living and of the immigrants believed to be organizing and thriving on the lucrative traffic in young white women.[13] "The best and surest way for parents of girls in the country to protect them from the clutches of the 'white slaver' is to keep them in the country," wrote one reformer.[14]

Police arrested prostitutes, but they also relied on them for information. In exchange for their help, police often looked the other way and tolerated prostitution in certain parts of the city. The close connection between politics and police also made brothels difficult to shut down because some madams served the city elites on whom officers relied for their jobs.[15] In Chicago, Carrie Watson's powerful clientele made her one of the wealthiest and most prominent women in the city. Her brothel, at 441 S. Clark Street, housed between twenty and thirty women and carried out its business openly: carriages lined the block out front. Watson had entered the business after surveying the labor market for women and determining that sin offered the best chance for advancement. She moved to Chicago from Buffalo and took a job as a prostitute at Lou Harper's Mansion to learn the business. Two years later, she set out on her own, buying a two-story brick building from Annie Stewart, a madam whose standing in the city plummeted after one of her girls shot a local constable. Watson raised the standards and elegance of the brothel. Her girls were well mannered and well dressed, and her house had a variety of other entertainment options, including a bowling alley, five parlors, a billiard room, and a three-piece orchestra. Despite several deaths in her house, Watson ran her business for twenty-five years, from 1868 to 1897.[16]

To cut off white slavers at the quick, reformers working primarily through women's organizations and clubs kept a constant eye out for girls traveling alone. In the 1880s and 1890s, they would greet female arrivals at city harbors and railroad stations to advise and direct them to safe housing. One investigator explained that the "watchers for human prey scan the immigrants as they come down the gang plank of a vessel which has just arrived and 'spot' the girls who are unaccompanied by fathers, mothers, brothers or relatives to protect them."[17] Even as they recoiled at the immigrant woman who became a prostitute, reformers placed the blame for her choice on the lack of protection afforded her by government and private agencies.[18]

Along with white slavery, criminology—specifically female criminology—became a late-nineteenth-century obsession. Working in a relatively new field, criminologists defined criminals as individuals who cannot or will not follow social norms. As such, some early theorists linked female criminality to expanding rights and freedoms for women, arguing that women's crimes were on the rise as women gained access to public life. Assaults and murders, crimes more often committed by men, were surely worse than theft and abortion—the most common female crimes—but they were perceived as more heinous merely because women did them.[19] British criminologist and former prison chaplain William Douglas Morrison wrote, "The more women are driven to enter upon the economic struggle for life the more criminal they will become."[20]

Some went so far as to blame women for all crime, not just the crimes they committed. Morrison claimed that poor mothering created criminals, and that the worst mothers of all were those who worked. This wasn't far off from the views expressed by pioneer policewomen. Asked why girls go wrong, Chicago officer Alice Clement answered, "Nine times out of ten it's her mother's fault." Alice Wells concurred. "As all the world knows, the perfect home training of every child would largely eliminate the need of police work," she proclaimed.[21] As family influence waned in the twentieth century, policewomen and many others blamed mothers for their lack of parental authority, failing to grasp the more fundamental social and economic changes at work.[22]

Cities also began turning to women to enforce morals and protect the virtue of local women during large-scale events like the world expositions, which drew large and potentially dangerous crowds. In 1905, officials in Portland, Oregon, hired Lola Baldwin to manage social conditions at the Lewis and Clark Centennial Exposition. Many worried that the influx of thousands of visitors to the fair, particularly single lumberjacks, miners, sailors, and other bachelors, would create an environment harmful to women and children. Baldwin was eager and well qualified for the job.[23]

She began her working life as a teacher in New York and later worked with delinquent girls and young women in other states, investigating homes and workplaces and conducting interviews with inmates to determine the best path for their moral salvation. When her husband relocated to Portland in 1904, Baldwin continued her voluntary investigative work there and served on the board of the local Florence Crittenton Home for unwed mothers.

With funding from the YWCA, Baldwin was placed in charge of a team of social workers and given police power for the duration of the fair. Baldwin was so effective that she persuaded the YWCA to seek donations to continue the program after the fair. When support dried up, in 1907, she appealed to the mayor and Portland City Council to support the city's straying daughters. To bolster her case, Baldwin reminded the council that her request for funds amounted to half of the six thousand dollars they had set aside for the city dog pound. Surely, the welfare of Portland's women counted as much as stray dogs.[24]

Baldwin won their support to fund preventative work, and she also scored 95 percent on a new civil service exam for "female detective." The city named her the director of the newly created Department of Public Safety for the Protection of Young Girls and Women, in 1908. The department supervised anti-vice activities, hunted for brothels, and kept women out of trouble, replacing much of the work done with YWCA funding. Baldwin was not known as a policewoman but rather as an operative.[25] This designation suited Baldwin just fine as she preferred not to be known as a police officer. "The effectiveness of the protective work is due to its quietness, lack of show or publicity and its sincerity and sympathetic approach," she said.[26] Her team wore plainclothes and worked out of the local YWCA so as not to embarrass or alarm their charges. Baldwin's hiring provided a boost to the policewomen movement.[27]

Several other cities created commissions to study and expose the vice problem in hopes of finding a solution—and they employed women to work for them.[28] The Chicago Vice Commission hired fifteen women investigators to go undercover as employees in department stores and mail-order houses. They gleaned information from female clerks, dressmakers, and other workers to uncover employment conditions and potential workplace conduits to prostitution. In 1911, the commission produced a 393-page report with the ominous title *The Social Evil in Chicago*, the contents of which were considered so shocking that the postmaster refused to send it through the mail. One thousand prostitutes were said to be working South Michigan Avenue alone, and arrests for prostitution averaged seven per day. For those who kept up with vice reports in the newspaper, the Chicago study was likely less of a shock.[29] A report from the US Immigration Commission, published the same year, seemed to solidify the link between prostitution and immigration in the public imagination.[30] A "large proportion of the pimps living in the United States are foreigners," the report stated, making special note of the ethnicities and religious groups most frequently involved in the trade of women. Among them, "the Jews" preyed "upon young girls whom they find on the street, in the dance halls, and similar places."

These reports increased pressure to hire policewomen. But even earlier, in 1907, prominent reformer Julia Goldzier collected more than five hundred signatures supporting the hiring of policewomen in Bayonne, New Jersey. She then published a pamphlet, *Policewomen: An Appeal to the People of Bayonne*, in which she argued that women would purify streets and businesses. She dismissed as "senseless twaddle" those who insisted that women belonged in the home, insisting that "healthful outdoor exercise as a policewoman with its limited hours and easy work will soon make our women strong and free as men."[31] She envisioned the policewoman uniformed in a dark-blue blouse and bloomers, patent-leather boots, and a blue hat complete with gold braid. Goldzier's plan called for the appointment of policewomen to "patrol the streets for the protection, assistance, and entertainment of our children while they are out of their parents' sight."[32] The Bayonne City Council could barely contain its laughter and ridicule when Goldzier presented her petition and plan. The *New York Times* reported that Bayonne's ninety-five policemen objected to the plan on the grounds that they "would have to stay home and do the washing and cooking if their wives landed their jobs." Of course, that's not at all what Goldzier had proposed.

Advocates for policewomen took pains to emphasize that women had no desire or intention of performing male police duties—nor would women replace men, as Bayonne's officers suggested. In a literary journal of the period, the *Nineteenth Century and After*, Maud Darwin stressed the difference between the two: "The policewoman has the same authority as the policeman; she can arrest people; but it is not her business to drag drunkards to the police station, to trap a burglar, or to direct traffic." That, Darwin declared, "is man's work."[33]

Los Angeles' Alice Wells argued that policewomen would protect male officers from potentially delicate situations with women that could cause permanent damage to both their reputations. The dual protection of women in custody and the male officers who came in contact with them had served as a rationale for the earlier hiring of matrons. In carving out a place for policewomen, reformers identified new crimes and abuses committed against and by women, and redefined the parameters of prevention to include adjusting the social situations of the most vulnerable members of society, women and children.[34]

Early policewomen like Alice Wells and Lola Baldwin had limited duties. They supervised entertainment venues to keep women from engaging in risky activities and dealt with prostitutes. Policewomen didn't protest their narrow role—it was largely the one they wanted. They saw policing as an extension of their cultural role as protectors of children and the home, and as guardians of morals. Policewomen served as mother figures with badges, providing gentle guidance and using moral persuasion to discipline and direct women and children. Police departments that hired female officers acknowledged the expanded role for women in public life, but their limited duties ensured that policewomen continued to perform "women's work," even in an unconventional setting. Most policewomen were indistinguishable from any other nicely dressed woman. She had a badge (that she often kept in her bag) but nothing else—no gun, no nightstick, and no uniform.[35]

After her appointment to the Los Angeles police force, Wells lectured widely and traveled almost continuously. Requests for advice flooded Wells's station soon after she took the job, many from cities considering hiring policewomen. She also fielded requests to speak to churches, women's groups, universities, and civic organizations. "I have spoken all the way across the continent and I shall speak all the way back," said Wells. "When I applied for my appointment in Los Angeles I thought chiefly of the immediate work to be done right there by a woman."[36] In 1911, she spoke in thirty-one cities in thirty days on a speaking tour organized by the WCTU. Her address before the session of the General Federation of Women's Clubs won more support for the presence of policewomen, which resulted in local clubs lobbying for their hiring. Although she spoke widely, Wells did not neglect policing completely. In her first year on duty, she logged thirteen arrests.[37]

Interest in Wells stemmed not only from her chosen profession but also that she spoke publicly about it. Though the sight of a woman lecturing was less scandalous in the early twentieth century than it had been in the nineteenth, and most audiences responded positively or at least respectfully to Wells's message, many Americans still believed that women had no place at the lectern. One New Orleans man begged to be arrested by Wells. In Grand Rapids, Michigan, in 1914, a heckler called for the patrol wagon to round up this "nut gone wrong."[38]

In one instance, at a City Club luncheon in New York City in 1912, the heckler was another policewoman. Isabella Goodwin was a police matron with the New York Police Department. She, like most matrons, worked twelve-hour days, seven days a week. But her rank changed when she found the key evidence that led to the capture of a gang of thieves who held up the East River National Bank in the middle of the day and escaped in a taxicab with twenty-five thousand dollars. It wasn't Goodwin's first case—she'd worked on special assignment for the Detective Bureau for more than a year—but it won her fame because of the public jest that was made of the official police for its inability to crack the case. The police believed that the two suspects frequented a boardinghouse of ill repute run by Annie Hall. Goodwin applied for a position as a domestic servant, and within a few weeks, she had won her employer over and secured enough evidence from Hall against the suspects to arrest them for the crime. For her effort, Goodwin was named New York's first woman municipal detective, in 1912.[39]

Goodwin was in the crowd at the City Club listening to Wells, billed as the first woman to serve on a "uniformed force" in America (though she herself had no official uniform). At the conclusion of Wells's talk, Goodwin was introduced to her as a detective rather than a member of the police force. Wells beamed at the news and said, "Now, if you were in our city you would be a regular police officer." Goodwin rose indignant, her cheeks pink.[40] Pulling out her badge, she replied, "I would have you understand that I am indeed a regular member of the police force. And what is more, before I became a Detective Sergeant, I was a member of the uniformed force and did the same work that you are supposed to be doing." Goodwin's retort to the constantly lecturing Wells drew whispers and laughs from the crowd, but before Wells could respond, the event organizer called for more questions, and Goodwin sat down.

Goodwin had entered policing around 1905, after the death of her policeman husband. With four children to support, she took the civil service examination to become a matron. Goodwin threw herself "body and soul" into the work.[41] Assigned to the Mercer Street Station because of its proximity to police headquarters, Goodwin attended to and searched all the female prisoners who came into headquarters. She soon became acquainted with all the notorious women criminals in the city. After fifteen years as a matron, though, with no prospect for advancement in that role, Goodwin began investigating clairvoyants and other swindlers for the detective bureau. "I have investigated hundreds of cases of fortune telling in all its varied forms, from common crystal gazing to the practice of tea leaves, cards, handwriting, and palm reading," Goodwin told the *New York Times*. As an official detective, Goodwin made headlines nabbing these charlatans, as well as ticket scalpers at the Metropolitan Opera. Positions like Goodwin's were rare in city police forces, though. Most women only detected on special assignment.[42]

Of course, apart from municipal policing, some women had worked as part of private detective agencies for years. Some even operated their own businesses. Around 1902, Miss Cora M. Strayer's Private Detective Agency opened in Chicago. Strayer had grown up in Elkhart, Indiana, and first found work in Chicago as a clerk, perhaps for a lawyer, as she later claimed to have drifted into detecting at the suggestion of an attorney whom she had assisted in an investigation.[43] Strayer's agency employed both male and female operatives, a fact that led to her inclusion in a newspaper story on "women who boss men." "I have about an equal number of men and women under me," she told a reporter. "The women are better in some things but, of course, men are absolutely necessary in others."[44] When her agency took on cases, Strayer studied each individually and provided instructions as to how her operatives were to tackle the case. While she took on many types of cases, Strayer marketed herself primarily to women. "Ladies, when in need of legal or confidential advice, why not confer with one of your own?" read one 1908 ad that included Strayer's picture.[45] Business must have been good because she opened a second branch in St. Louis that employed only female detectives.[46]

Chicago was also home to detective and fingerprint expert Mary E. Holland of the Holland Detective Agency. Holland ran the agency with her husband, Phil. They also published *The Detective*, a kind of catalog of criminological supplies and photo book of wanted criminals. Holland learned about fingerprinting from Sergeant John Ferrier, a fingerprint authority who had come from Scotland Yard to protect Queen Victoria's jewels, on view at the 1904 World's Fair, in St. Louis. Holland became an ardent convert to the new science and traveled throughout the United States teaching fingerprinting to police departments, as well as to the US Navy in 1907. She used her skill before the Illinois Supreme Court in a 1911 case involving defendant Thomas Jennings. Jennings was charged with murdering a man after he had been caught attacking the man's daughter, but the evidence against Jennings was slim. Holland served as an expert witness at the trial, analyzing the fingerprints that led to Jennings's conviction.[47]

The *Chicago Daily Tribune* featured some of the city's women detectives who "have accomplished feats that have baffled men" in 1908.[48] Among them was twenty-five-year-old Laura Maxey, who was hired by a prominent furniture maker to tail his wife, who he believed to be in love with another man. Maxey rented a room in the same house as the wife and shadowed her around town for days. Nothing seemed out of the ordinary until she stopped at a drugstore where Maxey was "witness to a most affectionate meeting between the woman and man who was not her husband." She notified the furniture maker that his suspicions were right, and divorce proceedings began.

Other private investigators did security work for department stores. Annie Aiger and Mayme Norton worked in a large store on Chicago's State Street, dressing like regular shoppers and carrying shopping bags as they made their rounds through the store. Aiger caught one woman stuffing a voile skirt and nine shirtwaists under her baby's long clothes. When Aiger confronted the woman, she began to sob. "I'm so sorry—so sorry! But I simply couldn't help it. My sister was going to get married, and, O, she needed some clothes so bad. So I thought I would help her out," cried the woman. Aiger and Norton sympathized with many of the people they caught. Norton recalled one elderly woman who'd nabbed five silk mufflers, a jewelry case, a fan, a cup and saucer, and a necklace around Christmas. "I never felt so sorry for any one in my life," said Norton. "She was a minister's wife and poor—desperately poor. It was the first Christmas that she had had nothing to give away." Both women found the work rewarding. "One is always on the alert. One must know instinctively whom to distrust," Aiger said.

According to the *Daily Tribune* story, private detection required a certain type of woman. "The woman detective, like the trained nurse, has no home life." She must be "intensely sympathetic" and must "instinctively understand the foibles of the women or men with whom she may be brought in contact." She had to be attractive and "magnetic," working her "way to the heart of secrets." Although the writer didn't say so, the tone of the story seemed to suggest that few women possessed these traits.

Chicago wasn't the only city where women worked as private detectives and operatives. In 1906, President Theodore Roosevelt sent federal agent William J. Burns to investigate the network of bribery and corruption between San Francisco mayor Eugene Schmitz and city political boss Abe Ruef.[49] Burns placed detectives in the field to search for evidence, among them a woman known only as "Mrs. R." To the shock of many, Burns had brought her with him from the East for the express purpose of "securing the secrets of a boodler [a person involved in bribery or graft] from himself" or "the female members of his family." Whoever Mrs. R was, Burns apparently considered her one of his most successful operatives and worth the expense of footing her cross-country travel.[50]

Private detection tended to offer women more opportunities to solve bigger, more high-profile crimes. These agencies also hired more women than police departments. (The same was true on the page, where more female detectives worked as contractors for hire or for private agencies than for city police.) But private detectives had to fight public perceptions of fraud and concerns about invasions of privacy that were harder to shake than they tended to be for police detectives, who were seen as public servants. Tensions also existed between public and private detectives themselves, in life and in fiction; one tended to find the other incompetent, arrogant, or both. The two functioned then, as now, under different parameters, with police detectives answerable to the common interests of society and private detectives to their own sense of morality and the needs of the individuals who hired them. And like many fields, detection soon had its share of entrepreneurial quacks setting up shop and minting detectives for five dollars a head.[51] Would-be "sleuths" received a tin star and official "credentials" in exchange for their money. Some shady detective agencies even offered photos of long-dead or imprisoned criminals for new detectives to claim as successes.

Sometimes the detectives themselves ended up behind bars. In 1896, Miss Fisher, a female detective with the Matt Pinkerton Agency, in Chicago, had taken a room at the Hotel Graylock adjacent to that of Mr. and Mrs. Bessenger.[52] With Mr. Bessenger out of town on business, Fisher knocked on Mrs. Bessenger's door and demanded three hundred dollars, claiming to have information against Mrs. Bessenger that Fisher would report to the police if she didn't receive the money. Mrs. Bessenger called her husband and told him that a woman purporting to be a detective had attempted to extort money from her. The next day, Fisher was arrested for blackmail. Fisher really was a detective, though, and had been sent to watch Mrs. Bessenger, but all the evidence of wrongdoing in this case was against Fisher.

Even with these moves into detection, by the early twentieth century, neither public nor private law enforcement agencies were overrun with women agents. Resistance to women's entry into law enforcement remained strong among city leaders and male officers. Though women's entry into the field was far from easy (and would only continue to be challenging), they had achieved some success, in part, because policing was a working-class field. Women would have had a much harder time had policemen been as well born (not to mention native born) and as well educated as themselves. The middle-class backgrounds of women entering the profession gave them psychological leverage in arguing for their place in law enforcement, a point that many did not hesitate to mention.[53] Alice Wells asserted that policemen "are not of our caliber or our character."[54] Edith Abbott, a University of Chicago social worker, warned that "the work of the policewoman certainly cannot be adequately performed by persons who have no more education than most of the men now filling positions in the police department."[55] No matter how much they were not wanted by men, pioneer policewomen saw little choice but to keep pushing. They hoped that making the streets safe for defenseless women would mean that all women would eventually be able to live in modern America in comfort and security.[56]

CHAPTER SIX

Girl Detectives

"**S**HE'S HERE!"[1]

Mr. Driscoll turned his opera glasses to a spot in the box near the proscenium where the young woman sat.

Surprised at who he saw through his glasses, Mr. Driscoll cried, "That yon silly little chit, whose father I know, whose fortune I know, who is seen everywhere, and who is called one of the season's belles is an agent of yours; a—a—"

Assured that she was the one—"a girl of gifts and extraordinarily well placed for the purpose"—Driscoll, with some lingering reluctance, engaged the services of the girl detective, Violet Strange.

Adventurous girls with unusual hobbies like Strange were common in the pages of early-twentieth-century books. These young heroines drove fast cars, piloted planes, and traveled the world as they sought out escapades. Already known for his Oz books, L. Frank Baum, writing under the name Edith Van Dyne, released the first of his Flying Girl series in 1911. Perhaps Baum felt that a pseudonym was necessary to win over young female readers, who might be skeptical of a man's take on their adventure, or, more likely, he may have been trying to dissociate these more commercial stories from the Oz books that had made him famous. The Flying Girl books featured the plucky Orissa Kane, who flies planes designed by her brother Stephen. Other popular series of the day included the Outdoor Girls, the Moving Picture Girls, the Girl Aviators, and the Motor Girls.

For parents who worried about the ill effects these books might have on their daughters, publishers assured them that the girls were of a "wholesome type." The heroines' ability to master automobiles and airplanes, as well as their appetite for action, marked these girls as modern. All the series assumed that girls were interested in and capable of activities outside the domestic comforts and obligations of home. That included detection.[2]

Although Strange wasn't exactly a girl (though the term often stuck to unmarried females well into adulthood), she was part of a new breed of young female detectives that would find its apotheosis in every girl's favorite young detective. Nancy Drew looms large in young-adult detective fiction, but she was not the first girl detective. In the late-nineteenth and early-twentieth centuries, there were a number of young female detectives who solved cases quite capably in their own right. Many were finished off not by the Reichenbach Falls, where Sherlock Holmes appeared to have been killed, but at the altar, a career-ending turn toward matrimony that reassured readers about the proper place of women and the primacy of family over a career as a detective.[3]

Violet Strange was the creation of popular mystery writer Anna Katherine Green, the author of the best-selling *Leavenworth Case* and the creator of spinster sleuth Amelia Butterworth. Published in 1915, *The Golden Slipper, and Other Problems for Violet Strange* introduced the wealthy debutante and favorite child of an opinionated father, Peter Strange. The girl's mother had died when she was a child, and her father gives Violet free reign over her life. She's young, likely late teens, with chestnut hair, a diminutive stature not unlike the flower of her name, and "a keen knowledge of human nature."[4] Her family home, on New York's Fifth Avenue, is luxurious, and Violet travels throughout the city to social events in a chauffeured limousine. But she also gets paid to detect as a member of a high-profile private detective agency. Like Butterworth, Strange conforms to type outwardly while rebelling within to live a life in defiance of expectations.

In her first case, "The Golden Slipper," Strange is hired by Mr. Driscoll to determine whether his debutante daughter, Alicia, is responsible for the disappearance of several household items, including jewels.[5] The girl's reputation and eligibility for marriage is at stake, so it is crucial that Strange be discreet in her sleuthing and that her presence in high society be accepted. The latter is easy for Strange, as an upper-class woman herself. In fact, Strange is welcomed into Alicia's group of friends and observes them while chattering away with them like a longtime pal: "Her satisfaction at entering this charmed circle did not take from her piquancy, and story after story fell from her lips." Strange makes no assumptions about the thief's identity but simply collects clues before setting a trap for the guilty party: in this case by putting on a pendant some Parisian paste that stains hands a vivid red. When the pendant turns up missing the next morning and Alicia's slipper is spotted on the ledge outside Strange's room, suspicion appears to fall on Driscoll's daughter once again. But Strange's dye reveals the true thief, a friend of Alicia's who sought revenge after Alicia stole her boyfriend.

As was the case with the fictional spinster sleuths, few took Strange's detecting seriously. She's variously described as "inconsequent," "infantile," and "quaint," and like the spinster, Strange uses this underestimation to her advantage. She flashes her dimples in timid smiles and opens her eyes wide in a show of guileless innocence as she asks questions and collects clues. Her behavior makes her appear unthreatening and hides her intellect and skills. Strange isn't above a little ribbing of other detectives either. Called in to assist with the investigation of a murder, Strange slyly remarks, "And not one of you knows who killed her. Somehow, I cannot understand that. Why don't you know when that's what you're hired for?"[6] The young sleuth, as always, solves the mysteries in the end, though without the final revelatory scene common to other detective stories. Rather than make her pronouncements public, at the very least to the affected family, Strange relays her solution to her employer with more self-deprecation than fanfare. She often heads home or to a party afterward while awaiting her next case.

Strange is so adept that some characters suggest she may possess supernatural skills, but Strange asserts that she is "nothing if not practical." She is unafraid of intellectual, daring work. Her detecting displays a talent for logic and mathematical puzzles, bucking the assumption that women were all emotion and intuition. Her clientele comes mostly from members of the upper classes, who trust her as one of their own, spending their time, as Strange often did, at "a tea, a musicale, and an evening dance." Strange's social standing also gives her insight into the mores of those she investigates.

Although she is often plagued by nightmares and sickened by the cases she investigates, Strange keeps accepting work until she reaches her stated monetary goal. Why she needs the money, though, is not revealed until her final adventure, eight short stories later, when it is disclosed that her income goes to support her musically gifted sister, Theresa. The girls' father, Peter, disowned Theresa after she married an Italian singing master, a "lowdown scoundrel," according to Peter. But Theresa's husband died soon after they wed, leaving Theresa penniless. Realizing her sister's talent, Strange offers to use her money earned from detection to help Theresa pursue a musical career. She's confident that her investment will pay off and that Theresa will become economically independent. While Strange detects to aid her own sister, a sense of sisterhood pervades all her cases, as nearly all of the people she helps are women.

Like many young women, Strange eventually marries and stops detecting. But she's chosen her husband wisely. Roger Upjohn appears to have few romantic illusions and little interest in controlling Strange or their marriage. When Strange despairs that her detecting career might have degraded her social position and made her unfit for Upjohn's regard, Upjohn reminds her of his own sordid reputation: Strange had helped him prove his father's innocence of the murder of the elder Upjohn's first wife. If ever a fictional woman had a chance at an equal partnership it is Strange. Empowerment for Strange comes from a successful career based on her own intelligence and self-sufficiency rather than through marriage, the typical route to fulfillment for women of Strange's ilk.[7]

But Strange was not like many of the earlier female characters. She was one of the "New Women" of the turn of the twentieth century. The term, coined by writer and activist Sarah Grand in her 1894 essay "The New Aspect of the Woman Question," became a popular catchphrase describing an intelligent, modern, emancipated single woman.[8] The New Woman lived boldly in a fast-paced urban environment. Well-educated, financially secure, and socially aware, New Women had no parental supervision and forged an identity based in self-expression. They danced, drank, and smoked. Some wore skimpy dresses and makeup, and cut their hair short, a style once reserved for prostitutes. They also rode bicycles. Pop culture popularized this image of modern womanhood as a symbol of urban energy and allure. *Harper's Bazaar* described the new woman as one "prepared to maintain her rights and claim her privileges . . . in whatever field she chooses to exploit her convictions or exert her abilities."[9]

The coinage "New Woman" was also a way of articulating very real shifts in the relative freedom and occupational choice available to young women going back to the 1880s. Though suffrage was yet to come and prejudice against women's incursions into public life persisted, by the start of the twentieth century, US women had penetrated many traditionally male bastions. Between 1880 and 1900, the number of women who worked outside the home doubled. The 1900 census counted five million women in the workforce. Women also went to college in unprecedented numbers. Nearly one-third of college students were women in 1880, a number that only increased in the 1890s after the introduction of home economics as an academic field.[10]

While most women still pursued marriage as their primary occupation, large numbers of women worked before settling down. Some even argued that this made them more fit and ready for marriage than the woman without work experience. "There is every reason to believe that a woman accustomed to regular hours, system, care of her income, and responsibility of many kinds, will make a successful home manager and wife," declared writer and educator Mary Eads in 1915.[11] These jobs became all the more important if the modern woman found herself dissatisfied with home life or unmarried by chance or by choice. A modern woman, Eads wrote, "has chosen her work, not as something to do until she marries, but as a field in which she may be happy all her life, in case she never marries."

The New Woman was, almost by definition, middle class since lower-class women had worked out of the home for decades and were not at liberty to shape their lives according to ideology and fashion. But even poorer women had new options during this period. The city offered jobs as shop girls, barmaids, waitresses, and work in other service fields. Women in these positions, rather than in the more traditional domestic occupations in private homes, were usually referred to by contemporaries as "working girls." Self-supporting women rejected the image of themselves as timid victims evoking pity. They repudiated their mothers' world because it offered an unmarried woman no options other than to move in with family as the spinster aunt or become a poorly paid teacher. They left their homes willingly for a life of excitement and adventure in the city that had not generally existed for women of their grandmothers' or even their mothers' generation.

The New Woman was not without her critics. The rising number of women in the workforce left many people uneasy, particularly as marriage rates dropped and divorce increased. Unmarried women raised alarms about "race suicide" as birthrates plummeted among white, middle-class women at the same time immigration from eastern and southern Europe grew. Repudiating their natural place as wives and mothers, New Women threatened the continuation of the white race.[12] American psychologist G. Stanley Hall claimed that the New Woman was selfishly expending her energy on intellectual endeavors rather than on her husband and children. "She has taken up and utilized in her own life all that was meant for her descendants," Hall wrote. "This is the very apotheosis of selfishness from the standpoint of every biological ethics."[13] Some more liberal reformers criticized the New Woman for using her hard-won freedom to pursue entertainment rather than political activism. Some criminologists even blamed the New Woman for the perceived rise in female criminality. In nearly all cases, the city and urban entertainment were blamed.[14]

Early policewomen were among those anxious about the New Woman. Middle-class interest in preserving female purity played a central role in the emergence of policewomen at the same time that gender roles and the customs of urban life were changing. Policewomen tended to equate the amusements that drew more and more Americans to the city with vice and immorality. What looked like fun to the young working woman looked like danger to policewomen, who fought for the right to contain it.[15]

The influence of this climate permeated fiction and influenced the rise of female characters. The New Woman of fiction fought against the traditional strictures that confined them to home. These women desired independence, adventure, fun, and personal fulfillment.[16] Some of them wanted to be detectives.

Anna Katherine Green was sixty years old when she published her collection of Violet Strange stories, but she had a daughter around the same age as her young sleuth, so she was likely familiar with the new generation of women. Green herself bridged the complex transition between the "true" woman of the nineteenth century and the "new" woman of the twentieth. The true woman was proper, timid, and humble, driven by the moral imperatives of piety, purity, and domesticity. The New Woman, on the other hand, was bold and independent. Green was a bit of both. She was college educated and had married late. The financial success of *The Leavenworth Case* and her subsequent titles, including those featuring the spinster sleuth Amelia Butterworth, allowed Green to hire help to care for her three children, releasing her from the domestic chores that could have impeded her writing in an earlier generation. But she was still a mother and wife who never repudiated domesticity. She gardened, attended church functions, and sewed her own clothes.[17] In 1917, Green even took a public stand against suffrage, claiming it would not help women.[18] She saw the confrontational tactics of the suffragists, including picketing the White House, as evidence that "the graces which once adorned [young women] are fading from our sight. Her modesty is already gone." Even Butterworth and Strange, Green's leading ladies, despite their independence and flouting of convention, solved cases primarily in private homes and in service to other women. Green deplored injustice and embedded the problems women faced in her fiction, but she also had a clear sense of the specific roles to be played by men and women. Her work asserted the traditional role of women as defenders of morality and family order.[19]

Green's contradictions made for media fodder. Writers loved to pit her murderous subject against her conventionally feminine demeanor. Some journalists expressed apprehension at the thought of meeting her and then relief at the woman they found. "She opens the door herself, a gentle woman," wrote one.[20] "It is a cozy, cordial room and all fear of the detective lady leaves you and you feel only an intense curiosity." The *American Magazine* even ran a photograph of her in an eighteenth-century style dress, trowel in hand, tending her garden. It wasn't unlike the "feminine woman in a masculine profession" coverage policewomen received.

Strange wasn't the first young and independent female detective. Daring young women took on detection in several nineteenth-century dime novels. As early as 1882, Edward L. Wheeler's pistol-wielding heroine Denver Doll was fighting crime, handily winning poker hands, and leading a band of adventurers known as the Red Shirts. Although her age is never revealed, Doll appears to be about eighteen years old with "rich brown hair" that fell in "rippling waves half-way to her waist. A plumed slouch hat of snowy white; an elegant suit of gray, and patent-leather top boots, with a diamond-studded 'boiled' shirt, collar, and a sash about her waist beneath the coat, made up her costume, and gave her an appearance at once dashing, and characteristic of the wild roving existence she led."[21] Doll has a particular talent for posing as a man, in one case disguising herself as a tough miner named "Glycerine George." Doll blazed through four stories, eluding capture by both criminals and love; in one, she saves the inheritance of a five-year-old from unscrupulous speculators and reunites the child with her mother. That Doll remains unmarried is a particularly rare feat for the young fictional heroine.

Detective Kate Edwards bounds through adventure in the most un-ladylike of ways in *Lady Kate, the Dashing Female Detective* (1886).[22] Edwards was the creation of Harlan Halsey, who also wrote the Old Sleuth series, one of the first dime-novel detective series. As a child, Edwards runs away from her orphanage and works a series of jobs before ascending to her chosen profession of private detective. She speaks multiple languages and dons disguises to uncover clues, ap-pearing as everything from an old woman to a tough-talking male sailor, successfully adopting the gestures and quirks of each of her guises. She knocks men to the ground and uses swords and pistols with skill. Trapped on a cliff at night during a storm, Edwards low-ers herself from a tree like a superhero, climbing limb to limb to the ground. She's not all brawn, though. In the most Holmesian of fash-ion, Edwards deduces the whereabouts of a suspect by examining the clay on his left-behind boots. No matter how independent, invulner-able, and strong Edwards seems, when it comes to love, she is the one knocked to the ground. Her detecting skills brushed aside by stereo-typical feminine weakness, Edwards quits her career for the love of the story's heroic villain, Arthur Everdell.

In those days, few female characters were allowed both a husband and a profession. Real women recognized the same limitations. Public opinion was generally hostile to married women who worked, though most policewomen were married, often to other officers. Detecting tended to belong to the young or the old woman: never the married.[23] Then there were those few women of marrying age who forsook mat-rimony for a career.

Among these was Catherine Louisa Pirkis's Loveday Brooke. Brooke was neither a sidekick to a male detective nor forced into de-tection to avenge a husband or other male relation. She detected to support herself, but her profession, like those of other New Women, was one she chose for herself after having enjoyed a privileged life and being "thrown upon the world penniless and all but friendless."[24] The circumstances of her change in position are never revealed, but she seems to have no regret. Transforming herself from an upper-class woman into a detective, Brooke is particularly adept at recogniz-ing physical deception in others. In one story, she identifies a young woman with short hair impersonating her sickly brother after dis-covering a lock of hair in an unswept fireplace. Her suspicions about people are inevitably proved right.[25] Most of the women Brooke helps are innocent, lower-class women without other means of protection, in contrast to Violet Strange's upper-class clientele, who can afford her skills and her discretion. In her early thirties, Brooke is older than some of her contemporaries but also more experienced, and she's emblematic of the new population of unmarried professional women, which came to cultural attention in the 1890s.

Brooke was Pirkis's last heroine. Born in London in 1841, Pirkis published her first book in 1877 and wrote thirteen more, many romantic melodramas. Pirkis stopped writing fiction in 1894 to concentrate on the organization she'd founded with her husband in 1891, the National Canine Defence League. Not surprisingly, given her devotion to animal welfare, Pirkis uses animal abuse as a clue to other kinds of cruelty among the characters in her Brooke stories.[26]

Several years later, in 1906, Reginald Wright Kauffman introduced another professional detective in *Miss Frances Baird, Detective*.[27] Kauffman claimed his detective was based on the experiences of a real female detective he first met "across the dead body of the murdered librarian Wilson, in the Philadelphia of 1897." Baird's story was supposedly told "as nearly as possible in the words in which you told it to me that summer evening," though it's surely fiction. Baird came to detection out of financial necessity, but she's not a widow or a spinster. She's an attractive woman with brown eyes and black hair who sometimes uses her appearance to gain an advantage. When a guard tries to stop her from entering a jail, Baird "flattered him first and impressed him with my position as a New York detective afterwards." But good looks are only one of her tools. Baird also carries a variety of scientific devices around with her, including a microscope and an apparatus for studying blood stains; a "scientific attitude," she declares, is indispensible to detective work. "All the available facts should be first gathered, and from them only should a theory eventually be erected," comments Baird. "No brief should be held, no cause espoused, save for the cause of justice."

Unfortunately, Baird appears to be a poor detective, especially compared to Brooke. The story opens with her castigation by the chief of the Watkins Private Detective Agency for letting criminals slip through her grasp. "Miss Baird," he begins, "I don't suppose it's necessary for me to tell you that I am very much disappointed in you—very much disappointed indeed." It's not clear how Baird ended up in detection since she seems to have limited talent for the job and no relevant skills from her years in boarding school and travel abroad. She sets off to redeem herself professionally, but continues to make mistakes. In one instance, a diamond necklace disappears during her watch, and in another, she inadvertently destroys evidence after being overcome at the sight of a dead body. When she messes up her testimony at an inquest, her initial instinct is to cry. "After all," she says, "I was a woman before I was a detective!" In another case, problems naturally arise when Baird falls in love with the principal suspect, a man she "knew to have committed theft and murder." She does finally solve the mystery, though more through happenstance and chance than the reason displayed by Brooke and later Strange. Although she's not notable for her skill, Baird did introduce a new type of female sleuth: the beautiful woman in over her head. Most fictional detectives were competent investigators, even if they appeared unsuited to the profession. Baird, buoyed by her good looks and youth, which the chief claims to value "only in a business way," keeps her job without much detecting success. Baird's type would reappear in various forms throughout twentieth-century detection.

In 1914, author Mary Roberts Rinehart introduced a detecting duo similar to Anna Katherine Green's Amelia Butterworth and Ebenezer Gryce, but with a heroine more on par with Violet Strange in age and temperament.[28] Rinehart's heroine, Hilda Adams, known as Miss Pinkerton when she's detecting, is a modern young woman trained as a nurse. Her profession allows her to learn a great deal from her patients, though often things she never wanted to know and is hesitant to exploit. Adams nonetheless uses this information to help catch criminals. A "nurse gets under the very skin of soul," where she "finds a mind surrendered," thinks Adams.[29] Her partner, Inspector George Patton, is, like Gryce, a professional detective, but he is also in love with Adams and proposes to her regularly. Adams, like Strange, is determined, smart, and brave, but unlike her, Adams is self-supporting and from a middle-class family in Chicago. The Hilda Adams stories were published over a span of nearly thirty years, beginning in 1914 with the serials "The Buckled Bag" and "Locked Doors."[30]

Rinehart was very familiar with Green's work. She, like Agatha Christie, acknowledged her debt to Green. Rinehart recalled picking up a copy of one of Green's books and noting the publisher, Bobbs-Merrill.[31] She sent her manuscript to the same publishing house, figuring she faced a more receptive audience for a female-authored mystery. By that time, Rinehart needed the money. Her husband's stock-market investments had tanked, and the economic panic of 1904 left them deeply in debt. To support a family that included three sons, Rinehart began to write long works that were serialized in popular magazines.

Her first novel, *The Circular Staircase* (1908), introduced the formula that grounded her success for forty years: a country-house setting that, like a Gothic, inspires fear and dread; a set of intertwined crimes or mysteries that make the solution hard, if not impossible, to guess; and an intelligent and witty female narrator. The inimitable opening line of *The Circular Staircase* sets the story rolling: "This is the story of a how a middle-aged spinster lost her mind, deserted her domestic goods in the city, took a furnished house for the summer out of town, and found herself involved in one of those mysterious crimes that keep our newspapers and detective agencies happy and prosperous."[32] Sensible, opinionated Rachel Innes is the main character. She's different from other spinsters in that she has dependents: her niece and nephew, Gertrude and Halsey, whom she adopted after her brother's death. With the young adults out of school and home for the summer, Innes decides to rent a country house for the family. Unbeknownst to them, the house they've chosen has a bad reputation. The first night, someone tries to break into the house. Then something (or someone) falls down the staircase. The next night, a dead body is discovered near the same set of stairs. Halsey is first suspected of the murder, then his friend, and then nearly everyone around them. Emblematic of Rinehart's style, a number of things happen that seem to have no clear connection to each other, including a butler dying of fright, the stable burning down, the discovery of a secret room, and the shaving of a mustache. These various strands do come together in the end, though with varying levels of plausibility, and in no way that readers could possibly guess on their own. Throughout the book, Rinehart drops broad hints of disaster with lines like "If I had only known" and "had we known." These backward glances became Rinehart's signature, a style characterized as the "Had-I-But-Known" approach to mystery writing.[33]

Rinehart's next mystery, *The Man in Lower Ten* (1909), became a runaway success and, coupled with *The Circular Staircase*, made Rinehart a household name. She is often called the American Agatha Christie, but her first mystery came out nearly a decade before Christie's, so perhaps Christie should be called the British Mary Rinehart.

Rinehart wrote more than just mysteries. During World War I, she convinced the *Saturday Evening Post* to grant her letters of introduction that would allow her to get behind the front lines in Europe. Her coverage of the war made her the first female war correspondent. Rinehart also wrote comic romances, nonfiction, short stories, and plays, some of which were adapted for film. At her death in 1958, Rinehart had written more than sixty books that had sold more than ten million copies.[34]

While most young female detectives chose marriage when the option arose, the decision was not made lightly. Dorothy Sayers's Harriet Vane, who was saved from a murder charge in *Strong Poison* thanks to the stalling tactics of spinster Miss Climpson, catches the eye of amateur detective Lord Peter Wimsey. Although Vane is not portrayed as beautiful, there's something about the gutsy and independent young detective novelist that grabs his attention. She refuses Wimsey's proposals for some time, concerned about the possibility of balancing a professional and personal life.[35] As the main character in a later Sayers novel, *Gaudy Night*, Vane spends several months investigating the threatening messages that have appeared around the women's college at Oxford University. It's a puzzle in need of a solution, but Sayers also uses the novel's setting to explore women's right to higher education. Sayers did not see herself as a feminist, but she did believe that women should have the freedom to do what they wanted with their lives, including pursuing a career. In the end of the book, Vane consents to leave her spinsterhood behind for marriage when she realizes that Wimsey will not attempt to stifle her ambitions and that theirs will be marriage of intellect as much as love.[36]

Vane was, in many ways, Sayers's fictional alter ego. The only child of an Oxford chaplain and headmaster, Dorothy Sayers was born in 1893. Like Harriet Vane, she studied modern languages and medieval literature at Oxford. Sayers did not care for academic life and worked as a copywriter at a London advertising agency, where one of her campaigns for Guinness with artist John Gilroy resulted in the toucan still seen in ads for the beer. Sayers fell in love with novelist John Cournos, who convinced her to live with him and then infuriated her by proposing marriage after she'd consented to the arrangement. Cournos explained that he had only been testing her devotion. Sayers left him, just as Vane leaves her lover after he backtracks on his opposition to marriage. Fiction did prove more sensational than life, however, as Sayers's lover did not then die of arsenic poisoning. Sayers later had an affair with a car salesman, which resulted in a son she supported though never acknowledged as her own. Worried about her ability to support herself and unsure of her marketable skills, Sayers began writing detective fiction in the early 1920s. She published *Whose Body*, her first Lord Peter Wimsey novel—and first detective story—in 1923. A few years later, she married Scottish journalist Oswald Atherton Fleming, known professionally as "Atherton Fleming." Like Vane, Sayers married a man who supported and encouraged her work. Besides mysteries, Sayers also wrote poems, articles, and plays. Her Anglican upbringing inspired her theological essays and books. Even with all her detective novels and the fame they brought, she considered her translation of Dante's *Divine Comedy* her greatest accomplishment.[37]

One fictional woman who did manage to marry detection to family with seemingly little anxiety was Mary Carner. Introduced in 1938 by Zelda Popkin, Carner works undercover at Blanchard's Department Store as the principal assistant to the head of store security, who also happens to be her husband. Most of her cases happen outside the store, however. Carner's husband praises his wife's skill and intelligence, even as he's left keeping the household running and caring for their daughter while she's out collecting clues. Carner's is the rare marriage. When she asks her husband for assistance, he helps without taking over the case and never intrudes without her invitation. And despite his wife's successful career, he feels no challenges to his masculinity or professional competence, as was commonly depicted in stories of independent women. The dynamic of the Carners' marriage was virtually unheard of in novels featuring women detectives or professional women of any kind at this time. The five books featuring Carner sold fairly well but did not inspire many imitators, even though Carner's work as a store detective was among the most common types of detecting for real-life female sleuths. Popkin herself was better known for her other books, including *The Journey Home* (1945) and *Small Victory* (1947), one of the earliest American novels to deal with the Holocaust.[38]

Detective Dorcas Dene also had an unconventional marriage: she's the family breadwinner. Her creator, George Sims, was well known for his poems, articles, lectures, and ballads on the plight of London's urban poor. But he was also intrigued by crime, especially the murders of Jack the Ripper. In 1897, he published *Dorcas Dene: Her Life and*

Adventures, starring a woman who moves with ease through London. With her distaste for intruding into the lives of others and apprehension about confronting suspects, Dene is initially uncomfortable at the idea of becoming a detective. But financial necessity forces her into the workforce after an illness leaves her artist husband blind and unable to make a living. A friend and retired police superintendent invites her to help him out on a case, assuaging her fears about pursuing an unwomanly profession by emphasizing the suffering experienced by a family. "That is surely a business transaction in which an angel could engage without soiling its wings," he explains.[39] Dene accepts. Most of her cases involve disruptions in domestic relationships, particularly inheritance fraud and domestic abuse. Like that of policewomen, Dene's intervention in troubled households helped to legitimize her endeavors: she is bettering the home life of others and safeguarding the domestic space. Dene solves cases by adopting disguises, spying through peepholes, and conducting stakeouts. Trained in the theater, Dene is particularly effective at impersonating characters and reading the performances of others. It's not surprising, then, that her first impersonation for a case is as an actress.[40]

Dene's a devoted, though childless, wife with a supportive husband, but she is clearly not the traditional wife. She's an autonomous wage earner with the determination and ratiocination skills of Sherlock Holmes (Arthur Conan Doyle was a friend of Sims). Dene also allies herself with a variety of men as she works with law enforcement to solve crimes. She frequently allows the police to make the arrest and dole out the appropriate punishment, recognizing the desire of the police to be the ultimate authorities in criminal cases and her own need to appear womanly. Sims seems to assume Dene's self-effacing behavior is natural for married women. She frequently relinquishes her independence to her husband, even though she's clearly proficient and good at her job. Her husband, on the other hand, has no detecting experience, and his blindness provides both a literal and symbolic obstacle to detecting. Sims's detective proved popular enough that he wrote a second collection the following year. Several silent film adaptations also appeared.[41]

While stories of girl detectives became more common in the early twentieth century, detective literature written specifically for young readers was slower to develop. Children's literature up to the mid-nineteenth century tended toward the didactic and moralizing. But in the 1840s, adventure and fantasy stories began to be seen as suitable material for children.[42] The morality tale still held sway, but it became less religious and dogmatic. The emerging books for children offered an escape from the turmoil and uncertainties of life, just as novels for adults did, but they also reflected changing attitudes toward childhood. No longer considered simply little adults, people grew more accepting of children's playful behavior.

Even without a specific line of detective books for young readers, elements of mystery and detection were important features of stories geared to a younger audience. Fairy tales frequently featured children victimized by unscrupulous parents, stepparents, and strangers, or children trapped in threatening situations. Hansel and Gretel, for instance, narrowly escape the clutches of a witch who hopes to eat them. They return home with her jewels to rescue their impoverished father.

In Britain, Robert Baden-Powell considered the ability to solve murders so important for children that he included it in his 1908 handbook, *Scouting for Boys*.[43] He provides instructions on what to do in case of finding a dead body, emphasizing the need to collect clues and make detailed notes if the body is to be removed. Baden-Powell recommended that boys could sharpen their observational skills by reading detective stories. Girl Scouts did not receive the same direct attention to crime as boys did, but the 1920 *Scouting for Girls* handbook for American scouts did emphasize the importance of careful observation. "Let nothing be too small for your notice . . . even a fingerprint which is almost invisible to the naked eye has often been the means of detecting a crime," the handbook read. "With a little practice in observation you can tell pretty accurately a man's character from his dress."[44]

It was the Stratemeyer Syndicate's Nancy Drew that brought the young female sleuth directly to children, though young readers had certainly read various detective novels for decades. Edward Stratemeyer presided over a novel-writing team that developed many of the most popular children's detective fiction series, including the Hardy Boys, the Dana Girls, Tom Swift Jr., and the Happy Hollisters. Nancy Drew first appeared in 1930 in *The Secret of the Old Clock*, written for the syndicate under the name Carolyn Keene.

Drew wasn't that different from her sleuthing peers. Though younger than many of her predecessors, the sixteen-year-old represented a version of girlhood that blended conventional femininity with the physical resilience, intelligence, and independence of the New Woman. Drew investigated mysteries that were closer to home than those of the Hardy Boys, but she still faced risks. She was bound, gagged, and locked up more than once.[45] Like Violet Strange, Drew had the financial means and freedom to travel to solve crimes, unencumbered by school (she was originally a sixteen-year-old high school graduate and later rewritten to be an eighteen-year-old graduate), family, or domestic responsibilities. Like Strange, Drew also lost her mother when she was young, and both young women had fathers who paid little attention to their whereabouts. Unlike Strange, though, Drew was not a professional detective—but she's treated like one. She navigates the adult world with ease while still going to malt shops and dances, just as Strange attends the society events of her peers. At the same time, Drew was child-like enough to be rescued and protected when necessary.[46] Over the course of the novels, Drew remained an adolescent, even as her gadgets, activities, and car changed with the times. Her formulaic adventures are consistent in theme: evil is always defeated by good. For young readers transitioning from childhood to adolescence to adulthood, this consistency offered a similar sense of reassurance that detection provided adult readers.[47]

Less perfect and less ageless than Drew was girl detective Judy Bolton. Created by Margaret Sutton in 1932, the fifteen-year-old Bolton grows up and marries over the course of thirty-eight books, while continuing to solve mysteries.[48] Marriage does not constrain her nor do the restrictions society places on women, despite her complaint early in the series that she wishes she were a boy "who goes into all kinds of dangers." Bolton later snaps at a man who seems surprised by her intellect: "Of course I'm thinking. What do you suppose my head is for, to decorate my shoulders?" In her day, Bolton was second only to Drew in sales and popularity, though she is less revered today.

Younger than Drew and Bolton was thirteen-year-old Trixie Belden, who lives on a farm in the Hudson Valley with her family. A tomboy with short hair and a tendency to snap at her brothers, Belden struck her many fans as more realistic than Drew. She struggles with school, complains about chores, and gets frustrated. Like other girl detectives, though, she solves mysteries that baffle the authorities, most in service to her family or neighbors. Belden surrounds herself with a diverse group of friends, from the wealthy Honey Wheeler to abused orphan Jim Frayne and reformed troublemaker Dan Mangan. They, along with Belden's brothers, form a club called the Bob-Whites of the Glen to have adventures. Belden appeared in thirty-nine books, starting in 1948 and stretching all the way to 1986.[49]

By the late 1930s, crime and detection stories had become a sweeping force in children's publishing. Like adult female detectives, these girl detectives engaged with the world in ways usually impossible for children. Detective stories were also some of the few books for young women where love was not the object. Nancy Drew has a boyfriend, but he plays a secondary role to detection. Cherry Ames, the creation of Helen Wells, detects while working a series of nursing assignments after finishing school, from cruise nurse to ski nurse, that take her around the world in twenty-seven novels published between 1943 and 1968. Wells broke ground in children's literature by depicting a woman with a career who is independent and willing to speak her mind. Ames changes assignments and locations with every book, and turns down proposals from young doctors in favor of her career. It's brainwork, not love, that drives the young detective.[50]

Young female detectives also found their way into broadcast media. From the 1920s onward, film, radio, and, eventually, television were obsessed with crime stories. Hollywood production codes governing morality and limiting sexuality on screen inadvertently facilitated the proliferation of independent career women. Detectives and girl reporters as detectives proved ideal heroines, keeping the focus on sleuthing rather than romance.

One of the most famous of these was Torchy Blane, played by Glenda Farrell in seven of the nine Blane films. One poster for the 1937 film *Smart Blonde* called Blane "a hard-boiled reporter with a soft-boiled heart!"[51] In the film, Blane chases a train on foot and lands on board the deck of the caboose like an action hero. She then straightens her coat and passes through the car like a respectable lady. In *Torchy Blane in Panama*, Blane parachutes out of a plane into the Atlantic Ocean and climbs a rope to sneak off a cruise ship. She also regularly wears trousers. Blane thrilled at murders and sets to work solving cases, excitedly calling her editor to report stories. Strong women like Blane reflected the independence of the New Woman and the reality of the Depression, which saw more women working out of financial necessity.[52]

As in novels of the day, these female detectives and detecting reporters were more interested in catching criminals than husbands, though many films ended with a marriage proposal. Not all women accepted, however, since getting married would end their careers as well as the film series. Both Hildegarde Withers, in *The Penguin Pool Murder* (a spinster in her late thirties on the page and slightly older on screen), and Sarah Keate, in *While the Patient Slept*, receive offers of marriage from the police detective in charge of the investigation, but both remain single throughout their respective six films. Reporter-detective Florence Dempsey, played by Torchy Blane actress Glenda Farrell, goes so far as to memorably declare to her friend Charlotte in *The Mystery of the Wax Museum*, "You raise the kids; I'll raise the roof!" She further proclaims that she "would rather die with an athletic heart from shaking cocktails and bankers than expire in a pan of dirty dishwater!" Unlike female detectives in books, women on the screen attracted men with this tough talk and their masculine careers. They could be outspoken and driven while also being valued and desired by men, something that took several more decades for women in books to achieve.[53]

A certain type of actress took on these bold screen detectives. The great film celebrities of the era, including Greta Garbo and Jean Harlow, never played detectives. The stars were instead character actors or B-film stars, many with a history of playing working girls who talked back and refused to be submissive. Glenda Farrell was the quintessential wise-cracking, fast-talking dame of the 1930s movie screen. She was even promoted during her years as Torchy Blane as being able to speak four hundred words in forty seconds. Actresses like Farrell had a strong association with the working class and seemed to embody the spirit of modern America and modern womanhood.[54]

Women also sleuthed on the radio, in detecting careers that lasted longer than their sisters on screen. Young sleuth Phyl Coe, a name derived from the show sponsor, Philco, a maker of batteries and radios, made her detecting debut in 1936. Described as "the beautiful girl detective," Coe starred in fifteen-minute episodes that invited listeners to solve each night's mystery using official entry blanks from their local Philco dealer. Coe lasted only one year. The next year, Philco decided to change the gender of its detective, turning feminine Phyl into masculine Phil. *Kitty Keene, Inc.*, a soap opera that centered on a former chorus girl turned detective in mid-life, joined Phil in radio detecting in September of 1937. The show ran for four years, the longest run for a radio female sleuth. Movie stars Joan Blondell and Dick Powell starred in the short-lived radio serial *Miss Pinkerton, Inc.*, in 1941. Blondell played Mary Vance, a law school graduate who inherits her uncle's detective agency and earns the nickname "Miss Pinkerton" from New York City police sergeant Dennis Murray, played by Powell. The year 1946 was a banner year for sleuths, with three women arriving on the scene. *Meet Miss Sherlock* played as much for laughs as detection, with ditzy amateur sleuth Jane Sherlock solving cases. *The Affairs of Ann Scotland* starred radio and stage star Arlene Francis as a sexy girl detective. Finally, real-life New York City policewoman Mary Sullivan inspired the series *Policewoman*, which dramatized cases from her career. Sullivan herself added postscripts to the episodes, enhancing the reality of the crimes depicted. This series marked the first pure female sleuth, devoid of comedy or the melodrama of soaps.[55] The glory days of the smart detecting woman did not last, however, as radio's last lady crime fighter went off the air in the early 1950s.

CHAPTER SEVEN

Breaking Through the Ranks

"**T**HERE'S A DEATH REPORTED FROM OVER HERE ON CLARK STREET,"
reported the station orderly to the captain and a lady detective
inside Chicago's police headquarters.[1] The victim was Eileen Perry, a
young woman of about seventeen or eighteen years old. Stricken by
typhoid, the girl appeared to have died from her illness.

The lady detective, along with a male detective named Williams,
left the station to have a look and were soon "ascending the steps of a
rickety building" past the gaunt, destitute figures of the other inhabitants of the tenement. When the detectives reached the top floor, they
found a janitor waiting for them.

"It's just a case of typhoid," said the janitor, moving toward Williams. "This little girl came here about six weeks ago looking for work.
She didn't find it. About two weeks ago she got sick. We did everything we could for her but there wasn't much money and we couldn't
find out where her folks were."

Williams looked around the room. Seeing nothing suspicious, he
concluded that the police had little to offer a case as obvious as this.

The lady detective, however, was less sure. Spotting a dulcimer in
the corner she asked who it belonged to

"Little Miss Perry, I guess," the janitor answered.

She picked up the instrument and ran her fingers up and down
the strings. She stopped and looked at her hand. The strings were

rough, but no rust was apparent. Taking her magnifying glass from her handbag, she examined the strings again.

After a quick look, the detective handed the instrument to Williams and ordered, "Take this to the microscopist."

"Now what have you got up your sleeve?" Williams asked.

"A murder case and a good one," the lady detective asserted as the two left the scene.

Investigating further, she discovered that the victim had inherited property in Colorado from her long-deceased father. She also found that Miss Perry had an aunt, a Mrs. Brent. The girl had known nothing of her inheritance, which had begun "pouring in money" after the discovery of gold on the property. Nor did she know of her relationship to Mrs. Brent, who had hired Miss Perry as a domestic to get close to the girl and her untapped riches. "An ordinarily good woman who had allowed greed to enter her heart and stifle all else," Mrs. Brent came up with a horrible scheme to claim the land deed for herself.

While on philanthropic business at city hall, Brent stole a tube containing typhoid germs from the public health laboratory. She then paid Miss Perry a visit. Brent found her alone in her room, playing the dulcimer that had once belonged to her father.

"I am thirsty," Brent said. "Could you get me a glass of water?"

The girl laid down the instrument and left the room. Brent drew the culture tube from her bag and applied some of the germs to the strings. She knew that Miss Perry often licked her fingers as she turned the pages of her music.

When the lady detective confronted Brent with her evidence, Brent's face "grew ghastly" at the allegation. She staggered forward and then fainted. When she came to, Brent admitted that money had driven her mad.

But before the detectives could take her to the station, "a wild scream interrupted." Brent plunged forward, "blood streaming from her throat, where she had pierced it with a penknife." She died a few minutes later.

The case, dubbed "The Dulcimer" by the press, seemed something straight from the pen of popular writers Agatha Christie or Dorothy Sayers. Yet the lady detective in the story was none other than Alice Clement of the Chicago Police Department.

Stories like this made Clement famous in the 1910s, while surely invoking the ire of many other pioneer policewomen who sought a quiet and unobtrusive approach to policing. Women had petitioned

Chicago city leaders for policewomen for several years but without success. They had succeeded in getting matrons, two per station, in 1885 but the workload quickly became too great for such a small force. By 1887, eight thousand women fell under matrons' care. Like matrons elsewhere, Chicago's matrons sporadically worked as detectives as well, going undercover to infiltrate brothels or to cozy up to the wives of suspected criminals, as Kate Warne had done for detective Allan Pinkerton's agency. In one instance in 1902, a matron at the Illinois Industrial School for Girls, a kind of juvenile detention center in Evanston, chased a man who kidnapped one of the students for several blocks until he managed to escape, eluding the matron and the male police officers who had joined the chase.[2] Chicago's first official matron-detective, Sarah Wheeler, lost her job after only one year when a new political administration cost her superintendent his job as well.[3]

Some progress was made in 1910 when Chief Justice Harry Olson of the Chicago Municipal Court appointed a committee of women trained in social work to make recommendations for how the court could better serve women and juveniles. The following year, a female social worker was placed on duty to deal with citizens' petty grievances. Visitors flooded her office.

Policewoman Alice Wells lent her support to reformers in Chicago on a lecture stint through the city in 1912. Finally, in December of that year, Chicago passed an ordinance authorizing the hiring of policewomen, but left the number of hires subject to budgetary constraints.[4]

Chicago mayor Carter Harrison recommended that the city council hire ten women for assignment to "bathing beaches, parks, and juvenile court work."[5] He argued that certain types of police work and activities were better handled by women because of the "greater care and appreciative attention to the morals and physical requirements of girls." The council passed the order, and Harrison appointed ten women to the Chicago Police on August 1, 1913: Alice Clement, Emma Nukom, Madge Wilson, Lulu Parks, Anna Loucks, Mary Boyd, Nora Lewis, Margaret Butler, Clara Olson, and Mrs. F. W. Willsey. They started five days later.[6]

The hiring of Chicago's policewomen created a media circus, likely due both to the size of the city and to the number hired at once. The ten women ranged in age from twenty-five to fifty. Of the ten, eight were widows. All were trained in social work. Police training consisted of two hours of instruction on their first day given by Chief James McWeeny. He mostly covered what they shouldn't do: "Don't stretch the truth"; "Don't be too strenuous, have compassion"; Don't be nosy"; "Don't use too much force in making arrests"; "Don't complain about long hours"; and "Don't talk more than necessary; let your command-ing officer do most of the talking." The women were then sworn in and given a whistle, fire and patrol box key (before telephones, a sys-tem of locked call boxes with levers sent requests and notifications of emergencies to police and fire departments), a rulebook, and badge. Guns were, as usual, not part of their uniform.[7]

Working in pairs, Chicago's policewomen visited dance halls, excursion boats, beaches, and train stations looking for suspicious people and girls in danger. Although they had the authority to make arrests, the policewomen were encouraged to gather information, "in-struct and persuade" rather than capture and discipline. The *Chicago Daily News* reported that hiring policewomen placed "emphasis upon sympathy and understanding instead of upon mere muscle" in law enforcement.[8] Even so, reporters followed the policewomen's every move, waiting breathlessly to report on their first arrest or, even better, a fight between officers and a suspect. Two days later, the newspapers had their story when a pair of policewomen arrested Nellie Cam-eron on charges of disorderly conduct. A crowd assembled to watch and applaud the policewomen. "Three cheers for the women cops and their first arrest," someone shouted.[9] That arrest was not their last: despite the directive to use persuasion over detention, in 1913 the policewomen arrested approximately ten thousand women.[10]

As Wells continued to travel the nation making the case for po-licewomen, several other cities began to act. Denver, Topeka, San Di-ego, and San Francisco were among those to appoint women to the force in the early 1910s. By 1913, the United States had thirty-eight policewomen. Two years later, the number had increased to seventy in twenty-six cities. Those cities without policewomen often increased the number of matrons and expanded their duties to include some police and detective work.

Even without the title "detective," policewomen performed an investigative function in their daily duties. They went to saloons and dance halls looking for evidence of proprietors serving alco-hol to children or men engaging in white slavery. In Chicago, the city's first African American policewoman, Grace Wilson, busted William New in 1921 after her investigation revealed that the "art gallery" New ran was actually part of a prostitution ring.[11] When girls (and sometimes boys) disappeared or ran away, policewomen gathered the evidence to locate and return them to their families. One Macon, Georgia, policewoman gathered evidence and tracked a missing fourteen-year-old girl named Helen Berry to a boarding-house in New York City, alerting her mother to Berry's whereabouts more than a month after Berry disappeared.[12] Policewomen mon-itored classified ads in newspapers for sexual harassers and fraud-sters offering nonexistent jobs as receptionists, clerks, and models, and apprehended the offenders by posing as applicants. In 1923, Los Angeles policewoman Lula B. Ditter used an assumed name to apply for jobs with agencies promising women movie careers. Most paid her far less than they agreed, if they paid her at all, while others billed her for photographs and makeup classes with vague promises of fu-ture employment that never materialized. These types of agencies placed women in brothels, not movies.[13] Policewomen worked on prostitution and abortion cases, arrested doctors and nurses illegally distributing birth control, and busted fortune-tellers and other swin-dlers. They investigated the home lives of troubled young women. These were not the cases of murder and robbery that fictional de-tectives tackled, but they constituted detective work nonetheless, requiring observation, the collection of evidence, and deduction in a protective function.

The appointment of black policewomen lagged behind that of white policewomen. Los Angeles appointed black men to the force beginning in the 1880s and gave them the same authority as white officers, including the ability to arrest whites. Women were another story. No one believed a black woman should have the power to arrest a white woman. Georgia Robinson joined the Los Angeles Police De-partment in 1916, likely the first black policewoman on a city force. Robinson worked closely with the underprivileged, often bringing women and children home with her for dinner. Tragedy struck in 1928 when a prisoner shoved Robinson's head into the bars of a jail cell, blinding her. The incident forced her retirement from the po-lice but not from social advocacy, and she continued to campaign for women and children's rights. Mary del Valle became the LAPD's first Hispanic officer, in 1917. Another Hispanic woman and two more black officers joined her in the 1920s.[14] New York City appointed its first black officer, Nettie B. Harris, in 1924, though black women had served as juvenile court probation officers since 1917.[15]

Shortly after the United States entered the First World War, in 1917, the federal government launched a vigorous campaign to keep soldiers from alcohol, prostitutes, and venereal disease while they trained for active duty in military camps. The potential for young women, even good middle-class white girls, to become involved with soldiers incited a national panic over "khaki fever." Sensational reports of prostitution and pregnancies out of wedlock in cities near military bases appalled an already anxious nation.[16] In one Illinois town rumors flew that half the graduating senior girls from a local high school had become pregnant after the opening of an aviation base. Anti-vice activities fell under the authority of the Commission on Training Camp Activities and its director, Raymond Fosdick, who sought to promote athletics and other healthy activities to young soldiers. Military-sanctioned activities certainly did not include dalliances with young women. Fosdick established the Committee on Protective Work for Girls and deployed local protective officers, who did much the same work as early policewomen. They kept prostitutes away from military camps, returned runaways to families, and patrolled dance halls and other places of amusement for immoral or suspicious activities. In Fosdick's hands, the eradication of vice became a patriotic cause, and women its foot soldiers.[17]

The war finally compelled New York City to allow women to join the police force. A volunteer Women's Police Reserve patrolled the city in search of potential criminal behavior, including violations of food and fuel rations. In the event an actual crime required physical intervention, reserve members called for the police. These women understood their role was temporary and supplemental: the end of war meant the end of the reserves.

But in January 1918, several months before the war's end, Commissioner Richard Enright hired Ellen O'Grady as a deputy commissioner to handle the hundreds of female lives wrecked every year by loafers, mashers, and white slavers.[18] He rationalized the decision by pointing to women's expertise in investigating youth and sex crimes. As the NYPD brought more women into wartime police work, some officials began to think that women could have a permanent if limited role in the department. Women, concerned about their status after the war and the men who might view them as a threat, embraced their femininity by emphasizing their caring and protective nature over women and children as a way to keep their jobs.

Detective Allan Pinkerton (seated, on the right) at Antietam during the Civil War. Standing behind Pinkerton holding the tent pole is believed to be Kate Warne, the first female detective in America, dressed as a man. (Circa 1860s)

Police matron Sarah Hill, who joined the police department of Davenport, Iowa, in 1893.

Anna Katherine Green, the "Mother of Detective Fiction." (Circa late nineteenth century)

Many people could not even imagine what a female police officer would look like, so this Ohio suffragist demonstrated how a policewoman would appear making an arrest. (Circa 1909)

The primary duty of policewomen was to prevent delinquency among young girls on city streets. (Circa 1910)

Ten women joined the Chicago Police Department in 1913. From left to right: policewomen Anna Loucks, Clara Olson, Fannie Willsey, Margaret "Madge" Wilson, Lulu Parks, Margaret Butler, Alice Clement, and Emma F. Nukom, as well as reformer Gertrude Howe Britton of the Juvenile Protective Association. Not pictured are Mary Boyd and Nora Lewis.

The second woman from the left is Georgia Robinson, the first black policewoman in the United States. She was hired by the Los Angeles Police Department in 1919.

Detective Mary Shanley of the New York Police Department pickpocket squad was well known for her skill with a revolver. (1937)

Anne Francis as TV's Honey West, with her pet ocelot, Bruce. (1965)

Angie Dickinson as Pepper Anderson from the 1970s TV program *Police Woman.*

Best-selling and highly praised author Phyllis Dorothy (P. D.) James rose to fame for her series of detective novels starring Adam Dalgliesh.

Carolyn Heilbrun, writing as Amanda Cross, was the creator of amateur sleuth Kate Fansler, an upper-class woman who uses her wealth to fund her cases.

Sue Grafton, creator
of detective Kinsey
Millhone.

Mark Coggins

Sara Paretsky, creator
of detective V. I.
Warshawski.

Steven Gross

Jacqueline Winspear created a modern "Golden Age" detective in Maisie Dobbs.

Detective Olivia Benson from *Law and Order: Special Victims Unit*, played by Mariska Hargitay, is one of the best-known female TV detectives. Pictured here with her partner, Detective Nick Amaro, played by Danny Pino.

The women proved their worth, and in 1920, the New York state legislature approved a bill incorporating women into the police department as patrolwomen. Applicants fell under the rules of the Municipal Civil Service Commission, which required women to stand at least five foot two, weigh 120 pounds, and be between the ages of twenty-one and thirty-five.[19] They also had to have some experience in social work or nursing. Enright issued his new policewomen revolvers and handcuffs, granted them arresting authority, and, remarkably, paid them the same as male officers, $1,200 per year.[20]

Among the women to lobby for policewomen in New York City was Mary Sullivan, the first female homicide detective.[21] Smart, cunning, and confident, Sullivan had entered the force as a matron in 1911 after the death of her young husband. She was twenty-six years old and had police in her family, from her uncle and three of her six brothers to a cousin who was an inspector for Scotland Yard and a sister who nabbed shoplifters in department stores. Precinct commanders asked for Sullivan's help in investigations. When a young woman was brought in for questioning about a neighborhood murder, the deputy commissioner asked Sullivan to intercede when the girl refused to utter a word. She soon had the girl talking and learned "everything she knew about the case."[22] Sullivan's success brought her more detective assignments, most of which required her to go undercover and interact with suspected criminals or their wives. This work made her realize "how much dramatic ability has to do with success as a detective."[23]

Sullivan's first big case came in 1912, after the murder of notorious gambler Herman Rosenthal. The case revealed the depth of corruption within the police department, with officers receiving payments from saloons, brothels, and gambling houses to stay open. Sullivan kept track of the wives and lovers of the suspects. She spent weeks with Rosie Harris, a prostitute and one-time companion of one of the alleged gunmen, to win her trust and, hopefully, information. Rosie introduced Sullivan to the wives of two other possible suspects, and the four spent many afternoons together in coffeehouses. The wives "were both bleached blondes, smothered in white fox furs despite the summer weather" and talked often of their need to move to keep ahead of the law.[24] Sullivan spent nights in cheap boardinghouses and opium dens in pursuit of evidence. Her skill and insightful reports won her high praise from the department and the district attorney, and led to the conviction of police lieutenant Charles Becker, the officer charged with ending vice in the city, who had orchestrated Rosenthal's murder.

Sullivan spent the next five years working as a detective in Harlem, working to foil quack doctors and fraudulent advertisers, and gathering clues in cafes and dance halls. However, Sullivan found it tough to disguise herself while working the same district and the same court again and again. So she bought several cheap evening dresses and wide-brimmed hats that she pulled over her face. She sometimes wore a pair of nonprescription glasses and, as she described it, tortured her hair into different styles. Sullivan also learned to mimic the foreign accents she heard around her.[25]

It was a life she kept largely separate from her family and friends. When asked about her detecting, Sullivan seldom offered anything "beyond a funny story or two." She preferred to keep her work at work for the sake of a normal life but also because of the kind of cases in which she was involved. Her dual identities as a police officer and mother became the underlying story of her 1938 memoir, *My Double Life*.[26]

In 1918, Sullivan was assigned to the Homicide Bureau as a second-grade detective, the first woman ever named a homicide detective. She later described the promotion as "one of the major thrills of my life."[27] Undercover work remained her primary function. One case had her locked in prison for two weeks so she could observe a female prisoner connected with the murder of a Mrs. Mary Hamil. Every two or three days, Sullivan was taken away from the jail under some false pretense to make her report to her commanding officer. In several other cases, she posed as a Board of Health inspector to get inside the homes of families in the tenements to uncover squalid living conditions.[28]

Like Allan Pinkerton, Sullivan had little patience with fictional detectives or their creators.[29] She contended that fictional crimes were far too complex to be real. "When one man sets out to kill another, he doesn't simply shoot him," she wrote. "He lures him into a swimming pool that contains man-eating fish or he arranges to have a medieval battle-axe fly out of the wall when a spring is touched in a room some distance away." Every bit of planning provided more evidence and made the case easier, not harder, to solve, she claimed. Sullivan was particularly exasperated by novels in which "a brilliant amateur solves the case after the professionals have proved themselves to be incredibly stupid." In Sullivan's experience, she had never known a murder case to be taken over and solved by an unskilled amateur. She certainly had a good point. Sullivan also objected to the bolt of inspiration that seemed to hit the fictional detective and lead to the solution to every case. "Murder cases aren't broken by a series of brain waves," Sullivan wrote. "Their solving is often the result of a patient drudgery that the inspiration boys wouldn't dream of following through." As detective stories with female sleuths became more common and popular, women often offered their services to Sullivan free of charge, claiming some special skill or psychic ability that would make them great detectives. "Though the Policewomen's Bureau is quite shorthanded," Sullivan commented dryly, "we wouldn't dream of admitting these romantic amateurs."

As more women joined law enforcement, many began to believe they needed a national organization to promote their cause and demand professional recognition.[30] "The need for policewomen is one angle of the very general need for women in lines of activity once wholly occupied, and without dispute, by men," declared Alice Wells before the National Conference of Charities and Correction annual meeting in Baltimore in 1915. "Always, women have cared for and protected the young; yet the police department which has charge of these strategic places where the young gather has been composed of men dependent upon the voluntary or collateral help of women, if any were given." With these words, Wells inspired the birth of the International Association of Policewomen (IAP), a professional organization, with Wells as its leader, designed to further the ambitions and, in some ways, correct the public image of female officers.

Policewomen faced continual critiques of their fitness for the job. Their physical strength was repeatedly questioned in regard to their ability to effectively police. In many instances, police chiefs seemed to set their policewomen up for failure. Chief James Gleason assigned several female officers to oversee a waitress boycott at a Chicago restaurant in 1914. Fights occasionally broke out between the police and picketers, drawing onlookers eager to see women coming to blows. The crowd grew so large that mounted police were called in to break it up. Gleason removed the policewomen from the scene and called the effort a failure, blaming it on the women's lack of physical strength. He grudgingly admitted that the boisterous crowd might have complicated policing for any officer, male or female, but he still concluded, "Policewomen are failures at handling disorderly persons of their own sex."[31] A reporter covering the event came to a similar conclusion, writing that the boycott demonstrated that "women will resist strenuously being arrested by a sister in uniform." Not only were women apparently physically incapable of being police officers; this incident also seemed to demonstrate that women could not handle other women, the foundation on which the policewomen movement was premised.[32]

Despite his condemnation of policewomen, Gleason swore in nine more women only a few days after the boycott fight. Recent events compelled him to order additional training for these officers, though: jujitsu. The New York Times reported the news with the headline "Policewomen to Wrestle."[33]

The IAP took an extremely negative view of the use of physical force in policing. Members may have been trying to avoid any appearance of competing with male officers, but force also conflicted with their perception of a woman's role. When asked why her division carried no firearms, Detroit's Victoria Murray, director of the city's policewomen, claimed that her officers "do not know what guns are" and "would not know what to do with them."[34] Some policewomen carried clubs or blackjacks, and a small handful carried weapons out of necessity as they patrolled potentially dangerous parts of town. But nearly all policewomen gauged their success not on arrests but on crime prevention. "A police woman will not receive credit by the number of arrests she makes. The few arrests the better, and we must get away from the idea of the strong-arm woman," explained Murray. Of course, the limitations placed on early policewomen and their narrow scope of duties also ensured they had fewer occasions for arrests. Policewomen specialized in comforting lost children, answering letters about missing persons, interviewing female victims of crimes, handling domestic disputes, and giving advice to parents about their wayward children. They were, in essence and in fact, mothers, who believed that the best way to practice their maternal brand of policing was in their own division, a women's bureau completely separate from male officers and male supervision. "Through love, sympathy, encouragement, and personal interest we try to teach children their duty to their parents and to society and by this same method awaken parents to their own duties and responsibilities," explained Los Angeles policewoman Aletha Gilbert.[35] Besides parents, Gilbert encouraged teachers, principals, and court officers to come to her for advice when their "boy or girl is getting beyond their control." Gilbert hoped that policewomen like her could be a "mother to the motherless."

Motherhood was one area where women laid particular and exclusive claim. As mothers, women had a credible reason to enter law enforcement, even if the mothering wasn't of their own children but of society's children. The actual marital and maternal status of policewomen never became central to the movement. While there was likely an expectation that women would leave work when they married, there was no requirement. The IAP chalked up the resignation of one policewoman to its "arch-enemy, matrimony," but the tone was playful rather than condemnatory.[36] Policewomen married but usually continued working. It was a rare instance of reality trumping fiction. Mothers and wives couldn't yet sleuth in fiction—detection on the page belonged to spinsters, girls, and, later, divorcees—but in real life, they might become policewomen.[37]

The Women's Bureau formed in 1918 in Washington, DC, partly in response to lobbying by reformers. The bureau was led by wealthy widow and suffragist Mina Van Winkle. She directed a group of four women that soon grew to twenty; two were African American.[38] The work was hard, the hours long, and the pay low. "It has been rather difficult to secure the full quota of policewomen allowed," Van Winkle said, because of "the desire of most women to have at least one day's rest in seven. The staff has never been large enough to have a special detail for nightwork. The policewomen who are on duty all day investigating and aiding in the prosecution of court cases are compelled to go on duty at night and remain out until midnight and after."[39] Like every other policewoman in the country, the officers in Washington wore no official uniform, though they did have a dress code: plain, dark suits with stockings and low, flat heels in gray, brown, or black. Unlike many other policewomen, though, Van Winkle trained her officers in the use of a revolver and rifle.[40]

Getting a separate women's bureau had involved one fight; keeping it became another for Van Winkle. This was true wherever and however departments organized its officers. Directors served at the discretion of the chief and could fall victim to internal or external pressures. Speaking in 1921, Van Winkle said she faced a "continuous struggle for existence against the forces of evil in the District of Columbia."[41] But it was a battle she believed worth fighting for the welfare of the city's young people. Her department devoted its energies to cases and preventative work involving women and children. Van Winkle asserted that separate bureaus were absolutely necessary because policewomen under the direction of men often had no control over the work assigned to them: "Usually he places her in some clerical position and nine times out of ten concludes before he sees the woman that she is unable to render any service in the police department."[42] Van Winkle argued that employing well-qualified women squelched any opposition to policewomen. "Vulgar, uneducated, untrained policewomen degrade the service in the eyes of both the public and the policemen," she declared.[43] That her own bureau faced continued challenges to its power suggested her blindness to women's struggles, particularly women not as well born and well off as herself. Few women could afford the education and experience required of officers under Van Winkle's charge, and even fewer were used to the privilege and deference afforded women of Van Winkle's status.[44]

Van Winkle's officers did more than just aid and advise. When a Russian countess rumored to be a spy checked into the Willard Hotel, just a few blocks from the White House, the Justice Department sent J. Edgar Hoover and twenty-four-year-old policewoman Imra Buwalda to work surveillance. Buwalda posed as a maid in the hotel and, as she cleaned rooms, observed the countess's movements. While the countess turned out to be innocent of espionage, Hoover and Buwalda did discover that "she had a most interesting sex life."[45]

Confrontations over jurisdiction and authority plagued Van Winkle's bureau into the 1920s. In February 1922, the police chief declared that, effective March 1, all matters relating to runaway children and women of any age would fall under the authority of the Women's Bureau. Previously, runaways had fallen under the purview of the Detective Bureau. On March 20, only a few weeks after the order went into effect, fourteen-year-old Jane Evans and sixteen-year-old Gwendolyn Pell ran away from their homes in Brooklyn. The girls had cut their hair short, wore boys' clothes, and were armed, one with a revolver and both with knives. A few days later, the girls, stranded at a train station in Washington, DC, with no money, called home for help. Their fathers contacted the DC Metropolitan Police Department, which sent male detectives to find the girls at Union Station. After taking their story, the detectives delivered the girls to the Women's Bureau in the middle of the night. The girls' fathers arrived the next morning and demanded the immediate release of their daughters. Van Winkle declined their request, saying she would have to verify the identities of the men first. Incensed by the delay, the fathers went straight to the chief of police to complain. Although Van Winkle soon released the girls to their fathers after confirming their identity, the chief charged Van Winkle with insubordination.[46]

Van Winkle felt she had done nothing wrong. How could she be certain these men were who they said they were and not white slavers? Protecting young women was the chief task of the Women's Bureau, and she had wanted to be sure these girls received adequate care. Van Winkle's trial before the police board brought much unwanted publicity to the department and drew representatives of women's organizations from around the country. More was at stake than simply Van Winkle's professional future and reputation. Many reformers feared that a guilty verdict would undermine the recognition of women's natural authority over women and children, which underwrote much of their work in social services. For policewomen, a guilty verdict might subject them to the whims of policemen or the elimination of their positions completely.[47] The trial board found Van Winkle not guilty but chided that she didn't seem to have a "proper conception of the cardinal principle of discipline . . . namely that the orders of a superior in rank must be accorded respect at all times."[48]

The conflict and Van Winkle's subsequent trial were not about the chain of command but about women's place within it. Van Winkle followed a social-work methodology rather than police protocol in handling the runaway girls. Policemen saw no reason to interfere with the demands of parents, while policewomen sought to safeguard homes, protect women, and defend morality. In the policemen's minds, Van Winkle had undermined the authority of the force. But female officers tended to privilege girls' interests over parental authority. Mothering meant listening to and protecting children. A runaway might be trying to escape an abusive home rather than simply acting out, they argued, and it was the job of policewomen to investigate the situation and find a solution.[49]

New York City established a Women's Precinct in 1921 and placed Mary Hamilton in charge of approximately one hundred women. The mayor, city officials, and leaders in social services attended its opening ceremony, on April 4, 1921. Located in a separate building in Hell's Kitchen and staffed entirely by women, the precinct contained a clinic, workroom, school, and temporary hospital to detain girls waiting for results from tests for venereal disease. The building required some work. Policemen had previously abandoned the space in the high-crime, poverty-stricken neighborhood after declaring it a "dingy, dirty rathole."[50] The patrolwomen of New York cleaned it up and redecorated to make it look as little like a typical police station as possible. They removed all the "earmarks of a regular police station" and transformed the space into a "center where a woman could seek information, advice or aid" from other women without "the grim atmosphere of the average police desk."[51]

The Women's Precinct kept runaways and other wayward girls detained without charges separate from the hardened criminals. These girls had previously stayed at private homes, often sharing rooms with women awaiting trial.[52] Hamilton stressed the importance of separate quarters to prevent the contamination of "innocent girls" by "immoral women."[53] Runaway girls were of particular importance to Hamilton because "every girl whether good or bad is a potential mother and in her rests the hope of the next generation."

A little more than two years after its heralded opening, however, the Women's Precinct closed. Hamilton mentioned nothing publicly or in writing about problems there—she went out of her way never to antagonize the male police establishment—but she almost certainly faced interference and hostility from male officers if other cities were any guide.[54] Like many of her fellow reformers, Hamilton had an idealistic view of what her precinct could do and the willingness of young women to seek out help. She exhorted her officers to use their powers of arrest only as a last resort, preferring, instead, to have men do the arresting so that the reputation of policewomen as a "friend and protector may be maintained."[55]

The precinct proved most successful in training its own officers and garnering national attention. Police from around the country visited to see how the facility worked. Precinct officers took courses in first aid, casework methods, detective techniques, and physical education and received guidance in working with delinquent girls. Physical tests required policewomen to jump three feet over a rope and to squeeze a machine with a force equal to a hundred pounds. Hamilton also advised her officers to wear a long pin in their lapel to use as a weapon if necessary.

With the closing of the precinct, Hamilton was transferred back to headquarters. In 1924, the welfare functions of the Women's Precinct were absorbed into a new unit, the Policewomen's Bureau, under Hamilton's supervision. The bureau performed regular policewomen duties but without the housing and training. Hamilton resigned two years later, however, replaced by Mary Sullivan, the first woman to become a homicide detective in New York City and later the subject of the radio program *Policewoman*. For Sullivan, it was a transition to a more administrative position. Now she did the assigning of police-women to cases requiring a female detective.[56]

The struggles of women in Washington, DC, and New York were not unusual. Policewomen succeeded in establishing women's bu-reaus in only a few departments. Most cities scattered policewomen throughout the precincts, often alone or in units under the direction of men, where the female officers routinely made arrests in addition to doing protective work. Perhaps none more so than in Chicago, where, in 1925, policewomen arrested and booked more than eighteen thou-sand women. This invited the criticism of female officers in other cit-ies, who pointed to the high number as evidence of their failure at preventative work.[57] Chicago's Alice Clement didn't care. She relished her skills with a gun—she even slept with it under her pillow.[58]

No cities hired policewomen of their own volition; all were hired after intense pressure and lobbying by women's groups. Men opposed to policewomen drove them out gleefully whenever they could. For-mer vaudeville performer Alma Longgale was pushed out of her job in Racine, Wisconsin, after a series of anonymous sources left mes-sages claiming she used her home as an illicit rendezvous spot for assignations with businessmen.[59] Opponents also distributed around town photos from her days as a vaudeville "strong woman" clothed in a tight leopard-skin suit. Another woman, Vera Bash, found herself out of a job in Portsmouth, New Hampshire, after opponents found her too attractive to be effective at policing. "Her beauty interfered with her work," reported the *Portsmouth Herald*. "The presumption is that no one had the hardness of heart to tell the young woman that beauty is not an asset to the Police Department."[60]

Outside the departments themselves, female officers in the early twentieth century generated a wave of satirical commentary and scornful caricatures. Cartoons of women dressed in some kind of paramilitary uniform and fully armed were common in newspapers and magazines.[61] In one unnamed city, around 1914, a reporter al-legedly found the police chief trying to teach six new policewomen to shoot pistols and handle an eighteen-inch club "without great suc-cess."[62] The scene was presented as the height of silliness. Soon af-ter her appointment, Alice Wells was portrayed by reporters in Los Angeles "as a bony, muscular, masculine person, grasping a revolver, dressed in anything but feminine apparel, hair drawn tightly into a hard little knot at the back of the head, huge unbecoming spectacles, small stiff round disfiguring hat."[63] This about a woman described elsewhere as "scarcely five feet in height, slender, with a mild, almost timorous voice and a pair of very round blue eyes" that make her "as formidable as . . . a kitten."[64]

The hiring of female officers stagnated in the 1920s and 1930s. Seeking efficiency and discipline, police departments began focusing more on crime fighting than social services, interventions, and mothering. New rank structures made officers accountable to police supervisors instead of politicians and, most importantly for women, the community they had long relied on for support. Women had always accounted for a smaller fraction of the total number of crimes committed, so with less attention paid to crimes against morality, the number of women booked dropped. With these changes, policewomen faced increasingly limited venues for exercising their authority as their unique occupational identity, which they had struggled for years to establish, shrunk to nearly the point of extinction.[65]

Women also faced increasing pressure to go home. By the 1930s, universities had earned the nickname "spinster factories," and women were urged to marry, have babies, and focus on their families instead of wasting time in college or pursuing a career. World War II marked a brief backpedaling on that front, as women were needed to fill jobs. Newspapers, magazines, and newsreels boosted the young, single woman's profile. But when the war was over, the men returned and women were guided back into the home by the same media that had called them strong, independent, and capable only a few years before.

One challenge for policewomen was that the crimes of middle-class and upper-class homes, which gripped readers in books, proved less appealing in real life. Many middle-class Americans balked at the possibility that an officer could investigate their parenting methods like a crime and render judgment on their ability to inculcate children with proper moral sense. The preventative rhetoric espoused by progressive reformers lobbying on behalf of policewomen was not meant for people like themselves—middle-class whites—but for control of the lower classes, especially immigrants. The thought that policewomen could intrude on middle-class private lives, and even go so far as to take children from their homes for investigation, pushed the limits of acceptance of police as a positive influence in family and community life. Policewomen themselves disagreed about the scope of their powers to inspect neighborhood conditions, crack down on fraudsters, and intervene in lives from the very beginning, divisions that split and limited the effectiveness of the movement.[66]

The women who entered policing in the 1930s were different from those of the pioneer generation. Economic necessity created by the Depression dispelled much of the idealism attached to the profession. Desperate for work, policewoman Helen Bauer said, "We didn't particularly want to become policewomen. We just took every civil-service exam that came along and prayed for a job."[67]

CHAPTER EIGHT

Hard-Boiled Heroes

F OR THE HARD-BOILED HERO OF THE 1930S AND 1940S, VIOLENCE CAME easily. It tested and revealed a man's honor, his moral code. It marked his masculinity. "Down these mean streets a man must go who is not himself mean," wrote Raymond Chandler in his classic 1944 essay "The Simple Art of Murder," originally published in the *Atlantic Monthly*.[1] "He is the hero, he is everything. He must be a complete man and a common man and yet an unusual man." Chandler's glorified hero was a lot of things but, above all, he was a man. Detective stories of this period were filled with tough men: cool, smart, and world-weary. The image of the lone private eye navigating a corrupt and criminal world guided by his own sense of justice became a hallmark of the hard-boiled detective genre—indeed, of the American crime story itself.

Yet down these same mean streets, women like Bertha Cool, Gale Gallagher, and Honey West stumbled over corpses, drank scotch, and carried guns. It turns out that, despite the stereotypes, some mid-century hard-boiled dicks were, in fact, janes.

The hard-boiled detective first emerged in pulp magazines. Named for the rough wood-pulp paper they were printed on, "pulps" filled with action-packed stories crowded American newsstands beginning in the 1920s and drew a new demographic of readers.

Until the late nineteenth century, only wealthy Americans read magazines. Monthlies such as *Harper's* and *Scribner's* featured articles on art, literature, European travel, and etiquette, which appealed to well-educated readers with the means to afford a cover price of up to thirty-five cents. Publisher Frank Munsey started a publishing revolution in 1893 when he cut the price of his *Munsey's Magazine* from twenty-five cents to ten cents and broadened the scope of its content. The low price and broader coverage attracted a new audience. Munsey's strategy was soon taken up by a whole generation of media entrepreneurs eager to reach a broader readership.[2]

The earliest pulps grew out of dime novels, which had fallen from favor as changes in postal regulations made it too costly to distribute them through the mail. Publishers moved to mass production, and in the early twentieth century, newspapers and magazines began to carry serialized fiction. Many publishers simply repackaged dime novels in pulp-magazine form. Pulps cost between five and twenty-five cents and were unmistakably trash—cheap to produce, written by professional "hacks," and designed for the garbage heap after reading.

Paid by the piece, pulp writers churned out tens of thousands of words with little editing and often under a pseudonym or several pseudonyms. It wasn't uncommon for a single issue to be produced by a single writer using a different name for each story. These writers earned little respect in the literary world because they seemed more like manufacturers than artists. Most lacked a college education. Editors cared less for the aesthetics of their fiction than for its quantity. Like their predecessors, pulps fed on the popular taste for escapist fiction and fantasy adventure.[3]

Intense competition and constant demand for innovation made the pulps highly responsive to shifting tastes. The wave of crime that accompanied Prohibition drew public attention to racketeering, corruption, and violence. Pulp writers and editors responded with a new type of detective story, which set aside the genteel features of the country estate and small town in favor of the grisly details of urban crime.[4]

Among the best of the new pulp titles was the *Black Mask,* first published in 1920. Its early banner promised "Detection, Mystery, Adventure, Romance and Spiritualism," but the magazine soon narrowed its focus to primarily "Gripping, Smashing Detective Stories." It was an accurate description as the *Black Mask* soon became synonymous with a certain type of crime story after the publication of Carroll John Daly's "The False Burton Combs," in 1922.

Although Poe had invented the modern detective story, its image in the twentieth century, largely promoted by Chandler, associated the genre with British writers and conventions. But this story elides the very real role of Americans, particularly women like Anna Katherine Green and Catherine Louisa Pirkis, in the development of detective fiction. The intellectual mystery in a mansion was just as much an American phenomenon as it was British. American detective fiction before the 1920s was diverse and responsive to cultural currents with urban and rural crimes, victims rich and poor, and detecting duos and singular heroes who were amateurs and professionals.[5]

But the tenor of American detection narrowed with the publication of "The False Burton Combs." Daly epitomized the pulp-industry hack, churning out hundreds of stories with confrontational, sardonic heroes that earned him a huge and devoted popular audience but little critical respect. Daly's hero, Race Williams, is a "man of action" who sleeps with a loaded gun.[6] In stark contrast to the rational detecting of Butterworth, Brooke, and, especially, Holmes, Williams declares, "I have brains, I suppose. We all have. But a sharp eye, a quick draw, and a steady trigger finger drove me into the game."[7] Williams lives up to that description. He's hard-talking and quick to pull the trigger to kill. Rowdy, gritty, and lower class, Daly's stories tapped into Americans' love for fiction that thumbed its nose at manners and refinement. His style inspired other writers, including Dashiell Hammett, Erle Stanley Gardner, and Raymond Chandler. By the late 1920s and 1930s, hard-boiled detectives ruled the pulps.[8]

Hard-boiled men tended to be terse and rude. They used slang and jargon. The unemotional, macho heroes bore names that reflected their spirit—Flashgun Casey, Tough Dick Donahue, Gravedigger Jones, and Battle McKim. More than just a name, the tough guy's power lay in his author's narrative voice. The prose was stripped down into short staccato sentences generally written from the perspective of the private investigator, rather than a sidekick or other narrator. Pulp writers adopted the style for its realism and connection to the working class. Their heroes were not gentlemen but loners completely dedicated to the work out of a nihilistic sense of duty.[9] Women who wanted to fit in and prove they belonged had to know the language. Even decades later, in Sue Grafton's B Is for Burglar, the elderly Julia tells detective Kinsey Millhone, "I'm going to start reading Mickey Spillane just to keep in shape. I don't know a lot of rude words, you know."[10]

Hard-boiled stories busted the polite conventions of the classic "cozy" story. They were American Westerns transported from the frontier to the city, with private investigators playing the role of cowboy. Bodies tended to pile up quickly, and villains ended up dead rather than captured.[11] In "The False Burton Combs," Daly's lone wolf shoots a man "right through the heart" but offers "no apologies, for it was his life or mine."[12] The stories took the corruptness of the rich and powerful as a given, and detectives operated according to their own code of justice and interest in self-preservation. The process of detection was no longer just the solution of a riddle but a quest for truth in a more complex, brutal, and ambiguous reality.[13]

These grisly narratives reflected the sentiments and interests of a drifting and changing urban American population, one more accustomed to the diversity and grunge of urban life than to the contained world of fashionable rural estates. For the working class, life had transformed between the wars. They could increasingly participate in mass consumer culture, shopping in department stores and attending movies, dances, and amusement parks. Skilled workers were increasingly being replaced by unskilled and semiskilled immigrant workers from southern and eastern Europe, as well as by African Americans and women. The autonomous craftsman of the past gave way to machines and managers. Hard-boiled detectives recreated the lone artisan who found himself increasingly at odds with the modern world. "To me, [Philip] Marlowe is the American mind," wrote Chandler of his iconic detective. "[He has] a heavy portion of rugged realism, a dash of good hard vulgarity, a strong overtone of strident wit, an equally strong overtone of pure sentimentalism, an ocean of slang, and an utterly unexpected range of sensitivity."[14]

Chandler called the classic mystery "too contrived, and too little aware of what goes on in the world."[15] It's true that the Depression, the lingering trauma of the First World War, and the rumblings of the second were almost completely ignored by writers of Golden Age detective fiction. They did so on purpose. Writers like Agatha Christie strived for puzzles that intruded on an ideal world but without the intensity that would cast doubt on its eventual solution and the resumption of regular life; they recognized their middle-class readers' desire for gentility and reassurance, and their yearning for a bygone time. What the classic cozy did well was trap some people in an old country house and let them stew within its walls. The story used its limited settings and a controlled and rather isolated set of characters to create tension.[16]

The details of death played a more minor role in detective fiction before the 1920s. Although the subject of all their books was murder, there was very little actual violence or blood in nineteenth-century novels or in those of the Golden Age. In Christie's *Murder at the Vicarage*, the vicar comes across the dead Colonel Protheroe "sprawled across my writing table in a horrible unnatural position."[17] A "pool of some dark fluid" surrounded his head and slowly dripped on the floor with a "horrible drip, drip, drip." Though Protheroe had been shot in the head, that's the only bit of blood—and it's not even identified directly as such—in the book. In these stories, death seems to happen with hardly a sound or mess. It's only in the wake of murder that distress and disorder appear, upsetting the balance of life in the village, home, and family. Hard-boiled writers, on the other hand, wrote stories, Chandler claimed, that depicted "the authentic flavor of life," giving "murder back to the people who committed it for a reason, not [just] to provide a corpse."[18]

Chandler's stance reflected not just the aesthetics of crime fiction but a real professional rivalry with the members of the London Detection Club.[19] Founded in 1928 as an informal social gathering, the club comprised some of the most significant British mystery writers of the time, including Agatha Christie and Dorothy Sayers. Its members were well organized enough to devise a constitution, in 1932, and to write three collaborative novels, each chapter written by a different author, to raise funds for the club. Club members also formulated rules (largely adapted from writer Ronald Knox's 1928 "Ten Commandments of Detection") about what should and should not be done in detective stories.[20] Among the rules, club members agreed, were that it was bad form to rely on coincidence or intuition rather than reason to solve crimes, to withhold clues from the reader, to swear too much, to use humor, and to overuse gangs, ghosts, lunatics, and evil twins. The club emphasized, above all else, that detection was a game. These rules became the initiation oath for members. The London Detection Club soon had rituals as well. The club president wore a red robe and the presided over a host of props, including black candles and a human skull called Eric with red bulbs in its eye sockets. Both Christie and Sayers served terms as president. The club and Eric are around to this day.

Despite the club's social underpinnings, its members were serious about their work and the integrity of the detective genre. Though their work was far from homogenous, club members produced novels that came to epitomize the detective story in its purest form, codifying the genre for decades to come and influencing writers on both sides of the Atlantic.[21]

The London Detection Club was not the only group organizing for detective writers. The Mystery Writers of America also formed during the Golden Age era. Together, these groups signified a growing sense of professionalization on the part of crime writers.

That the best-selling British mystery authors of the 1920s and 1930s were predominantly women—Agatha Christie, Dorothy Sayers, Patricia Wentworth, Margery Allingham, to name a few, was not unnoticed by Chandler and his hard-boiled brethren. These men wrote heroes based on masculine stereotypes that seemed to fulfill fantasies of male strength. That's not to say there weren't any successful male writers of the classical story or even as members of the Detection Club: Anthony Berkeley was instrumental in setting up the club, and G. K. Chesterton, A. A. Milne, and Ronald Knox were among its members. But even so, mystery writing often seemed a particularly feminine occupation due to the popularity of its women authors (even though most created male detectives).

Hard-boiled writers broke the rules of the London Detection Club with abandon (so, too, did members of the club, for that matter). Chandler wanted his books to sell as well as Christie's and the other women he derided as silly, so he went to great pains to separate the two styles.[22]

But the differences were more of substance than form.[23] The hard-boiled and classical detective story shared a similar formula. Both move from the introduction of the detective and the presentation of the crime through the investigation to a solution and apprehension of the criminal. Differences appear in the way this pattern is worked out. Rather than the charming and elegant home of Amelia Butterworth or even the amiable bachelor apartment of Holmes and Watson, the hard-boiled detective belongs to a broken-down building on the sordid margins of the city. In the classical story, the actual capture of the criminal is less significant than the explanation of the crime. The victim is a relatively minor character and the story emotionally detached from the crime itself. The hard-boiled story, on the other hand, often features multiple victims, usually including one close to the detective, not unlike the older Gothic style; the culprit is frequently tied to a larger criminal underground. The solution to the case usually ends with a violent confrontation and the detective forced to come to terms with his own sense of justice.

Despite their claims to a more realistic style, however, hard-boiled writers had little more experience with crime than the writers they sought to displace. Dashiell Hammett had been a Pinkerton detective before beginning his writing career, and he included in his writing details that he learned on the job. But he was an exception. Most hard-boiled writers drew as much from urban folklore and newspapers to craft their corrupt metropolises as the writers dreaming up secluded mansions in picturesque English villages drew on rural folklore and mythology.[24]

On the surface, Amelia Butterworth or Miss Marple would seem to have little in common with Race Williams and Philip Marlowe. But the spinster sleuth served a similar function in her own fictional realm: she, too, navigated a world filled with insincere and dangerous people that she must expose and punish. She's driven by an ethical attachment to right and wrong to work outside the strictures of regular society (and regular womanhood) as an amateur investigator. Her challenge might be greater, however, as she must discover subtle clues and crimes that lie cloaked beneath respectable ordinariness. One expects criminal activity on the "mean streets"; few suspected the horrors hidden within benign country homes.[25]

And though she may not have sought her loner status, the never-married woman has a detachment from regular society that allows her the same objective perspective as the hard-boiled male. Both thrive on the misconceptions and assumptions that come with their roles. The nosy spinster is considered annoying but harmless, preoccupied with gossip, birding, and knitting rather than reasoning. When artist Joyce Lemprière proposes forming a mystery club with her friends, in Christie's story "The Tuesday Night Club," she counts everyone in the room as a member except Miss Marple.[26] "You have forgotten me, dear," Miss Marple calls out. Lemprière, taken slightly aback, conceals her surprise quickly. "I didn't think you would care to play." Miss Marple responds, "I think it would be very interesting, especially with so many clever gentlemen present. I am afraid I am not clever myself, but living all these years in St. Mary Mead does give one an insight into human nature." It was an understatement of her skills that Miss Marple would use to her advantage again and again.

The hard-boiled detective, with his physicality and ties to the working class, is assumed to lack intelligence. "There's very little to tell. I'm thirty-three years old, went to college once and can still speak English if there's any demand for it. There isn't much in my trade," says Philip Marlowe describing himself to General Sternwood in *The Big Sleep*.[27] Hard-boiled detectives may be physically impressive, but their ability to solve crimes goes beyond violence. He is a thinking man who, like the nosy spinster, uses the successful manipulation of stereotypes to great success.[28]

But spinsters don't inhabit the urban world of pulp detectives. The women who appeared in early hard-boiled stories tended toward the amoral femme fatale or predatory vixen. They certainly were not professional or even amateur detectives. In part, this reflected a cultural tradition that defined women by their relationships to others. The female loner was seldom seen in life or literature, so such women seemed incompatible with the urban crime fighter. Most men likely agreed with Race Williams: "I never took a woman seriously. My game and women don't go well together."[29] Part of what made the femme fatale so dangerous to the hard-boiled man was that she threatened his isolation and mastery of emotions. Others were hostile to women. In Chandler's *The Big Sleep*, Philip Marlowe tears apart his bed after a woman has lain in it, declaring the next morning, "Women made me sick."[30] Mickey Spillane's Mike Hammer finds pleasure in hitting women. In these stories women were treated as objects, only redeemable by their submission to male authority.

Some of this spiteful attitude toward women on the page reflected a cultural discomfort with real-life women and their expanding role in society in some quarters of American society. Nearly all the hard-boiled detectives of the 1920s and 1930s were unmarried, and most of the women they met were unprincipled, selfish, and greedy. In the hard-boiled crime world, men were men and women were dangerous.[31]

But even if women played only minor roles on the page, it did not stop them from writing for pulp magazines or creating detectives. Hard-boiled fiction was marketed as particularly manly fare, so women often used pseudonyms or only their initials to conceal their gender. Like many female detective writers of the time, they created mostly male protagonists.[32] In 1936, the *Black Mask* hired a woman, Fanny Ellsworth, as its new editor. Ellsworth was already the editor of another pulp, *Ranch Romances*, which blended the Western with romance and often starred a female heroine. So as to not alienate the magazine's male readers, Ellsworth used her initials rather than her full name on the masthead. Even if some could not believe that a woman would want or be well suited to editorial oversight of such a masculine magazine, Ellsworth was not such an odd choice for editor, as the *Black Mask* had initially published romance stories alongside those of detectives. And women did read the pulps, even if their existence as readers might have been treated as an anomaly. Nearly a quarter of the names listed as contest winners in the *Black Mask* in the 1930s and 1940s were women. But in the minds of industry leaders, the audience for pulps was divided by gender: romance for women and detection for men.[33]

Strong female characters weren't uncommon in the pulps, even if they were seldom seen in hard-boiled detection or marketed as such. In Victor Maxwell's 1926 story "A Good, Smart Girl," Maisie Belknap outwits a disguised murderer and disarms a jewel thief while running a cigar stand in the lobby of a fancy hotel. Women even appeared in magazines like *Gangster Stories* and *Gangland Stories*, often as reporters, mob bosses, and even detectives. C. B. Yorke's heroine Yola Yates is a female detective with her own agency in the story "Hot Numbers," in the May 1931 issue of *Gangster Stories*. Yates carries a gun and does not shy away from confrontations, shouting, "Gun 'em, guys!" after discovering mobsters. Another female detective appeared in the "Ex–Dick, Feminine" stories of Margie Harris in these gangster pulps. These stories of bold professional women appealed to the newly working, urban woman of the 1920s.[34]

A few tough-talking female investigators did appear in detective novels in the late 1930s and 1940s, all by men. Bertha Cool was an overweight, middle-aged widow with a penchant for smoking, fighting, and swearing. Erle Stanley Gardner, best known for the Perry Mason series, created Cool in 1939, publishing under the name A. A. Fair. Gardner described her as possessing "a bulldog jaw, little glittering, greedy eyes," with a temperament just "as hard and tough and difficult to handle as a roll of barbed wire."[35] Unlike many of her contemporaries, Cool is not only a professional but is in charge of her own agency. Some clients hesitate to hire her as a result: "He got afraid I'd be too soft and easy because I was a woman."[36] For enough money, Cool was willing to overlook intimations that women couldn't detect as well as men. She does not detect alone. Young Donald Lam starts as her employee but then moves up to junior partner in her firm. Even though she's in charge, Lam narrates and does most of the legwork to solve cases. Cool offers primarily comic relief, uttering phrases like "Kipper me for a herring!" or "Peel me for a grape!" as she banters and bickers with Lam. Gardner won a loyal following with the series, which stretched to twenty-nine titles.

Similar to Cool, Sam Merwin Jr.'s heroine, Amy Brewster, introduced in 1945, is a cigar-smoking, three-hundred-pound-lawyer who became a detective at the urging of friends. Both Cool and Brewster were everything the genre's typical woman was not: tough, large, and masculine. Their unwomanly appearance and behavior made them far less threatening to men and all but eliminated the possibility of the romance that derailed many other female sleuths. These women were such anomalies, however, that they did not produce notable imitators.[37]

More genuinely hard-boiled than her predecessors was Gale Gallagher, created in 1947 by the team of Will Oursler and Margaret Scott, who wrote under the pseudonym "Gale Gallagher." Gallagher (the detective) heads the Acme Investigating Bureau. She's in her late twenties, single and attractive. "I guess the boys figure the average girl is detective enough without marrying a professional," Gallagher jokes with a friend about being unmarried.[38] Her clients and suspects often insist she looks nothing like a private investigator, likely because few expect one to wear a beaver-fur coat and silk dress to a crime scene. But she trained at the police academy and is competent in the use of firearms, though she rarely carries a gun. Gallagher learned the basics of police work from her father, a New York City policeman killed in the line of duty. He's never far from her mind as she regularly recalls what her father would likely do or say in a certain situation. Walking the streets of Manhattan, Gallagher encounters the standard challenges of the hard-boiled detective—dead bodies, dangerous criminals, and gunfire (she fires back). She's particularly skilled at finding missing persons.[39]

Gallagher is hardly the tough and cynical loner of her male counterparts, though. Her reliance on her late father's wisdom and her boyfriend, the handsome painter Bart Crane, whose cat she feeds in his absence, show her to be connected to family and friends. She, like many of the hard-boiled women who will follow her, relishes her independence while also maintaining personal relationships. Gallagher also pays close attention to her clothes, and she longs for a better wardrobe and perfect makeup. While the authors may have intended this to signal the femininity of their detective, vanity was not an unusual trait among twentieth-century detectives, male or female. Many detectives demonstrated a particular concern with their clothing, hygiene, and physical appearance.[40] The original hard-boiled writers made the physicality of the detective so central that it could border on the ridiculous. Philip Marlowe describes himself as "six feet of iron man. One hundred and ninety pounds . . . Hard muscles and no glass jaw."[41] Marlowe's description reassures the reader that he's man enough for the job. These men also dressed to impress. Marlowe itemizes his wardrobe at the beginning of *The Big Sleep*: "I was wearing my powder-blue suit, with dark blue shirt, tie and display handkerchief, black brogues, black wool socks with dark blue clocks on them." Gallagher with her fur coat wanted to look her best just as much as Marlowe.[42]

Candy Matson was the first hard-boiled woman on the airwaves, in 1949. Sassy, sexy, and sensible, Matson carries a gun, never hesitates to enter the lowliest dive bar for a case, and doesn't take anyone's guff. Monty Masters created Matson and cast his wife, Natalie Parks, in the lead role. Every thirty-minute episode opens with a ringing telephone answered, "Hello, YUKON 2-8209. Yes, this is Candy Matson," followed by the swell of the theme song. Matson's work took her from her apartment on San Francisco's Telegraph Hill to real locations around the Bay Area. Matson works with her best friend and sidekick, Rembrandt Watson, though he is not a doctor like the most famous Watson and provides more comic relief than actual help. Her boyfriend, San Francisco police lieutenant Ray Mallard, continually underestimates her skill, even as she reliably solves cases before him. The show ran on various NBC stations until 1951.[43]

By then, the Cold War had brought spies and scientists to the shadowy forefront. Stories of espionage, technology, and science challenged the popularity of the mystery novel and old-style detectives like Miss Marple and even Sherlock Holmes. The arrival of television as a mass medium also familiarized the public with police methods, forensics, and criminal behavior.

The police-procedural story was one result, a style that aimed to bring realism to the genre of detective fiction by showing policemen solving authentic crimes according to actual police methods. Contrary to the consulting detective of fiction, the real-life private detective rarely investigates murder and is often prohibited by law from doing so. Most spend their time locating missing people or serving court orders and other legal documents. Writers lived with these inconsistencies for decades (they still do), while others developed more credible styles.

The men and women in these stories were strikingly different from the great detectives of fiction and film, who cracked cases only they could untangle using their own eccentric or idiosyncratic techniques. Everyday police work was no place for these singular figures. The restrictions of the job and the police's obligations to society required accessible and human characters, willing and able to collaborate. Detective fiction didn't die out with these transformations, but it did have to adapt to new forms and incorporate new faces for a modern age, including those of women. And because women were employed in many city police forces, they also began to appear in police procedurals.[44]

Jennie Melville, the pseudonym of Gwendoline Butler, wrote one of the first police procedurals with a female protagonist in *Come Home and Be Killed* (1962).[45] The book, the first in a series that continued for nearly forty years, featured working-class Scottish police detective Charmian Daniels, who primarily investigates violent crimes against women in Deerham Hills, outside London. She joins the force because she wants a career "where she could use her sense of justice and order." She's also ambitious, remarking, "There is only one more fearsome thing than a Scotsman on the make . . . and that is a Scotswoman."[46] Like many policewomen of her time, Daniels is first given menial typing and filing tasks, along with monitoring women and children in the stationhouse. But her inquisitiveness is rewarded, and she soon receives promotions and more challenging cases, which garners some resentment from her male colleagues, even many years into her career (and many decades into the series). Daniels remarks in *Footsteps in the Blood*, that "in her profession you were allowed to be a woman, but not too female."[47] In *A Death in the Family* (1994), Daniels considers how to listen in on the questioning of a suspect without being given "the frozen treatment" by her fellow officers for inserting herself where she isn't wanted, even though her rank meant "she could not easily be moved out."[48] The difficulties Daniels faces navigating a male-dominated police department reappear throughout the series as she rises to become a superintendent in the force, much like the trials faced by Jane Tennison in the TV series *Prime Suspect*.

The second-wave feminism of the 1960s brought a reexamination of gender and of the social conceptions attached to women. It also put a gun in the hands of an independent, beautiful, and sexually active woman—the kind of woman who might have been a femme fatale in the 1930s but for her warmth, honesty, and morals.

Honey West is a hard-boiled detective who manages to lose her clothes nearly as often as she uncovers a corpse—"Honey! Where are your clothes?" is a recurring question. West was the creation of Forrest E. Fickling and his wife, Gloria, writing under the name G. G. Fickling between 1957 and 1971. West becomes a detective after the murder of her father, Hank West, and takes over his agency. Her career choice is not without its complications, most particularly due to her physical attractiveness. She's five foot five, with blue eyes, "taffy colored hair," and a small mole on her left cheek. She carries a pearl-handled .22 revolver in her garter. Many people believe that her good looks preclude a detecting career and attempt to steer her to jobs they consider more suited to a woman of her ilk: stripper, movie star, beauty contestant, and, of course, wife and mother. That she ends up disrobed in the course of nearly every book did little to dispel these perceptions. In *Dig a Dead Doll*, West's pursuit of Mexican criminal mastermind Zingo leaves her strung naked from a tree, a situation that leads her nemesis and sparring partner lieutenant Mark Storm to comment, "You seem to be naked more time[s] than you're clothed." In the 1960s, her carefree sexuality marks her as adventurous and puts her in league with hard-boiled men, pursuing sex without relinquishing her detecting career.[49]

Despite her sexual freedom and frequent disrobing, West is tough and competent. In eleven novels, she outmaneuvers police and outsmarts those who underestimate her.[50] West knows what she likes: "masculine men, martinis on the rocks, fast cars, black silk stockings, water skiing, rare steaks, Hemingway, Roquefort salads, dancing, sour cream and chives, apple turnovers and baseball."[51] She fearlessly confronts those who question her right to detection. In *This Girl for Hire*, when Lieutenant Storm asks what she's trying to prove, West heatedly proclaims,

> You've got a lot of guts to tell me what I ought to do—where I ought to get off! Sure, I'm a woman! I act like a woman, think like a woman, look like a woman, but I'm mixed up in a rotten dirty business that men think they own by right of conquest! But you've never stopped to consider that half the crimes in the United States today are committed by women, and half of those committed by men are provoked

by women. So where does that leave you? In a business operated seventy-five percent by females! All right, so you don't think I'm nice. What are you going to do about it?[52]

She also gets into brutal fights. Her father had trained her in judo, which she uses to good effect, winning nearly every contest, despite often enduring savage beatings.[53]

Honey West became a short-lived television series in 1965, starring Anne Francis and produced by Aaron Spelling for ABC. The TV West differed from the woman in the books. Onscreen, she had a pet ocelot named Bruce and a parcel of James Bond–like gadgets, including an exploding compact and a lipstick microphone. She also kept her clothes on. Although the show didn't last, *Honey West* anticipated the glamorous appeal of female detectives yet to come, like Diana Rigg's Emma Peel in *The Avengers*.[54]

Even as these early hard-boiled women appeared torn between traditional female roles and the demands of their profession, they shared some similarities with their male counterparts. Both lived and navigated a similar urban landscape, and they demonstrated an extensive knowledge of street names and city landmarks both major and minor. Neither was afraid of physical force or guns. But the challenges for hard-boiled women were greater. Although they saw themselves as professionals, doing a job they chose, they continually had to overcome obstacles specifically related to being female before they could tackle the obstacles that detection itself entails. Women had to prove themselves able to meet the mental and physical demands of the job, while also maintaining enough of their femininity to combat allegations of being ashamed of their gender—of suggestions that the only people who can perform the role of detective are men or women adopting masculine traits. Male detectives could simply step into a ready-made formula of lone warriors and epic heroes, while women had to battle again and again to prove their right to adopt the role.[55]

Although the professional hard-boiled private eye was clearly an American invention, Phyllis Dorothy James, known as P. D. James, introduced a British version with Cordelia Gray, beginning with *An Unsuitable Job for a Woman*.[56] With her sexual naiveté and innocence, Gray is a far cry from Honey West. Gray inherits a detective agency at age twenty-two after her mentor, Bernie Pryde, commits suicide. Rather than sell the business, she decides to keep it going, despite it being an "unsuitable job for a woman." The novel's title reflected the common opinion of women in detection, though in Gray's case, the slight seems justified, at least at first. Working-class Gray endured a difficult childhood, including a dead mother, a neglectful father, and a series of foster homes, but she's young, charming, and smart. At the same time, she has no investigating experience or particular sleuthing qualifications. She's originally hired as a temporary typist for the unprofitable and struggling detective agency. When she takes over Pryde's agency, she lacks confidence and is tentative but becomes more methodical and skilled as her first case progresses. Like the many young detectives who preceded her, Gray is rarely recognized as a detective. She looks younger than her age and worries that her behavior might strike others as unprofessional: she usually has to tell people she's a detective.[57]

Gray is never fully free of James's more established male detective, Adam Dalgliesh. He lurks in the background throughout *An Unsuitable Job* and even makes a cameo in the final chapter. But Gray doesn't need his help and proves herself capable of solving murders on her own. Still, Gray doesn't get another chance to detect until 1982, in *The Skull Beneath the Skin*, and then never again on the page.[58]

Not until the 1970s did the female private investigator match the style and characteristics of her hard-boiled male peers. The women's movement of the 1960s and 1970s influenced a new generation of writers and readers eager for strong female characters. Facing a lack of empowering female role models in masculine detective fiction, the women who took up detective writing in the 1970s and 1980s forged a new kind of hard-boiled sleuth, one who proved far more influential than Gallagher and West. Writers such as Marcia Muller, Sara Paretsky, and Sue Grafton grew up reading detective stories and were excited by the tough language and daring of the male adventurers. But they also found these stories unsatisfying in their treatment of female characters, who tended to fall into two basic camps: nonsexual secretaries or hypersexual femme fatales. The classic story, with its genteel old lady solving crimes between cups of tea and the clacking of knitting needles, also did little to excite readers hungry for smart, urban, and adventurous women. So these and other writers set out to create a new kind of story that blended the hard-boiled conventions of an independent, professional hero with the social consciousness and relationships that defined women's lives in this period.[59]

Marcia Muller avidly read private-eye novels but found particular inspiration in the work of Margaret Sutton, whose girl detective,

Judy Bolton, is tough and self-sufficient.[60] Unable to find an adult female character to match the girls or the hard-boiled men she read about in novels, Muller set out to develop a quick-thinking female investigator. She created Sharon McCone in 1972, but it took five years to find a publisher interested in a female detective with a strong, anti-authoritarian nature. McCone had much in common with Bolton. Both are intelligent and unyielding to authority. They also have their faults—stubbornness, irritability—which get them into trouble but also make them seem more human. It was Muller's style—an adult take on the teen Bolton—that would influence a new generation of crime fiction.[61]

This new approach to female private investigators caught on quickly with other writers. Sue Grafton's heroine, Kinsey Millhone, introduces herself in A Is for Alibi (1982) with "The day before yesterday I killed someone and the fact weighs heavily on my mind. I'm a nice person and I have a lot of friends."[62] The loss of life is expected of hard-boiled detectives, but the mention of friends clashes with the image of the loner sleuth. These hard-boiled women were independent, bristling at authority just like the men, but they defined their freedom differently. Much of it came from their refusal to fit stereotypes of traditional femininity. A female detective is isolated not from other people but from assumptions about women's place in society.[63]

Like their male peers, female private investigators take a physically active approach to urban crime. They carry guns, get in fights, and kill if necessary. But they do not glorify violence or tend to use it without careful consideration of its implications on their targets or on themselves.[64] These women also reveal the difficulties they face as investigators in a male-dominated criminal justice system. This new crop of female detectives told stories from their own perspective, transforming and taking ownership of the iconic voice that characterized the hard-boiled style. Although they reflected the male hard-boiled tradition, the women were also following the path of earlier female detectives, who ventured boldly into seedy and dangerous neighborhoods.[65]

The female detective in these modern stories, unlike the male detective of old, has a past as well as a present. Her relationships, with family, friends, colleagues, and even lovers, are important and impact the meaning and often the direction of her life. Countless women in fiction and fact became private investigators or police officers because of a family member, many who, particularly in fiction, had been killed in the line of duty. The difference in connectedness is, in part, because of gender. The nature of the work marginalizes and isolates hard-boiled men from relationships, whereas women face marginalization within detection because of their gender. Women still can and do form mature relationships. Hard-boiled men like Sam Spade have no past and no family. The people in his life seem to have no impact on the meaning of his life. He arrives on the page as fully formed as he will be when the story ends. He is a detective with no other possible lives.[66]

Sara Paretsky's V. I. (Victoria Iphigenia) Warshawski, introduced in the novel In Indemnity Only, in 1982, by contrast, is a divorced former public defender turned private investigator based in Chicago. Warshawski's previous involvement in political feminist work often leads her to cases that challenge patriarchal institutions like government, corporations, and the church. She takes society to task for its mistreatment of the less fortunate, elderly, minorities, and working class. Like her fellow female sleuths, Warshawski experiences abductions and violence, carries a gun, and is frequently told that detecting is no job for a woman. Warshawski lost her parents as a young woman, but she's not without family, creating a familial circle with childhood friends who shape her development and career. She also strives to live up to her mother's mission of helping the less fortunate through her work.[67]

Marcia Muller's heroine Sharon McCone, whom we first meet in Edwin of the Iron Shoes (1977), is one of five children and rebelled against the chaos of her rowdy San Diego childhood. She lands in San Francisco, where she discovers her knack for detection, giving up her dream of becoming a social worker. She joins the All Souls Legal Cooperative, an organization that gives her a sort of ready-made family so, as Muller explained, she "wouldn't just be sitting in an office with a bottle in the desk drawer."[68] She hasn't left her immediate family behind, however, and continues to interact with her parents and siblings, who struggle to become responsible adults. In Eye of the Storm, McCone investigates a case for her sister Patsy to help her move past her troubled teen years. In a later story, Where Echoes Live, McCone asks her mother's advice about a man only to be shocked by her mother's announcement that she's left McCone's father after forty years of marriage. Not only that, she's got a new boyfriend. This news forces McCone to redefine her relationship with her mother.[69]

McCone's personal experiences imbue her with a tremendous store of empathy for the lives and traumas of criminals and victims alike. It's in these discussions of family and personal history that the heroine's path to a career in detection is often revealed.[70]

Among all these relationships, the protagonist's marital status often occupies the most space. Where spinsters and unmarried younger women dominated earlier women's detective stories, allowing the authors to skim over love, female PIs in the late twentieth and early twenty-first centuries have more complicated love lives that frequently included divorce. Grafton's Kinsey Millhone is twice divorced by age thirty-two. In many cases, the woman's job was the primary cause of the marriage's disintegration. These divorced women do not spend their time searching for new husbands, though. The wrenching experience of the breakup of their marriages often leaves them cynical and reluctant to jump into another serious relationship. They are not unwilling to date or sleep around, but the nature of their jobs tends to leave them with few prospects. Several women become involved with fellow investigators, who understand what they face—violence, danger, death—on a daily basis. That these women are successful as single women also repudiates the traditional notion that men are necessary for their happiness or economic security.[71]

Patricia Cornwell claimed forensic detection for women through the introduction of forensic pathologist Dr. Kay Scarpetta in the 1980s.[72] But the scientific detective was neither new nor unique to Cornwell. Scientific detectives had first appeared in the late nineteenth century. The invention of the lie detector in 1895, along with refinements in fingerprinting, made science appear increasingly useful for law enforcement by real—and fictional—police forces. Some writers experimented with how small or insignificant a clue could be.[73] In Hugh C. Weir's *Miss Madelyn Mack, Detective* (1914), the key evidence was a small, hollow silver ball. "How often must I tell you that nothing is trivial—in crime?" exclaims Mack.[74] The ball had rolled off the windowsill in the room of the missing Norris Endicott on the morning of his wedding. Endicott is feared dead, but Mack's identification of the ball as the head of a pin, and then her scientific reading of the ashes in Endicott's room, leads her to a solution. Mack discovers that Endicott was very much alive and that he had, in fact, saved his bride from ruin after her first and long-presumed-dead husband reappears and threatens her future.

Cornwell had personal experience that allowed her to incorporate realistic details into her writing. She worked for a time in the office of the state medical examiner in Richmond, Virginia, and also joined a volunteer police force, which gave her direct experience with urban crime. Cornwell's heroine is the chief medical examiner for the state of Virginia, based in Richmond. Divorced after a brief marriage, Kay Scarpetta is devoted to her job. She sees her mission as restoring some measure of dignity for the victim, because doing her job well means that a killer will be punished. The work often has her dealing with gruesome murders and brutal crimes, while also facing extra scrutiny as one of the few women in the country in her high-level position.[75]

Though not a police officer, Scarpetta is written in the police-procedural style that became more common for women writers in the 1980s and 1990s. These stories showcase female characters at work in the official "masculine" system. Many explore how state authority can be more complicated for women than men, and deal with conflicts over the "proper" place of women. Another non-officer in a procedural series is Manhattan prosecutor Alexandra Cooper, the creation of former sex-crimes prosecutor Linda Fairstein. Like Cornwell, Fairstein used her own experience as head of Manhattan's District Attorney's Office's sex-crimes prosecution unit to craft her character, inventing what she has called her "fictional alter ego" in Cooper.[76] Fairstein inspired the character of Alexandra "Alex" Cabot, played by Stephanie March, on Law & Order: SVU (Special Victims Unit).

Margaret Maron's Lieutenant Sigrid Harald is a more traditional heroine in a police procedural. She's a veteran police officer with the New York Police Department whose policeman father was killed in the line of duty when she was a child. In eight books, from 1981 to 1995, Harald wins grudging acceptance from her male colleagues for her dedication to the job, but she's well aware that deference can disappear in an instant. Most of the officers she works with think she's cold because of the rational and unemotional approach she brings to her cases. But Harald understands, as many detecting women do, that to show emotion would leave her open to the contempt and mistrust of other officers. Harald often finds herself overcome by the scenes she witnesses on the job, but she hides her feelings and, as a result, is misunderstood by those she works with. A man becomes more human if he sheds a tear, but a woman is scorned. Like female officers both real and fictional, success in a man's world does not entail simply doing the job as well as a man. Gender often comes before the uniform in cultural attitudes toward women in authority.[77]

For women who are part of large police systems, friction with male colleagues, suspects, and the public is a daily obstacle. Cornwell's Kay Scarpetta wins respect for her expertise in the field. She sets out to succeed in a male-dominated profession as an act of revenge against all of the men who stood in her way or did not take her seriously. Scarpetta must also play a more political role than most female investigators because her job falls under the jurisdiction of elected officials. These politicians are guided by their need to retain the favor of the voting public, so Scarpetta must play politics with the men who control her job, in addition to examining bodies.[78]

The modern hard-boiled woman does not look or dress like Gale Gallagher or Honey West. Millhone is generally uninterested in her physical appearance—she cuts her hair with nail scissors, wears no makeup, and owns one dress in a serviceable black—but she does place a premium on physical fitness. The mundane activities of daily life—waking, showering, dressing, eating—receive great attention and provide clues that reveal the person. Sigrid Harald dresses plainly and functionally to win respect as a police professional, but it's a style that causes many to wonder about her personal life and femininity. Beneath it all, and hidden from view, she wears lingerie. Harald's external aspect is a mask for who and what she is inside. V. I. Warshawski dresses for practicality and professionalism, wearing dark clothes and heavy rubber-soled oxfords as she prepares for a potentially violent confrontation.[79] Hard-boiled women dress to demonstrate that they are capable of fulfilling the role of detective, skirting the line between tough guy and woman. The gap between expectations of feminine appearance and those connected to traditionally masculine professions has long been an issue for women. Fictional female sleuths understand these expectations and manipulate their image accordingly to play a certain role. Right or wrong, how a woman looks says a lot about what a woman can do. Millhone has a supply of costumes that she uses as disguises. An unflattering blue-gray uniform with a patch that reads "Southern California Services" and thick, black shoes allow her to "pass myself off as just about anything."[80] That appearance and abilities are strongly correlated makes it no surprise that physical presentation plays such a strong role in the novels.

Like their real-life counterparts, fictional female detectives often carry guns in their purses. It's not without its complications. Purses are easily misplaced, stolen, or lost, and it's difficult to pull a gun quickly from a handbag. Millhone struggles to keep track of her purse in *G Is for Gumshoe* after her car is run off the road and rammed by a truck, sending the bag and the gun inside sailing from the passenger seat.[81] Dr. Scarpetta owns a Ruger .38 revolver and several times a month visits a shooting range for practice. Her cases often put her in contact with extremely violent criminals, including serial killers, so she tends to feel more comfortable when she has a weapon close at hand. But she, like many other female sleuths, almost never uses deadly force.[82]

Women's advancement into less traditional occupations was not just evident on the page. Although fictional women have long been more likely to be employed than the average woman in the United States, by 1980 more than half of the women in the United States, even mothers of infants, were working outside the home.[83] As women's employment numbers changed, so did the work history of fictional sleuths. Many of the detectives in the earliest stories were spinsters who appeared to have never worked or young socialites who did not need to. The elderly sleuth continues to detect in newer works, but she now often is or has been employed. She's been joined by women of more varied backgrounds, including working mothers.[84]

P. M. Carlson created perhaps the first working-mother detective with her Maggie Ryan series.[85] It starts with *Audition for Murder* (1967), when Ryan is in college, and continues through her marriage and then parenthood, as she and her husband adjust to their changing roles. Another fictional detective was Blanche White, a black domestic worker, mother, and amateur sleuth, created by Barbara Neely in the 1990s. At the end of the first book, White has the opportunity to leave her job as a domestic, but she likes the work and the independence that comes from being self-employed.[86]

While the modern professional female private investigators have grabbed most of the attention, amateur sleuths have also seen a revival in recent decades. Prior to the boom in women's mysteries in the 1980s and 1990s, female amateur sleuths were primarily nosy spinsters in the Miss Marple mode. But the renewed popularity of women's mysteries opened the field and created a revolution in the variety and diversity of women taking on detecting, particularly as a sideline career. Many of the new women's authors had grown up reading Nancy Drew and sought heroines older than Drew but younger than Marple to connect with a life of adventure and mystery. The amateur sleuth often appears ill-suited to detecting, but like the spinster and girl sleuths of the past, the amateur often succeeds in spite of her lack of training and criminal mindset. She typically has little, if any, experience in law enforcement and little contact with violent people. The crimes these amateurs take on are not the anonymous shootings or crime syndicates of the front page, but more localized crimes of relationships gone wrong, expectations unfulfilled, and passions unmet. As a result, they experience minimal violence compared to the professional female investigator.[87]

Amateur sleuth Kate Fansler bridges the gap between upper-class woman of leisure and working woman, with echoes of Dorothy Sayers's Harriet Vane. Created by Carolyn Heilbrun, writing as Amanda Cross, in 1964, Fansler was born to wealth but becomes a professor of Victorian literature at a prestigious university in New York City. Fansler cherishes her independence and her work, while also using her family money to travel as her cases demand. She believes, like Vane, in the importance of women's work and is active in causes related to women's rights. Fansler has a taste for martinis, whisky, brandy, and steak. Unlike many female sleuths, Fansler marries about halfway through the series, but she wears no ring, does not take her husband's surname, and does not rely on him financially. Her husband has his own life and career that provides them a modern, companionable union; it's what Vane hoped for herself when she consented to marry Lord Peter Wimsey. Fansler married too late to have children, which she considers fortunate. And, like Vane, she resembles her creator.

Heilbrun became the first female tenured professor of English at Columbia University, in 1972. A specialist in modern British literature, Heilbrun was an outspoken feminist and critic of male dominance in academia. Like Fansler, she maintained her independence in marriage, keeping her own room and even her own house, which she lived in alone, though she and her husband had three children. Heilbrun's creation also inspired a later set of academic sleuths, like Theodora Wender's Gladiola Gold, Joan Smith's Loretta Lawson, and Sarah Caudwell's Hilary Tamar.[88]

Kathy Reichs mixes the scientific, procedural style of Kay Scarpetta with the academic sleuthing of Kate Fansler in her series crime solver, Temperance Brennan. The divorced and recovering alcoholic Brennan is the director of forensic anthropology for the province of Quebec, as well as a professor in North Carolina. She first appears in *Déjà Dead* (1997), where she studies the dismembered body of a woman found in an abandoned monastery in Montreal. Brennan becomes convinced that the woman is the victim of a serial killer, despite the skepticism of the detective in charge of the investigation. Her expertise and investigating finally convince the detective, while also putting herself in danger. Reichs is herself a forensic anthropologist and professor and decided to write fiction as a way to bring her science to a broader audience. As a result, Brennan's solutions are science-driven rather than based on instinct or even legwork by the detective. It's a point of pride for Reichs, who has taken other mystery writers to task for incorrect or sensationalized science, particularly Patricia Cornwell. Many of the fictional cases Brennan tackles are based on Reichs's real investigations. Reichs herself became the inspiration for the TV show *Bones*, in which the main character shares the name of her fictional character, Brennan, but is based more on Reichs.

Laura Lippman's detective, Tess Monaghan, begins as an amateur sleuth in her debut book, *Baltimore Blues* (1997), but has become a licensed private eye by her third outing, *Butchers Hill* (1998). Monaghan is a star reporter in Baltimore who suddenly finds herself out of work when her newspaper folds. Desperate for anything that will pay the rent, Monaghan takes up detecting and soon finds herself a new career. She also eventually has a family, including a young daughter and a partner who works nights running a bar, leaving Monaghan to juggle her detecting with parenting. Monaghan is physically tough—she's an avid rower on Baltimore's Patapsco River—and retains a reporter's eye for detail. She works cases involving the disenfranchised that would likely not have made headlines in her former job, such as the identity of a young girl who had escaped from an institution for women with eating disorders, or the woman in a green raincoat Monaghan sees walking her dog every morning until one day she doesn't. Monaghan's inquisitiveness usually leads her deep into people's past crimes and troubling deaths and disappearances.

Other writers cast strong women in stories with sensation and Gothic overtones. Mary Higgins Clark turned to mysteries after the poor sales of her first novel, a historical romance about George and Martha Washington called *Aspire to the Heavens* (1969). Encouraged to keep writing, Clark turned to the suspense stories she loved as a child. Her first suspense novel, *Where Are the Children?* (1975), became a best seller and launched a career that now includes more than fifty books. Clark's stories typically feature beautiful and ambitious women in danger who often save themselves using their own intelligence and quick wits. These women are not detectives, though, but characters caught up in a nightmare that they must navigate to survive.

Another spunky woman appears in Janet Evanovich's romantic adventure series featuring Stephanie Plum, a former lingerie buyer turned bounty hunter in Trenton, New Jersey. Plum has no idea what she's doing, but she's determined and manages to take down criminals, though not without a bit of chaos and car wrecking in pursuit of sleazy characters.

Detective stories by women and starring women boomed in the 1980s and 1990s. So much so that it can be hard to remember a time when women were not leading investigations. No longer confined by the Golden Age cozies and the hard-boiled male private eyes, women writers introduced new female voices. They weren't the only ones. Men also began to write popular series with female detectives for the first time since the nineteenth century.

Among these new sleuths was the first female private detective in Botswana, Precious Ramotswe. The creation of Alexander McCall Smith, Mma Ramotswe first appeared in 1998 in *The No. 1 Ladies' Detective Agency*, where she sets up her business at the foot of Kgale Hill with income from the cattle left to her by her father. Although she lacks a formal education, Mma Ramotswe is endowed with common sense, good instincts, grit, and well-attuned empathy. Many of her cases involve missing or unfaithful husbands and other domestic disputes, rarely violence, and the various town characters play nearly as much a role in the stories as the mysteries themselves. Mma Ramotswe has a folksy way of problem solving that draws heavily on what she refers to as old-fashioned Botswana morality, often dished out over a steaming cup of red bush tea. Another of the new male-authored female sleuths was Jasper Fforde's Thursday Next. First introduced in *The Eyre Affair* in 2001, Next lives in an alternate Britain within a world obsessed with literature. Next works as a literary detective, tracking down forgeries, unauthorized works, and policing the text and characters through time and space.

Computer hacker and all-around tough woman Lisbeth Salander teams up with disgraced journalist Mikael Blomkvist in Stieg Larsson's Millennium Trilogy. The twenty-four-year-old Salander grew up terrorized by an abusive father. Seeing that the police and social services could do nothing to stop him, she set her father on fire to stop his attacks on her mother. Salander ends up in a mental institution, only to be raped by the guardian assigned to protect her after her release. Traumatized, she's become emotionally detached, defensive, and vengeful. And with her piercings and tattoos, Salander looks as tough as she is fierce. In the series' first book, *The Girl with the Dragon Tattoo*, Salander's work as a hacker leads her to Blomkvist, who hires her to help him investigate—and, for Salander, avenge—atrocities committed against women. Salander even saves Blomkvist from being murdered in the course of the story, becoming a sort of superhero with her physical prowess and personal moral code.[89]

The hard-boiled heroine reflected, in many ways, the feminist ideal of the late twentieth century. She was self-reliant, educated, physically tough, and independent. The conventional image of women as weak and ineffective in physical confrontations is exposed as a ruse in contemporary crime fiction. Grafton, Muller, Paretsky, and countless others put their detectives in situations that require mental and physical agility, and the women triumph. They work in a profession dominated by men, but they make it because of their intelligence, stamina, grit, and determination.

Even Raymond Chandler, with all his macho men, could imagine the possibility of a tough-talking woman. Anne Riordan, the cop's daughter in his 1940 novel *Farewell, My Lovely*, is a strong, restless young woman with a gift for sniffing out clues and an insatiable curiosity that leads her to take chances that few other women would. She's professionally independent, working as a freelance writer for newspapers, and frequently finds herself involved in matters that don't really concern her. Wisecracking and smart, Riordan easily matches wits with men.

She's hardly the typical Chandler woman. Riordan perhaps speaks for all hard-boiled women when she exclaims, "Who the devil cares what I do or when or how?"[90]

CHAPTER NINE

From Mothers to Crime Fighters

POLICEWOMEN SWORN IN TO DUTY IN NEW YORK CITY IN 1939 WERE warned of the many pitfalls they might encounter on the job, but none weighed so heavily as weight itself. "We don't want to see you taking on weight too rapidly—or at all," Commissioner Lewis Valentine told the women.[1] They were instructed to take the stairs over the elevator, to watch their diet, and to exercise regularly. Mayor Fiorello La Guardia echoed Valentine's sentiments, remarking that the day of the helmeted, handlebar-mustached, fat policeman was over. "There are no fatheads in this department—not now."

Regardless of the fatheads, the force these new recruits were joining was changing—as were the women entering police work. "A day in the life of a policewoman is lively," Mary Sullivan, head of the NYPD Policewomen's Bureau, told the *New York Times* in 1932.[2] She favored younger women as officers because she believed they were better able to enter into casual conversation and pick up the "friendly gossip" vital for prosecutions in dance halls and speakeasies. "We need the girl who can look harmless when sent to investigate," Sullivan explained.

Not every police department agreed with Sullivan. In cities across the country, policewomen performed duties that ranged from filing reports and facilitating the weddings of unwed mothers to arresting fortune-tellers and white slavers. Department-store detective and pickpocket-squad officer were two of the few jobs offering women a consistent opportunity to lead investigations. These disparate conceptions of women's functions and abilities, coupled with the lack of a national leader, weakened the movement and fragmented policewomen's identity in the 1930s.

Outside forces did little to help the policewoman cause. After winning national suffrage in 1920, white women leaders entered the new decade with optimism about their enlarged political responsibilities and possibilities for reform. But the more prosperous, consumer-oriented society that arose in the 1920s fostered an atmosphere less hospitable to change. Americans focused more on leisure and entertainment than on lobbying and petitioning, as reform movements of all kinds lost steam.

At the same time, the women's movement had itself split. Before national suffrage was achieved, women could put aside their differences to unite behind the idea of "votes for women." But after gaining the vote, reformers splintered. Women continued to be active in reform but in more specialized efforts rather than with the single-minded fervor of the late nineteenth and early twentieth centuries. These reform efforts stagnated for a time, along with the economy, during the Depression. With jobs short, women's entry into the job market—even in roles as sharply circumscribed as women's policing—was viewed harshly, particularly for married women. The collapse of the International Association of Policewomen (IAP), in 1932, came partly as a result of the organization's inability to anticipate and adapt to these changes in society and the women's movement.[3] In a declining economy, policewomen lost recognition and the status they had gained since Alice Wells took the oath in 1910.

Those few who did speak for policewomen clung to their vision of separate work. In Detroit, Eleanore Hutzel turned her city's Women's Bureau into a national model. Thirty-nine policewomen, three female sergeants, and, remarkably, three male detectives reported to her.[4] Seeking to standardize procedures for women, Hutzel wrote a manual in 1933 called *The Policewoman's Handbook*, which became the standard guide in police departments for a quarter century. In this how-to book of fieldwork, Hutzel supported minimum educational standards of high school graduation, plus at least two years of social work or nursing.[5] Standards were even higher in Hutzel's own force, where she required women to have college degrees and at least one year of social-work experience. Hutzel believed that policewomen were best suited to dealing with complaints concerning juvenile girls, boys under age twelve, and older women requiring no court action.[6]

"Women tramps, drug addicts, and beggars are usually handled by men officers," wrote Hutzel. "These women are usually older women who do not respond to constructive efforts toward rehabilitation and are not primarily a problem for the policewoman. She should, however, offer assistance at any time that it seems needed."[7]

Female recruits continued to be better educated than their male peers, but they were not the same upper-middle-class, college-educated, and social service–oriented women as the founding generation. As civil service exams became standard, aspiring policewomen could substitute other experiences for a college education, including previous employment in service or clerical positions, or military service.

Beginning in 1934, female applicants to the New York City Police Department took the same civil service exam as male applicants.[8] The city had configured the work of its female officers in several ways since their initial appointment in 1918, from a welfare bureau and then a women's precinct to a women's bureau and crime prevention unit that eventually became the juvenile bureau. Once hired, women received the same academic training as men but not the same physical and practical training, because regular training was seen as irrelevant for women.

Some women were taken prematurely from the academy or immediately after graduation for so-called "special" assignments, which ranged from typing to undercover work. Women qualified for these assignments simply by being women: an investigation might need a female decoy, for instance, or an assignment could benefit from some supposedly innate female quality, like emotional warmth. These were specialized jobs that departments claimed women performed more adroitly. While the work appeared glamorous, decoys offered little prestige because the women served primarily as bait and the men as law enforcers.[9]

New York created a special civil service test for female detectives in 1938. Mayor La Guardia had helped push for the test as a way to increase the number of women fit for undercover work, a growing need in the city. Women who did not meet the physical requirements for policewomen could still become detectives under the new requirements by virtue of their previous experience as actors, newspaper reporters, nurses, stenographers, or social workers—all skills that could prove useful for undercover detection. Physical requirements were less important for undercover work, claimed Paul J. Kern, president of the Municipal Civil Service Commission, because of new "scientific crime-detection methods" that relied more on brains than brawn.[10] Perhaps New York hoped to follow the lead of the police force in Lancashire, England, which established an official women's detective unit with specially trained officers in 1921. These women worked in collaboration with the male detectives on every case, not just those deemed appropriate for a woman.[11]

Controlling crime became a hot political issue in the 1920s and 1930s and changed the orientation of policing. Everywhere Americans turned, they heard politicians, police officials, and social commentators warn that the country was going through the worst crime wave in American history.[12] Radio, one of the new consumer products of the era, brought reports of graft and corruption into the homes of millions of listeners.[13] Some blamed Prohibition for boosting criminal activity by outlawing something nearly everyone consumed. These reports, along with detective dramas and fact-based dramatic series like Phillips Lord's 1935 *Gangbusters*, based on FBI activities, made the public more aware of and more concerned about crime and the police response.

American anxiety about crime pushed police toward reform and new crime prevention programs that activists had fought for for decades. Berkeley, California's police chief, August Vollmer, rallied police officials around the idea of reform in the 1920s and 1930s.[14] He urged departments to professionalize and promoted a focus on criminal law that emphasized police as law enforcement rather than keepers of public order. Many reformers hoped to finally sever the tie between politics and police, and to institute more stringent hiring methods, better training, and higher pay. The use of the civil service system became one way to remove patronage from policing. Departments also moved toward a military-rank structure to standardize work, enforce discipline, and recognize merit and experience.

Fighting crime became the key measure of police efficiency and success for both the force itself and politicians trying to make cities safe. The importance of the "crime fighter" was emphasized in 1931 with the findings of the National Commission on Law Observance and Enforcement, better known as the Wickersham Commission. Charged with examining rising crime rates in the United States, the Wickersham Commission recommended that police officers should focus primarily on crime control to alleviate mounting crime.[15] This approach required a more active role for police in preventing crime. But rather than try to reform would-be offenders, as policewomen had long advocated, officers would instead aggressively confront criminals in a show of force that demonstrated the severe punishment they faced for law breaking.[16]

These reforms did little to help policewomen. The social services that women performed became less associated with the police, as agencies created for specific health and communal welfare purposes became part of the urban landscape. The "mothering" that policewomen provided now appeared amateurish and useless.[17] Paradoxically, professionalism didn't foster appreciation for the higher educational standards and specific preventative training that women brought to the job, despite the emphasis that Vollmer and other reformers placed on increased standards for officers. Part of that was due to the economic climate of the 1930s. With jobs short, police work, with its job security, pensions, and fringe benefits, became a desirable profession for educated, middle-class men who had previously scorned it. This did not last long, though, as policing again became a refuge for the working class and immigrants by World War II. With these changes, policewomen saw their role in crime prevention pushed aside and ignored.[18]

Fewer women were coming to policing from social work, as well. No longer an emerging profession, social work had become a recognized field, with graduate degrees and authority in private and state welfare agencies. Social workers had, to some degree, surpassed policewomen in legitimacy. They concentrated instead on working with, rather than joining, law enforcement. Members of the IAP had noted the growing lack of interest in policing among social workers in the mid-1920s, but they attributed this to the job's long hours rather than to shifts in the professional field. As fewer social workers entered policing, some social workers came to see policewomen as encroaching on their domain.[19] Imra Buwalda, a policewoman in Washington, DC, chastised social workers for failing to acknowledge the importance of the police function. "The juvenile bureau was not an intruding and competing new welfare agency for treatment, but a police unit with a social welfare point of view."[20]

The appointment of policewomen stagnated during the Depression. Some women found positions as part of crime-prevention or juvenile delinquency–prevention bureaus, which formed on the assumption that delinquency posed a major threat to cities, particularly during times of economic crisis. Policewomen generally opposed these units because women were not in charge—most fell under the jurisdiction of male officers—even though these units provided most of the job opportunities for women.[21] Chicago, which had ignored demands to create a separate bureau for its women officers for decades, succumbed to the recommendations of a reform committee and established a crime-prevention bureau in 1931. As a result, the number of policewomen in Chicago actually increased, from 30 in 1929 to 61 in 1938, at a time when numbers elsewhere had ground to a halt or declined.[22] Crime prevention received far more attention from reformers and community leaders than within police departments, however. Most of these units had few male officers and were composed primarily of policewomen.[23]

Bucking trends, some cities hired their first women officers during the Depression. Fort Worth, Texas, appointed four women in 1930. The division was organized and the officers trained under the supervision of Sergeant Rhoda Milliken, a Washington, DC, officer on loan to the Texas city. The two policewomen appointed in Richmond, Virginia, in 1930, traveled to Washington for two weeks of training in Milliken's unit. Phoenix, Philadelphia, and Shreveport, Louisiana, were among the other cities to counter the declining numbers of policewomen with new appointments.[24]

Undercover work, particularly to catch shoplifters in department stores, like the fictional detective Mary Carner did, also resisted downward trends. In December of 1938, New York City pickpocket detective Mary Shanley, with her pistol drawn, chased a male suspect down Fifth Avenue, dodging automobiles and disregarding a red light.[25] The assailant, Charles Herbert, was a known swindler. Shanley overtook him after three blocks and brought him by taxi to the station. The experience wasn't new to Shanley, who was known as a particularly tough street cop. She'd tracked down and fired at a larceny suspect a year earlier and chased down two other criminals on city streets before. Earlier in 1938, she'd halted a robbery by smashing her pocketbook in a suspect's face. Shanley had joined the Special Frauds Bureau in 1935 and rose quickly to first-grade detective. Unlike other female officers, Shanley preferred to use her gun on the job, earning her the nickname "Dead-Shot Mary" and comparisons to Annie Oakley. But Shanley's gun fancy also landed her trouble. In 1941, Shanley fired while off-duty and intoxicated at a bar in Queens. She was demoted to policewoman and suspended, but she returned to active duty only a month later. She was later promoted to detective again. When she retired in 1957, Shanley had halted more than a thousand pickpockets, shoplifters, and swindlers. Once, she'd even accompanied actress Grace Kelly on a shopping trip down Fifth Avenue, when Shanley had sensed trouble in the large crowd forming around Kelly. Women like Shanley were likely just the type Mayor La Guardia hoped his city's new civil service exam for detectives would attract.

Even as women struggled to make gains in police departments, one woman revolutionized the study of crime scenes in much the same way Mary Holland popularized fingerprinting in the early twentieth century. Frances Glessner Lee was a wealthy Chicago heiress with an unconventional hobby: investigating murder using miniature dollhouse-like dioramas.[26] The child of industrialist John Jacob Glessner, who made his fortune as a cofounder of International Harvester, Lee was educated at home, learned interior design from her mother (a skill she put to use later), and married at nineteen. Though she had three children with her husband, Lee eventually divorced him, in part to pursue her creative and scientific interests.

Constructing miniatures was a pursuit that many affluent women enjoyed, but Lee used her skills to explore homicide investigation and forensics.[27] Her brother's friend, George Magrath, who later became a professor of pathology at Harvard Medical School, introduced her to the field. Lee began to throw lavish dinner parties for detectives and scientists, who would share the intricacies and problems of their professions with her. At the time, local coroners, responsible for determining cause of death, were not required to have medical training, and without the methodical study of crime scenes, many deaths were wrongly attributed. So, in 1936, Lee used her fortune to endow Harvard's Department of Legal Medicine, what we would today call forensics, and made later gifts to fund seminars in homicide investigation, some of which she taught herself. Her conversations with police officers and scholars impressed upon her the value of careful crime-scene evaluation and inspired her to create what she termed "The Nutshell Studies of Unexplained Death."

These lovingly crafted scenes of domesticity featured blood-spattered walls, upturned chairs, and beds littered with corpses. Her first, "The Case of the Hanging Farmer," took three months to assemble and included wood from a hundred-year-old barn. The crimes were composites of actual cases, though the room decor was Lee's invention. With her upper-class background, Lee made certain assumptions about the tastes of low-income families, often depicting seedy spaces with tawdry decor. Each model was incredibly detailed:

The lights worked. Drawers opened to reveal linens and clothes. Lee knitted and sewed all the clothing and painted the faces of the victims with details of decomposition. The scenes were intended to hone an investigator's powers of observation. For each model, she devised a case with a beginning, middle, and end, as well as a solution.

Lee used the dioramas as teaching tools in her seminar at Harvard where she lectured to police officers (all men) who eagerly signed up for her course. She advised students to investigate spaces in a clockwise spiral to catch every detail.[28]

In 1942, Lee was named captain of the New Hampshire State Police, an honorary position, and her Harvard seminar was later given her name, the Frances Glessner Lee Seminar in Homicide Investigation, a title it still carries. When Harvard's Department of Legal Medicine closed, in 1967, Russell Fisher, a former student of Lee's at Harvard, transferred the "Nutshells" to the Office of the Chief Medical Examiner in Baltimore, where they are still used to teach homicide investigation techniques. Students study the models in groups and present their theories and conclusions. The methods of gathering evidence have changed since Lee created her models, but her approach to interpretation remains the same. And though she referred to herself as a "hobbyist," Lee's work made her one of her era's most innovative and astute criminologists.

The onset of another war renewed outcries against prostitution and immorality, and reopened a place for women to guard against them. But this time, rather than being hired to mother and protect errant girls, policewomen were urged to watch and punish them. Fulfilling the role that the Committee on Protective Work for Girls had provided during WWI was its WWII equivalent: the Social Protection Division. Led by former Prohibition special agent Eliot Ness, the division investigated vice in its efforts to safeguard the health and morality of soldiers. Unlike during World War I, however, the Social Protection Division did not hire its own female protective officers but rather broadened the scope of misconduct subject to police action. Prostitution now meant not only sex for hire but also "promiscuous intercourse" without the exchange of money. Disorderly conduct now included activities that endangered morality. Other laws cracked down on lewd speech and on couples falsely registering at a hotel as married. Concern about venereal disease created positions for policewomen, but Ness did not see them as vital to enforcement. He was a crime fighter, not a reformer, like Raymond Fosdick had been, lobbying for the appointment of female officers. Instead, Ness urged cooperation between the police and social workers, without mentioning policewomen.[29]

Even so, the number of policewomen around the country increased in the 1940s. In Detroit, the number of policewomen grew from thirty-three in 1932 to fifty-four in 1942. New applicants tended to be in their twenties and were required to weigh at least 120 pounds and be at least five feet two inches tall. Although a college degree was not required to join the force, women needed two years' experience in social work to qualify.[30]

Detroit's policewomen in the Social Protection Division detained women suspected of immoral behavior. The women were questioned, tested for venereal disease, and held, often for several days, without charges until the results were obtained. All young girls and first-time offenders were interviewed for possible referral to a social-services agency. In 1943, policewomen in Detroit detained nearly nine thousand girls between ten and seventeen years old; at least half had committed no crime or were released with a warning.[31]

Arresting girls ran contrary to the idea of prevention and protection promoted by pioneer policewomen. Early policewomen operated on the assumption that female criminals were an aberration and their crimes avoidable. But by the 1940s, the crime-fighting ethos made law enforcement, not intervention, the focus.[32]

Policing itself changed little for women during WWII. Their gains were in numbers rather than function. Even when faced with the loss of men to war, police departments rarely allowed women to step outside their traditional roles, as women did in other industries. This had one benefit, though: at the end of the war, policewomen did not lose their jobs like those women employed in factories and other businesses. Cities retained the policewomen they hired and even increased the number of women in crime-prevention bureaus.[33]

Washington, DC, officer Imra Buwalda encouraged police departments to hire returning servicewomen.[34] She argued that these women were already in good physical condition, had experience working with men, and had received training in specialized fields appropriate to dealing with criminal girls and women. Rather than coming from social work, as they traditionally had, the women who entered policing after the war often had broader life experiences, including military service. These women were not reformers; they came to policing to earn a living as much as they did for the good of the community. And in the coming decades, they would be willing to give up their specialized role as policewomen for the possibility of full equality with their male peers.[35]

Indeed, even many decades after they first entered the force, policewomen still attracted media attention, though less as objects of curiosity than as attractive professionals successfully managing family and career. Most newspapers and magazines in the 1940s focused on how these women managed to stay feminine in a masculine profession. In 1942, the *American Mercury* described Detroit's policewomen as "young, attractive, refined," and, in case there were any doubts, "thoroughly feminine." Writer Karl Detzer proclaimed, "The modern policewoman bears about the same relation to the old-fashioned burly, lantern-jawed, middle-aged police matron as an up-to-date G-man does to a Keystone cop."[36] Still, stereotypes persisted. Detzer accompanied a few of the women on their evening rounds: "Our two policegirls are ready to start—flashlights tested, handbags stuffed with leather billies, patrol box keys, lipstick, violation blanks, police whistles, gold badges, dainty handkerchiefs. . . . Neither carries a revolver, although some members of the division always go armed." An officer based in Texas, "Sis" Dickerson, "who was sworn into policing in 1940 to fill the term of her late father, has been reelected twice, [and] has been involved in a number of dangerous situations," liked nothing better "than to come home and busy herself with needle and thread."[37] One reporter blamed the resistance to hiring policewomen on the popular image of "a broad-shouldered, heavy-handed lady-flatfoot in navy blue."[38] These stories conveniently overlooked the role the press played earlier in the century in creating and popularizing these caricatures of policewomen as club-wielding monsters. The press also communicated the message that the value of these women lay not in their policing skills but in their domesticity—and that's what they were hired for.

The 1943 federal guidelines on the use of policewomen were little better than the views of the popular press, presenting women with a contradictory view of their role. *Techniques of Law Enforcement in the Use of Policewomen with Special Reference to Social Protection* asserted that a policewoman was "first and foremost a police officer" with "all the same privileges—including salary, rating, and promotional opportunity—as male officers who are doing the same type of work."[39] This was not true in any department. At the same time, the authors also described a policewoman as neither "over-feminine, nor, on the other hand, aggressively mannish" in her work and attitude. She must "hew to the line between being either sentimental and soft or callous and indifferent."[40] Like earlier guidelines for women in police work, this report shored up the purview of the policewoman to what it had been in 1910: protecting youths, investigating sex crimes, and monitoring dance halls, theaters, and amusement parks.[41]

Early in the policewomen movement, the image of women training in marksmanship was used to highlight the ridiculousness of the new profession. But by the early 1940s, policewomen in several major cities, including New York, Detroit, and Los Angeles, carried weapons.[42] New York police commissioner Lewis Valentine had issued women .32 caliber firearms in 1934 and instituted regular pistol practice. Rather than carrying their guns in a holster, policewomen used regulation pocketbooks with a special gun compartment. Detective Mary Sullivan observed that most of the women were "surprisingly efficient" marksmen.[43] A decade later, in 1944, Mayor La Guardia issued a combination gun and makeup shoulder bag that contained a holster, red lipstick, a compact, and a case of rouge, reportedly advising his policewomen to "use the gun as you would your lipstick. Use it only when you need it, and use it intelligently. Don't overdo either one."[44] Weapon use varied widely though. Some women were ordered to carry firearms, while guns remained optional for others.

Still, the popular impression of armed policewomen was one of charming ineptitude, which betrayed the lack of seriousness accorded them. Certain themes came to dominate media portrayals of women and guns: women overreact; they cannot operate guns when they are excited; and they disregard public safety. The *Saturday Evening Post* told of two New York City policewomen investigating complaints that a tailor was showing obscene pictures to women who applied for a cashier position in his shop. One of the policewomen posed as an applicant. When the tailor made a pass at her, she flashed her badge. The man ran outside where he was confronted by the other policewoman, who shouted, "Stop or I'll shoot," while pointing the barrel of the gun at her own stomach. Despite the lack of threat posed by a misdirected gun, the tailor stopped fleeing. When they brought the tailor into the station, the female director of policewomen added to the ridiculousness of the scene: "You can give a woman a badge, a gun and all the professional training in the world, but she remains a woman at heart." The story seems highly unlikely, but it played to popular perceptions of women in law enforcement.

Even the sleuthing daughter of famed New York detective Mary Sullivan seemed to emphasize glamour and femininity over detecting skills to solve crimes. Grace Marie Legay was one of nine house detectives—and the only woman—employed at the Commodore Hotel in New York City. Although she knew jujitsu, Legay told the *New York Times* in 1950 that she found her "large blue eyes more useful."[45] The photo accompanying the article showed an elegant woman with upswept brown hair, a diamond choker, and finely arched eyebrows over a shrewd expression. Married with children, Legay decided to enter policing during World War II and trained at the police academy under her mother. Legay spent most of her day at the hotel "cruising," riding the elevators, walking through corridors, and mingling with guests with an eye out for suspicious behavior. Special assignments, usually protecting mink coats and fancy jewels, called for formal dresses and hats, the latter of which she called her "particular weakness." She detained criminals with a "few phone calls," no force and certainly no gun. Legay didn't ignore all her training, though. In her off hours, she worked as a private detective in an agency with her mother.

Policewomen were often complicit in stereotyped portrayals of themselves as uncomfortable or ill suited to the job. Many officers described their discomfort with carrying guns. They preferred to keep them tucked away in their handbags, though even this could cause trouble. New York policewoman Marjorie McCarron described her gun as "a nuisance at parties and dances. I can't just put my bag down and forget about it. I have to carry it or keep it in sight, which isn't easy during a mambo or the Lindy."[46] In the 1940s and 1950s, *Spring 3100*, the official magazine of the New York Police Department named for the department's old phone number, which had long depicted women in cartoons as sexual objects, provided policewomen a regular column called "Strictly for the Girls." Ostensibly a forum to address the concerns of female officers, "Strictly for the Girls" focused almost exclusively on marriage, morality, and housekeeping. Its writers did not contemplate the idea of new or different roles for women in the NYPD.[47]

Police administrators, who had once been upper-middle-class, educated men, were, by the late 1940s, more likely to be working-class men who had risen through the ranks. These new careerists tended to resent outsiders, especially women, even though women's ability to follow a similar career trajectory was impossible because of a lack of promotional opportunities and limited duties. August Vollmer, a national leader in law enforcement and one-time police chief in Berkeley, California, gave lip service to the benefit of policewomen but did little to actually advance their cause.[48] He continued to see them only in very limited roles, more like social workers and mothers than police and detectives. Of policing as a career for women, Vollmer said, "I can imagine no finer career for young women than in the police field where they have the opportunity of helping to save some of the 10 million children now in school who otherwise are destined to crime."[49]

Vollmer's student and the influential criminologist O. W. Wilson, on the other hand, wrote about the work of policewomen as if it required no skill at all.[50] Wilson had built his reputation on championing police efficiency and the use of patrol cars with two-way radios, which allowed officers to arrive at crime scenes faster and more dependably. A force built on crime-fighting speed had little place for policewomen. Wilson advised that departments could use a secretary or matron for detective work if no policewoman was available. He further recommended that policewomen's downtime be devoted to clerical work. Wilson strongly believed that men, not women, should head juvenile divisions because men had a better understanding of the different law enforcement divisions, were physically and emotionally more equipped to withstand the pressures of the job, and, perhaps most galling of all to pioneer policewomen, were better supervisors of women. Wilson stripped women of their authority over children and each other, assigning them a place defined not by their moral superiority but by their biological inferiority. By the 1960s, this attitude had become entrenched in police administration and law enforcement literature.[51] *Police Juvenile Enforcement* declared that while a policewoman could be an asset, "a female officer is not a necessity."[52]

Some even went so far as to suggest that male officers could simply dress as women for undercover work. In 1962, eight male officers did just that in order to trap muggers and rapists in New York City. "We want our men to look like housewives, not like Hollywood stars," explained Inspector Michael Codd, head of the tactical force. Twenty-seven-year-old patrolman Victor Ortiz wore white sandals, orange tapered pants, and a beige padded sweater on top of a bright print blouse. On hand to help the officers get ready were two policewomen, Caryl Collins and Dolores Munroe. The women stood by in their official uniforms as the men posed for the TV and newspaper cameras. Why teaching men to wear heels and put on lipstick was deemed more useful than simply deploying policewomen seems a question the reporters never asked. It's true that decoys did get attacked as part of these operations (that was the point), but all officers worked in teams with detectives standing by to apprehend suspects. In this instance, two of the disguised policemen had their purses snatched in Central Park and seven people were arrested in the overnight anti-mugging operation.[53]

As they long had, pickpocketing, theft, and fraud remained areas where women continued to detect in fairly large numbers. Washington, DC, got its first female detective in 1938. Cecelia A. Clarke began as a matron after the First World War. She became particularly adept at catching shoplifters, like real-life store detective Mary Carner, and was named a detective at age sixty-two.[54] In New York, fifty-eight women worked as detectives. Though they could work any case, including murder, women usually specialized in cases that the department believed could be done better, or only, by women. The biggest demand for women detectives was in the Missing Persons Bureau, Narcotics Division, and Special Frauds Squad (usually dealing with pickpockets and confidence men). Some women spent years posing as drug addicts or visiting palm readers for cases. Laurette Valente began as a policewoman in the late 1940s and had risen to detective first-grade (the highest such rank) by 1960; she specialized in pickpockets, averaging 250 arrests a year. Before entering the force, Valente had served two years during WWII with the WAVES, working on ballistic calibration at a US Navy proving ground and then as a mathematician with the Atomic Energy Commission. She entered the police force against the wishes of her mother and found she was good at the job. She met her husband, a fellow detective, during a stint in the Narcotics Division. Not all the work was enjoyable, though. Valente disliked decoy work, walking down deserted streets late at night, waiting to be attacked while other detectives watched from the shadows. She told a *New York Times* reporter:

> Then, out of the corner of your eye you see someone moving toward you. You can't really see him, and you can't hear him, either. You just sort of feel him getting nearer and nearer. You don't know whether he has a gun or a knife, or whether he is going to hit you on the head or just grab your handbag and run. You don't dare turn your head or try to look or do anything else to give it away. Your

hand is on your pistol in your coat pocket and your palm begins to
sweat because you know you'll never get it out fast enough if he has
a gun or a knife. And all you can do is keep walking as though you
didn't sense a thing. And with every step you pray those detectives
are close, real close.[55]

But in many cases, this type of undercover work remained a special
or occasional assignment rather than a regular position for women.

The Chicago Police Department, which had long gone its own
way in deploying women, established a women's bureau in 1947,
more than thirty years after reformers and the International Association of Policewomen had pressed for one. In 1931, the Citizens' Police
Committee of Chicago delivered a scathing attack on the treatment
of women in police departments, emphasizing the need for a separate
policewomen's bureau. The committee noted that because civil service requirements were the same for policewomen and matrons, the
distinction between the two positions were often "totally disregarded
and the policewomen . . . allotted duties within the normal scope of
a matron's limited qualifications."[56] Integrated into the Chicago force
under the command of men, policewomen's duties varied widely, from
regular police duties to detection to clerical and other non-police
work. This, the committee argued, demoralized policewomen and,
worse, threatened community safety. The committee strongly recommended the creation of separate bureaus "until there is an almost
complete reversal in the attitude of many of the district commanders
toward policewomen."

The city finally gave in and formed a bureau under the supervision
of policewoman Ruth Beiderman. Part of the crime prevention division, the women's bureau was largely responsible for the women's jail.
How much this new bureau actually changed policewomen's work
is unclear, however. Women continued to work out of different precincts rather than together in a central headquarters, and officers and
matrons were still used interchangeably, even when counted separately
on personnel lists. Department reports also tended to list the women
as part of crime prevention, rather than the women's bureau.[57] And as
they long had, Chicago's policewomen continued to outdo their peers
in other cities by making many more arrests of women and the men
who harassed them. Among those arrested was Mrs. Margaret Reilly,
a small, auburn-haired woman with an impressive record of theft in
Chicago and elsewhere, more than sixty offenses, mostly of women's

purses left carelessly on store counters. Caught in a department store, Reilly was searched by matron Mary McKune, who found two bundles of money—one of ninety-five dollars and the other of thirty-five dollars—hidden in the knots of her hair. Responding to the reading of her record at the stationhouse, Reilly retorted, "And why not? If I don't take the purses, somebody else will. It teaches those women a lesson. Finders keepers, losers weepers—that's the way I feel."[58]

But attitudes toward the separation of male and female officers were changing. The 1949 Labor Department bulletin suggested that women's bureaus provided a surer path to advancement, but only a few years earlier, a study of the profession by a policewoman concluded that women's future lay in integration with the rest of the department.[59]

Policewomen themselves remained conservative about their role. Many adhered to the position of the 1961 *Policewoman's Manual*, which maintained that police work would always be men's work. Criminologist Evabel Tenney, of the California Department of Justice, asserted that men and women should work not as rivals but as a harmonizing unit, though she placed the onus on women to fit in.[60] Portland sergeant Mary Anderson warned women that they might be pinched or patted by male officers, so they needed to be sure not to wear flashy makeup or suggestive clothing that might invite that behavior.[61] Even those women rallying around equality were generally only interested in promotion and equal pay. Policewomen tended to stay out of the discussions of structural inequality that animated the women's liberation movement of the 1960s and 1970s, even as its efforts helped produce a new social climate that ultimately helped policewomen advance.[62]

In 1956, policewomen reestablished the International Association of Policewomen (IAP) as the International Association of Women Police (IAWP). Rather than revive the old name, the association chose a new name, in part over concerns that "policewoman" was too narrowly defined and would disqualify women from positions as troopers, sheriffs, detectives, or marshals. The IAWP chose as its first president Lois Lundell Higgins, a policewoman from Chicago. It was an ironic choice given Chicago's historic dissociation with the original IAP and its preventative ideology.[63] Higgins sought to integrate women more fully into policing, while maintaining a gender-based role. She embraced an image of womanhood that was committed to family and was morally pure, respectable, and content with playing a supportive role to men. Higgins conceded that women occasionally made headlines with a sensational arrest or especially lurid case, but these were rare. The daily work life of a policewoman was largely "concerned with everyday problems of normal families."[64]

Membership in the IAWP was limited to women with full police authority, not the crossing guards, traffic officers, and other women who were often called police and wore police-style uniforms but were not sworn officers. Higgins also sought a closer relationship with the International Association of Chiefs of Police (IACP), an organization in which she was one of few female members. She hoped that this relationship would give policewomen greater recognition as law enforcement professionals and colleagues.[65]

By the 1950s, though, the moral authority leveraged by pioneer policewomen carried little weight, particularly as the number of women held in custody and juvenile detention grew. Though some women, particularly those in the IAWP, clung to their vision of a specialized role, newer policewomen saw work with women and juveniles as limiting. Like their male colleagues, they saw their future in diversified assignments within their departments and the opportunity to rise through the ranks. Demands for equality usually came from women in larger cities. New York City policewoman Marie Cirile recalled that the so-called "special qualities" women brought to the job were more handicap than help, leading to sex-based segregation and isolation within departments.[66] Others, even while still preferring separate work, changed the way they described the work of female officers. Theresa Melchionne, director of the New York Policewomen's Bureau from 1952 to 1963, wrote articles promoting policewomen's skill at decoy work, surveillance, and interviewing victims of sex crimes. It was a fairly predictable set of tasks for policewomen, but Melchionne made no claims to moral authority or efforts toward social redemption. She attributed women's skills less to innate qualities than to the available role models women had: mothers and teachers.[67]

But even as policewomen moved further away from their original role as guardians of women and children, assignments to a greater range of activities was still largely based on gender—this despite major changes to the image of male officers, which complicated the divide between male and female officers.[68] An article in *This Week* magazine described the cop of old as a caveman whose "requirements in the brain department were less than exacting."[69] By the 1950s, the trend was "toward brighter men and better training to enlist the smartest men and teach them more." A 1958 recruitment flyer from the New York Police Department stressed the multiple, interrelated roles of the policeman as "a family figure who used his mind and kindness to achieve his goals. He was a husband, father, taxpayer, a neighborhood boy, a teacher, clergymen, and brother."[70] If a patrol officer required less physical prowess than previously thought, then perhaps that officer could just as easily be a woman as a man. Younger women became convinced, as their foremothers had not, that segregation hampered their chances for authority and mobility. So, in the 1960s, women began to sue for promotion.[71]

Civil service exams for promotion were closed to women in New York City, even as the number of women in law enforcement grew. A record number of women joined the force in 1950 but with no opportunity for advancement.[72] "Regardless of her effectiveness, her self-dedication, or her accumulated skill and experience, a worker in the Juvenile Aid Bureau can anticipate no monetary reward nor change in status for the seventeen years between becoming a policewoman first grade and eligibility for retirement," wrote New York City officer Felicia Shpritzer in the *Journal of Criminal Law and Criminology*.[73] The only promotion a policewoman could hope to achieve in a regular career was an appointment to detective, but even that position offered no further place for women to go.

New York City was not the only city lacking promotional opportunities for women into the 1950s. Of the hundred largest cities, only twenty-eight provided promotions to women, nearly half of which was only to sergeant. Female lieutenants worked in Chicago, Philadelphia, Cleveland, Pittsburgh, Minneapolis, New Haven, and Washington, DC.[74] A handful of cities had female captains. Prohibiting women from promotional opportunities precluded competition between men and women in the regular police ranks.[75]

In 1961, Shpritzer sued the city on behalf of all women for the right to take the examination for promotion to sergeant. New York had one of the most restrictive promotion policies in the nation. Shpritzer, a college graduate with two master's degrees, had joined the force in 1942 and worked in the youth division since 1943. When she applied to take the sergeant's examination in the late 1950s, the civil service commission denied her request on the grounds that statutes prescribed one rank for policewomen. Shpritzer first appealed through administrative channels before abandoning that course for an order from the New York Supreme Court. She appealed to the

Mary Hamilton served as director of the New York Police Department's Women's Precinct (later the Policewomen's Bureau), charged with crime prevention and the protection of women and children. (Circa 1920s)

GO SLOW
and see our town

GO FAST
and see our jail

Three motorcycle officers with the Los Angeles Police Department on duty. From left to right: Hildur Fleming, Myra Richardson, and Beryl Wilson. (1927)

IAWP for help, but the association declined to openly support her case. Although sympathetic to her goals, the IAWP refused to jeopardize its relationship with the men of the IACP.[76] In 1962, the Appellate Division of the New York State Supreme Court declared that women could not be "arbitrarily denied the right to take the examination for Sergeant because of their sex, and no reasonable grounds have been shown to warrant the 'sex selection' evidenced."[77] Although New York City officials appealed, the State Court of Appeals upheld the decision of the lower court. Shpritzer had won. Her battle was one of the first by a policewoman to achieve equality through the courts. The following year, 126 women took the sergeant's exam. Two passed. In 1965, Shpritzer and Gertrude Schimmel became the city's first female sergeants; Schimmel later became the first female captain, and in 1978, the first woman to rank as deputy chief.[78]

Before she took her case to court, Shpritzer had tried to allay men's fears about women's promotion in a 1959 article, writing, "Obviously, it would be misuse of policewomen sergeants to assign them to a precinct to direct uniformed men on patrol duty." Yet by 1976, when Shpritzer retired, she was doing exactly what she had once called a "misuse of policewomen"—supervising male and female officers on patrol.[79]

Even with this win, many policewomen still struggled to perform police work at all, much less be eligible for promotion. In the early 1970s, seventy of New York City's 350 policewomen did clerical rather than police work. More than half the officers in Indianapolis, including most of the five female sergeants, were used as secretaries. In small departments, women often performed wildly different jobs. Limiting women's duties led many to conclude that this was all they could do. England and Germany passed strict rules prohibiting the use of policewomen for typing, switchboard, and other non-police work, but no such laws existed in the United States.[80]

Before *Roe v. Wade*, abortion investigations provided women a rare opportunity for promotion. In New York City in the 1950s, abortion came under the purview of the Policewomen's Bureau. Men had handled these investigations, but did so ineffectually and had a weak arrest record. Bureau director Theresa Melchionne, in her efforts to expand policewomen's domain, helped to push the issue to put women in charge. Women, even those dying from botched abortions, would rarely help the police, so policewomen went undercover. In 1954, Melchionne had supervised a decoy operation that uncovered an abortion ring in several counties. The women used wiretaps, walkie-talkies, long-range cameras, and other surveillance techniques that had long been the exclusive realm of the detective division. The operation resulted in 22 arrests and 203 indictments. More importantly, for the officers, four women received promotions to detective third-grade. In 1968, Officer Olga Ford was transferred from the Policewomen's Bureau to narcotics, where she rose to an investigator (detective) thanks to her experience investigating abortions.[81]

Many departments still required higher educational standards for policewomen than for policemen. The force in Portland, Oregon, required a four-year college degree for women but only a two-year degree for men. Because the openings for policewomen were few, departments rationalized the disparity on the grounds that they were hiring only the best women. Many departments also provided separate training to male and female recruits. Examinations for promotion could also differ by gender. Women in Philadelphia were required to take both an oral and written examination for promotion, while men had only a written exam.[82] Officer Ruth Wells challenged the practice in 1967, but the Pennsylvania Supreme Court ruled in favor of the different practices, since men and women had different duties. "Many of the tasks performed by the police force are of such a nature, physiologically speaking, that they cannot and should not be assigned to women," read the decision.[83]

While Shpritzer's case accelerated change in New York, social and political changes outside policing also helped policewomen. In the 1960s, violent-crime rates were on the rise. In many cities, riots broke out over civil rights, gender equality, and the Vietnam War. These incidents brought widespread attention to police practices that were illegal and brutal. Americans, as they had in the 1920s, once again were becoming increasingly frustrated with the police.

In 1967, the President's Commission on Law Enforcement and Administration of Justice (known as the Crime Commission) found that police appeared to have little ability to prevent, reduce, or deter crime with their current methods and pointed to the huge gulf separating police departments from the communities they served.[84] The report called for greater attention to police-community relations and for the subordination of aggression to emotional sensitivity and intelligence. Women received only scant mention in the report. The Crime Commission observed that policewomen were largely performing the duties they had always done in service to women and children. Rather than maintain the status quo, however, the commission suggested expanding their duties, so that women served "regularly in patrol, vice, and investigative divisions." The commission also recommended that cities hire more highly educated and more diverse recruits, noting that the height and weight requirements in use almost everywhere eliminated many qualified female applicants. Despite devoting three pages to raising educational standards (policewomen got five paragraphs total), the report did not mention the higher qualifications already expected of women in most cities.[85]

Legal efforts to achieve gender equality in policing picked up in the late 1960s and 1970s. In 1972, Title 7 of the Civil Rights Act of 1964 passed, extending the ban on discrimination on the basis of sex, race, color, national origin, and religion to public-sector employees, including those in police departments. But banning discrimination based on sex was still a long way from instituting equality. In 1973, Congress passed the Crime Control Act, banning, among other things, sex discrimination by law enforcement agencies receiving federal aid. The Law Enforcement Assistance Administration (LEAA) administered money and required departments with fifty or more employees and receiving a minimum of $25,000 in grants toward plans to ensure women's equal opportunity.[86]

New laws meant that police departments faced not only political pressure and lawsuits but also financial cuts if their hiring practices proved unlawful. These laws ended separate educational requirements for male and female applicants, separate promotion lists, and some height and weight requirements. Many departments dropped "policeman" and "policewoman" and adopted the gender-neutral title "police officer" in the 1970s, as legal changes mandated the hiring of women and men on an equal basis. Some cities had already abandoned these discriminatory practices, but discrimination remained deeply entrenched in many police departments.

Cracks were beginning to appear in male-dominated forces. In Indianapolis, officers Betty Blankenship and Elizabeth Coffal (later Robinson) successfully agitated for regular patrol duty. The two had sought patrol assignments from the beginning of their careers, suggesting the idea to Sergeant Winston L. Churchill as recruits at the academy. When Churchill became chief, in 1968, the women reminded him that he had promised to put women on patrol were he ever in charge. True to his word, Chief Churchill transferred them out of the Juvenile

Division and sent them out on patrol in September of that year.[87] However, he gave them only twenty-four-hours' notice. Blankenship and Coffal had no additional training; even male rookies straight out of the academy had some training specific to patrol. Dispatchers sent calls selectively. Some male officers ignored the women completely, while others sent them only the most awful cases. Women dispatchers tended to send them as many calls as they could. Set up to fail, the officers succeeded nonetheless, learning patrol through trial and error, but not without substantial risk to themselves and to others.[88]

Experiments showing that women could handle patrol, as Blankenship and Coffal demonstrated, did little to force departments to act, however. Women had to prove themselves again and again.

Not all policewomen wanted to go on patrol. Many had joined the department on the assumption of doing a particular type of work and were not ready for the drastic change in duty that uniformed patrol represented. When the chief of the Miami Police Department proposed sending women on patrol in 1967, half of the fourteen female officers opposed the plan and questioned its legality. Age was often a factor, with younger women seeking equality and older women seeking to retain their traditional role. Some women quit. Others adapted to keep their jobs.

Others, even as they took on more duties, insisted on a gender-based division in policing. In Chicago, policewoman Cindy Pontoriero qualified for promotion to the rank of detective in 1971, placing eighty-first among more than two thousand candidates, mostly men, in the department exams. Pontoriero had already worked for several years as an investigator on shoplifting and pickpocketing assignments downtown. Of her high score on the exam, which made the local news, Pontoriero asserted, "I'm not trying to compete with men. There is a distinct difference between men and women, and I want to do a woman's job in this department."[89] The newspapers hailed her as the city's first woman detective, though that was far from true. Alice Clement had held the title of detective decades earlier, and policewomen had investigated cases involving women and children, in addition to undercover work, for much of the century. Two years after her initial promotion, Pontoriero became a homicide detective, working the four-to-midnight shift with a male partner. It was a department position that Pontoriero had requested because she thought "the homicide detail might be able to use a woman in its investigation of cases involving sex offenses."[90] Her perspective was not all that far removed from that of the pioneer generation of female officers more than half a century earlier.

Clothing remained an issue for women. Chicago introduced uniforms for policewomen in 1956. It consisted of a regulation navy-blue skirt and jacket, light-blue shirt, man's tie, and navy-blue leather pumps and shoulder bag. Many departments required women to wear a skirt and pantyhose, despite their obvious unsuitability for police work.[91]

By the 1970s, male and female patrol officers in New York City wore identical uniforms: a light-blue shirt with the badge and name tag over pockets, dark-blue pants, sturdy black shoes, and a Sam Browne belt (named for a nineteenth-century British army officer and the utility-type belt he devised for himself in India), which held a revolver, Mace, a baton, handcuffs, and keys. Supervisors urged the women to remain ladies, even as they also demanded a professional demeanor that skewed masculine: short hair and limited makeup and jewelry.[92]

Clothing malfunctions were a frequent feature of media stories and profiles of policewomen. Reporters described how officers in Miami ruined several pairs of pantyhose exiting their patrol cars as though it were news. In Los Angeles, an officer nearly lost her skirt scaling a wall, while another officer in Irvine struggled in her tight skirt to climb a hill to assist an accident victim.[93] Few if any stories informed readers that policewomen were not allowed to wear pants or holsters, and that pantyhose and skirts were required. Tight clothing never seemed to slow down TV detectives Honey West or Diana Rigg's Emma Peel. When the press wrote about female officers wondering where to pack their guns and choosing their purses, it illustrated how ridiculous policewomen were considered, as well as ambivalence about women's role as an authority figure. It took years for women to acquire proper attire and equipment, which was another way for departments to delay putting female officers on the street.[94] Even so, putting women in uniform did not guarantee their acceptance. "A female is a female. Nobody can say that to look at her that she is a police officer—she's not. She's still a female, no matter what she is going to be wearing, and she's going to be wearing the same uniform as me," said one officer.[95]

Patrol remained vital for promotion, but most departments continued to resist giving women these assignments. Ellen Helsel, an officer with the University of California at Irvine Police Department, could just as easily have been speaking in 1872 when she made the case for women on patrol in 1972. "More women are going out alone at night and are becoming victims of crime, and more women are committing crimes. So it seems obvious that more women should be hired to help the victims and stop the female criminals," Helsel said, though she was quick to add, "But that doesn't mean we should be limited to working just with women."[96] Policemen insisted that women could not perform uniformed patrol and that a gender-integrated force would cause chaos in departments and on the streets—this despite the fact that policewomen had patrolled since their earliest days and had used cars once they became commonplace. What distinguished these two types of patrol was what officers were looking for: policewomen concentrated on potential problems with women and juveniles, while policemen focused on law breaking and enforcement. The real issue came down to whether women should, or even could, physically and emotionally handle male criminals. Most policemen said no.[97]

Though most could, generally, acknowledge women's intelligence, policemen continued to see their physical strength as a requirement and superior asset. Sergeant Leland Bowers of Garden Grove, California, asserted, "A woman cannot possibly hold her own in wrestling a brute to the ground. All the defense techniques she learned at the academy don't work when a guy is physically stronger than she is."[98] An article in Police Chief claimed, "As a woman she probably has not been socialized to engage in physical violence with fighting men . . . [she may] unconsciously revert to her female role by standing by, not intervening in the fight."[99] Another asked, "How can a five-foot woman possibly handle a man who's six-foot-five and weighs 250 pounds?"[100] Many male officers felt women could not handle the job because of their size, ignoring the fact that a 250-pound man would be a challenge for any officer to handle alone. Some men argued that chivalry would lead them to protect their female colleagues while the criminal went free. Claims about women's physical strength—or lack of it—were taken as givens, even though no one had any data to back them up.[101]

Women had, in fact, demonstrated their ability to perform physical tasks multiple times. In 1948, police rookie Lorette Ingram tossed her lieutenant, a woman much taller and heavier than herself, over her shoulder and onto the mat during training, a feat that earned notice in the newspaper.[102] In 1956, New York City held a physical test for potential recruits. Joseph Schechter, chairman of the Civil Service Commission, welcomed the candidates with a speech typical in its condescension: "I must confess that you young ladies have put to shame the people who have labored under the illusion that a woman must be husky looking to become a policewoman. Some of you look more like Hollywood studio models than young ladies who might be tangling with violators of the law."[103] Of the 132 women who tried out, only ten failed to pass. The police commissioner drew the applause of the women when he proclaimed his intention to "ask for an increased quota of policewomanpower" based on the results.

Those opposed to putting women on patrol had trouble describing what exactly made women ineligible. Height and weight requirements for patrol varied among police forces; they were consistent only in describing a person bigger than the average woman. Those protesting the constitutionality of hiring practices argued that a police force should reflect the racial breakdown of the population it policed; somehow, no one thought to suggest that the police force should also reflect the gender breakdown of that same population.

In 1972, Washington, DC, police chief Jerry Wilson decided to put women's strength and fitness for patrol to the test. He had indicated his determination to use policewomen throughout his department, including on patrol, soon after his appointment in 1969. Wilson issued guidelines for the equal treatment of male and female rookies but left implementation in the hands of district supervisors, some of whom opposed the use of women on patrol and sought to undermine them. The nonprofit Police Foundation studied the two groups of officers for one year. Four months in, initial results found that "men and women officers were observed to obtain similar results in handling angry or violent citizens. There were no reported incidents which cast serious doubt on the ability of women to perform patrol work satisfactorily."[104] One difference the researchers did find was in officers' training and work environment. Several women received different instructions from the men, and faced informal opposition and hostility as they attempted to do their work. These issues were often not brought to the attention of supervisors by the female officers out of fear of repercussions. On the job, the women made fewer arrests and gave out fewer traffic citations. Even before the final report was issued, in 1974, Chief Wilson declared the experiment a success and announced his intention to hire men and women for all positions, including patrol. The only disadvantage the final report cited for hiring women was the additional monitoring required to "insure that women are given the opportunity to perform the work."

Other smaller studies followed, and by the 1980s, much more research had been done on female officers. Women proved as capable as men in all of these studies. Female officers required no additional assistance from supporting units and worked as well with their partners as male officers. That women tended to have a lower arrest rate may have had more to do with the greater number of women working inside duties, despite so-called equal treatment. Whether more arrests represented better policing went unquestioned.[105]

No matter how many studies declared women fit to serve as officers, opinions of policewomen among male officers remained low. Perhaps that's why the creators of the fictional female detectives in the late 1970s and 1980s emphasized the physical fitness of their heroines. Kinsey Millhone may not be glamorous, but she's certainly fit. In 1971, before an audience of a hundred policewomen, Los Angeles police chief Edward Davis asserted that women's physical and biological makeup limited them to their traditional duties. Women did not belong in patrol cars, he stated, adding that they could not be trusted with guns "during that time of the month."[106] He also refused to hire anyone under five foot eight, a restriction that remained in place until 1981. Many cities hired female officers only under court order. Average citizens seemed more likely to support women on patrol, affirming their belief in women's skill and ability to bring empathy and comfort to victims. Female officers were becoming a staple of fiction and TV, which undoubtedly helped accustom many Americans to the sight of a woman in uniform. But at the same time, many people expressed attitudes that reflected traditional notions of women's place, particularly in regard to the potential dangers women faced on the street and their ability to physically handle violent criminals.[107]

Others argued that women on patrol would have a calming effect on offenders and the police system. According to psychologist Lewis J. Sherman, "There is some good reason to believe that police work could be still more peaceful and less violent than it is at present if women were recruited for it in large numbers."[108] New York City officer Patricia Thornton claimed that violent criminals often apologized for their behavior when she and her partner showed up to arrest them. It was an argument that early policewomen had made more than fifty years earlier. At the same time, Thornton also declared that she doesn't really think about her gender while on duty. "You react first as cop, only later as a woman," she said.[109]

The number of women officers more than doubled between 1960 and 1980.[110] By 1980, women were employed in virtually all federal law enforcement agencies, from the FBI to the US Customs Service and the National Park Service, just as they were in fiction. Even so, women constituted less than 4 percent of police personnel. The growth came when recruitment among men lagged or after lawsuits. To boost the number of female state troopers, in 1980 New York's State Police Academy hosted a women-only training class. Although the academy had offered co-ed classes since 1974, only two women had graduated to become officers. The rest left for a variety of reasons, including intimidation in the predominantly male atmosphere.[111] The New York City Police Department added detective classes for women in 1977, hoping to add them to the all-male homicide, robbery, and burglary detective squads. The force already had sixty-eight female detectives, but none served on these specialty squads. Chief John Keenan said the move was prompted by a belief that women could improve the effectiveness of the team, though it may also have been tied to the complaint lodged by the Policewomen's Endowment Association, which accused the department of discriminating against its 450 female officers. A lack of female recruits wasn't the only problem. Many departments struggled to find qualified male applicants as well, due to the poor public image of the police, low salaries, and deplorable working conditions.

In 1979, Helen Kidder and Peggy York became the first female homicide team in California, a real-life Cagney and Lacey three years before the TV show debuted.[112] Many speculated that the show was, in fact, modeled on the officers. Kidder and York paired up because no man wanted to work with either of them. But the women quickly won the accolades of their supervisor, Lieutenant Ernest Curtsinger, and contributed to the unit's high "solve rate" on murders, more than 80 percent. Kidder and York's male colleagues remained somewhat skeptical, however. The other officers often commented on their clothing and made them feel that they did not fit the image of a homicide detective, particularly with their predilection for nice clothes and sandals. "Sometimes I simply lose my sense of hearing to ignore sexist shoptalk from the male officers," said Kidder. Suspects and the families of murder victims also sometimes expressed surprise at the team assigned to their case. Like other female detectives, Kidder and

York declared the work hard and exhausting with little of the glamour seen on TV or in books, but well worth the effort.

But a lack of glamour among female detectives got the TV show *Cagney & Lacey* into trouble with viewers in the 1980s.[113] Its tough and abrasive female leads, described by one CBS official as "too harshly women's lib," led many to believe the detectives were lesbians and caused the network to order a retooling of the show. The response to the series generated significant debate over the meanings of femininity and masculinity. As the only female homicide team in the country, Kidder and York were asked to comment on the show and its portrayal of female detectives by TV critic Harold Rosenberg in 1982. "I watched the show once and I was so turned off," said Kidder.[114] "They looked rough and tough, and they weren't terribly feminine, just in the way they dressed and acted." York declared the show featured "two women trying to do exactly what men do." Cagney and Lacey's wardrobes particularly turned off Kidder. "Peggy and I wear good suits, nylons and pretty shoes, silk blouses, the hair, everything," said Kidder. Neither detective believed that the reboot of the show, including making the women more feminine, would make the show more authentic. Echoing the sentiments of real officers on their fictional counterparts, heard since the nineteenth century, Kidder declared, "They never care if police shows are accurate."

Policing became particularly attractive to African American women in the 1970s after educational requirements for men and women equalized. Black female high school graduates earned more money as police than they could in just about any other job, and their percentage in all departments far exceeded that of African American men. Even though they experienced more discrimination than white women, African American women couldn't get the same pay and benefits elsewhere. Hiring men and women on an equal basis allowed departments to hire women whose class and schooling were more similar to their male colleagues as well. These women sought police work for the same reasons men did: salary, benefits, and job security.[115]

African American women were not new to policing, though. Los Angeles hired the nation's first black policewoman in 1916.[116] Washington, DC, hired its first black female officer in 1919, and by 1949, the city's eight black policewomen accounted for one-third of the department's women.[117] Substantial numbers of black women made up the force in Indianapolis and Philadelphia as well. African American policewomen were the logical extension of the rationale that early reformers made for policewomen: a person who reflects the community she patrols is more effective.

Despite their numbers and presence among the pioneer policewomen, African American women remained largely invisible. Early policewomen worried that publicizing the presence of black women on the force would disrupt the image of social order and moral stability women (meaning white women) brought to law enforcement. One Los Angeles policewoman remembered that the only minority woman included in a 1947 press photo was fair with blue-gray eyes.[118] "She could have been . . . anything. She never denied—but she never made a point of saying anything about it either." A 1972 Police Foundation survey did not include any black women in its photographs of policewomen.[119] White policewomen also demonstrated little knowledge of race relations when they cited the characteristics that would make African American officers effective in the inner city. Whites failed to understand the distrust and fear within communities terrorized by police and racism.[120]

The idea of black women patrolling public space challenged white prejudice. The primary goal of protecting girls from white slavers in the 1910s had been the shielding of girls from men of other races. Even though most African American officers had their primary policing duties in black neighborhoods, full police power enabled them to arrest white women and children, too. At the same time, those raising alarms about the safety of white policewomen on urban streets did not seem to consider the safety of black women of equal concern. According to one African American officer, it was because of popular perceptions of black women: "The Joe Public—when they think of danger on this job, they may be thinking of a Caucasian female; they think that she's not gonna handle it. They're not gonna think that way about a Black female police officer. . . . A Black female officer can be in as much danger as the white female officer. But people think we Black women are warriors anyway, so we should be able to take care of it."[121]

But black women officers began to make major inroads in the late twentieth century. Helena Ashby joined the Los Angeles Sheriff's Department, the largest in the nation, in 1964. In 1995, she became the first African American and first woman to reach the rank of chief.[122] Police work hadn't been her initial goal. She had wanted a job that would allow her the flexibility to go to college and one that paid more than clerical work. Ashby applied for and passed all of the exams for deputy sheriff. She'd held a range of detecting jobs through-out her career, but as chief, she assumed leadership over the depart-ment's Detective Division. Ashby led investigations in commercial crimes, homicide, juvenile investigations, and metro vice until her retirement in 2000.

By the 1990s, the most successful homicide detective in New Orleans to date, solving 98 percent of her cases, was a black woman named Jacklean Davis. She had a tough childhood. Raised by her great-aunt, who worked as prostitute, Davis suffered sexual abuse and a teen pregnancy that found her on welfare at a young age. She knew some people in law enforcement and decided to try it herself as a way out of her situation. But when she took the examination for the po-lice academy, she failed. She took it again and failed. And again. And again. Davis finally passed on her fifth try and volunteered for duty in one of the highest-crime areas of New Orleans. She earned a good reputation for her relationship with neighborhood residents. After her work on a rape case that ended with the capture of a serial killer, she became a homicide detective, though not without considerable harassment from her peers. "On the majority of homicide units I've seen," she said, "recruitment is not always fair. You have to get past the stigma of being a female—let alone a Black female."[123]

Beverly Joyce Harvard became the first black woman to run a ma-jor police department when she was appointed Atlanta's police chief in 1994.[124] Harvard had joined the force in 1973 after betting her husband, Jim, that she could graduate from the police academy. Jim had argued that a woman officer would have to be big and strong, not small and quiet like his wife. Harvard had no particular interest in law enforcement at the time, having graduated from college with a degree in sociology. But she set out to prove her husband wrong and soon discovered that her sociology skills and interest in public service served her well in policing. The pioneer generation of policewomen would likely have agreed. Harvard focused on community policing as a way of preventing crime during her eight-year tenure as chief. She was criticized internally for her lack of patrol experience, a not uncommon accusation leveled at the first generation of female chiefs. But street-patrol experience was still hard-fought ground for women of Harvard's generation.

In fiction, a few black women took up detection, though it was a white woman, Susan Moody, who created the first black woman detective in 1984, the amateur investigator Penny Wanawake. As a white, British woman, Moody did not explore the issues of race that became integral to later stories featuring black detectives. It wasn't until the late 1980s that black women published stories with black heroines. The first detective novel by and about an African American woman is Dolores Komo's *Clio Browne, Private Investigator* (1988), set in St. Louis. Browne is well aware of her difference from detective heroes of the past, often contrasting her own thinking and behavior with detectives like Sherlock Holmes. She relies on her friends and family for support, and works from gut instinct to determine guilt.

A few years later, Nikki Baker, the pseudonym for novelist Jennifer Dowdell, created a sexy lesbian sleuth named Virginia Kelly in 1991 with *In the Game*. Kelly is a successful Chicago investment banker who detects on the side. Eleanor Taylor Bland introduced her detective, Marti MacAlister, in *Dead Time* (1992). MacAlister is a streetwise widow raising two children and solving cases in the small town of Lincoln Prairie, Illinois. She's paired with a Polish American male partner, who has some outdated ideas about women and race. Like MacAlister, detective Tamara Hayle is a savvy single mom trying to make it on her own as a private investigator in Newark, New Jersey. Created by Valerie Wilson Wesley, Hayle made her first appearance in *When Death Comes Stealing* (1994).

But even with these pioneering sleuths, the number of fictional black detectives remains small to this day, even as the number of black women in real policing grew.[125]

As women took on more policing duties, including street patrol, they also faced more dangers. In September 1974, twenty-four-year-old Washington, DC, officer Gail Cobb became the first policewoman killed in the line of duty. She had joined the department nearly a year earlier and had been on patrol only five months at the time of her death. She was writing a traffic ticket when a citizen informed her that an armed man had run into a garage. Cobb followed and confronted him. The man had been part of an attempted bank robbery that had been foiled by officers only minutes earlier. Cobb ordered the suspect to place his hands on the garage wall. As Cobb called for assistance over her radio, the suspect spun around and fired at Cobb. More than two thousand police from around the nation, many of them women, attended her funeral. The job had never been without its risks, though. Inmates attempting escape had killed five matrons by the early twentieth century. In 2014, the National Law

Enforcement Memorial listed 280 women who had perished in the line of duty.[126]

Few could have predicted women's advances in policing, least of all policewomen themselves. The women of the International Association of Women Police saw patrol as a step down rather than up on the career ladder. Patrol officers were generalists rather than experts in handling specialized cases, they argued. As some women demanded patrol and detecting assignments, sometimes even going to court to get them, others resigned or retired rather than accept these assignments. In Washington, DC, all but eight of the twenty-five women who had been in the bureau before Chief Jerry Wilson came on board in 1969 resigned rather than accept their new role. Many IAWP members also failed to see crime fighting as a role for men and women to undertake on equal terms. The organization continued to stress work with juveniles and women, and fell out of touch with the crime-fighting mentality of the new generation of policewomen. Not until the 1980s, with a leadership change, did the IAWP promote the full participation of women in policing.[127]

In 1952, Lilian Wyles, one of the first sergeants of the London Metropolitan Police Force, wrote, "Prejudice dies hard in police circles: it has been dying these thirty years, and is not quite dead today."[128] Wyles foresaw a day when the "convulsive shudder" of opposition to policewomen would be dead and buried. More than half a century later, that day has still not come.

CHAPTER TEN

Women Detectives Today

"**T**ELL ME, MISS HOLT, HOW DID YOU BECOME A DICK?" ASKS THE JEWEL thief in the premier episode of *Remington Steele*, in 1982. The question makes clear that even though women have detected on television since the 1950s, and on the page since at least the 1860s, a woman's legitimacy as a sleuth remained questionable in the 1980s. Detection belonged to men.

Yet today, the fictional female detective has become nearly a genre of her own, with a fan base hungry for the next book or television series. Crime fiction has offered women writers a home from the very beginning, even though they were, until the twentieth century, largely excluded from professional careers in crime. By the early 2000s, women were regular members of investigating teams on television, working as private investigators, cops, forensics experts, sheriffs, and federal agents in more than a hundred crime series. Some have called it a new golden age of detective fiction, as women have changed the gender—and, to a lesser degree, the race—of the quintessentially everyman white male private eye or homicide tec.

Women writers in the 1970s and 1980s steered crime writing and the female detective in this new direction. They successfully appropriated and reformulated the genre and the hard-boiled style to fashion tough female private eyes who reflected the lives and experiences of actual women—even though the sight of a real female detective still makes headlines to this day. Signs of the capable and self-reliant female sleuth appeared much earlier though in women like Harriet Vane, Amelia Butterworth, Loveday Brooke, and the crinoline-dodging Mrs. Paschal. These were fictional women who, in their own ways, chose unconventional lives and pursued destinies other than marriage. They sought adventure and independence over passivity and dependence. Undoubtedly, the image of women entering male strongholds—saloons and prisons, for instance—and taking charge constituted a large part of the appeal of early women's detective stories. The improbability of a female investigator preoccupied women's detective fiction for decades.

The interventions of these early detectives (and their creators) in the genre laid the groundwork for the female detectives who have upended and reimagined the possibilities for women in mystery fiction. There is no Jane Marple, Kinsey Millhone, Temperance Brennan, or Precious Ramotswe without Amelia Butterworth and Loveday Brooke. Literary critics have generally considered the detective genre conservative and formulaic, with its artificial restoration of order and prescribed characters (detective, victim, suspects). But writers since the late nineteenth century have often paid little more than lip service to the formula. They nod toward the conventions of the genre while making use of detection for their own literary purposes.

While the hard-boiled style remains incredibly popular, in recent years, some notable series detectives have harkened back to the genre's Golden Age. One of the first was Amelia Peabody, an Egyptologist and amateur sleuth first introduced by Elizabeth Peters, the pen name for Barbara Mertz, in the 1975 novel *Crocodile on the Sandbank*. It's 1884, and the thirty-something Peabody, a wealthy, self-proclaimed spinster, sets off to indulge her passion for ancient Egypt, a parasol firmly in hand. There she meets an archaeologist who ends her spinsterhood, and she finds a sideline career as a sleuth investigating shady antiquities dealers, murders, and sabotage. Nineteen books follow Peabody from 1884 to 1923 as she marries, has a child, and gathers a large circle of friends and allies. Nearly all the stories are set in Egypt, with the excavations providing the backdrop to the mysteries. Peabody's creator, Barbara Mertz, was herself an Egyptologist, pursuing a doctorate in the field in the 1950s, a time when few women sought such opportunities. Unable to find a job in academia, she turned to fiction, weaving her interests in history, ancient Egypt, and archaeology into her stories. Mertz adopted several pen names to distinguish her fiction from her scholarly work. Peabody was only one of the female sleuths Mertz invented. She also wrote six mysteries featuring art historian Vicky Bliss, whose work puts her in contact with forgers, art thieves, and killers; the sleuthing Jacqueline "Jake" Kirby, a librarian turned romance novelist, turned detective in four novels.

On the other side of the world, Phryne Fisher is a wealthy detective in late 1920s Melbourne, Australia.[1] She wasn't born to wealth but inherits her title and money after all the male heirs in her family are killed in World War I. Even with her money, Fisher's background makes her empathetic to the less fortunate and the problems of others. She's adventurous—she can fly a plane; cosmopolitan—she can speak several languages; and bohemian—she sometimes sports trousers—while still managing to maintain her elegant style and class. Fisher is single but boldly sleeps with any man she finds intriguing with no regrets, a marked departure from the well-known lady detectives created in the 1920s. Overt sexuality was a regular part of films in the 1920s and early 1930s, before film production codes reined them in, so Fisher is, in some ways, true to her era. The character first appeared in Kerry Greenwood's 1989 novel *Cocaine Blues*, which finds Fisher bored with high society in London and willing to try her hand at detection when asked to investigate the mysterious illness of the daughter of a family friend in Australia. Fisher soon finds herself embroiled in several different problems and manages to solve each one. But because she can't be a detective in the Australian police force—women are only allowed to be policewomen, never detectives—she forms her own private investigation business. As usual with female sleuths, the police find her troublesome, but they also know they wouldn't solve half their cases without her. The series became an Australian television drama in 2012, starring Essie Davis as an especially glamorous Fisher.[2]

Another modern Golden Age–style detective is Maisie Dobbs, the creation of Jacqueline Winspear. Dobbs is a World War I field nurse turned detective, similar to the path taken by fictional detective Cherry Ames in the Second World War. Becoming a detective wasn't Dobbs's first career transformation. Born working class, Dobbs worked as a servant in a London mansion until her employer, Lady Rowan Compton, catches her reading philosophy in the library and sends her to Cambridge University. War breaks out soon after Dobbs finishes her degree, so she enlists for nursing services overseas. Years later, after an apprenticeship with a former Scotland Yard officer, Dobbs sets up her own detective agency, where she works as both an investigator and a psychologist. But she soon discovers she can't escape the war and her first case, a seemingly ordinary assignment to investigate an infidelity case, introduced in *Maisie Dobbs* (2003), plunges her back into the horrors of the Great War. The lingering trauma of war on both individuals and society is a theme that appears again and again throughout the series.

Then there's Mary Russell, who is fifteen when she stumbles—literally—over a retired Sherlock Holmes tending to his bees near Sussex Downs in *The Beekeeper's Apprentice* (1994). Russell's keen observations on Holmes's efforts to replenish his stock of bees impresses the great detective and launches a partnership that finds Russell first as Holmes's protégé and then his equal in detection by the time she enters Oxford, in 1917. The series, the creation of Laurie R. King, mixes the Victorian style of Holmes with Russell, an adventurous New Woman of the twentieth century. Orphaned after her parents and brother are killed in an automobile accident, she lives with her aunt, who is jealous of the trust left to Russell by her parents. Despite the regular presence of Holmes, Russell is the narrator and voice of the stories. She is just as frank and intelligent as Holmes but with the humanity and emotion that Holmes lacks. The two decide to marry in 1921, and they keep detecting, often guided by Russell's various passions, particularly theology. She investigates a Christian feminist sect in her second story, *A Monstrous Regiment of Women*, after the death of three followers who willed their fortunes to the group. A different case has Russell investigating a letter written by Mary Magdalene, and another finds her hunting for spies in post-WWI Palestine.

But even with the soaring success of women's detective fiction in recent decades, women writers have struggled with discrimination and acceptance, too. The genre has not always been a comfortable place for women, despite their presence in crime fiction from the very beginning, and despite surveys showing that far more women than men read mysteries. To promote the cause and address the unequal treatment of women mystery writers, Sara Paretsky, Margaret Maron, Nancy Pickard, and other writers formed Sisters in Crime in 1986. Members expressed concern over the sadistic violence inflicted on women in some novels; the dearth of women winning major honors like the Edgar awards, named for Edgar Allan Poe; and the disproportionate amount of critical attention paid to male writers in book reviews, a point argued by women authors outside crime fiction as well.[3] To that end, Sisters in Crime organized the Media Monitoring Project, an annual effort to track reviews of women in major newspapers and journals and awards won. The number of women reviewed in 1985 averaged 15 percent at a time when women wrote 40 percent of the mystery novels. The numbers have improved: in 2013, women hit 36 percent in national newspapers.[4]

Sisters in Crime, as well as mystery bookstores, fan conventions, increased media attention, and, of course, the authors themselves, have helped women recognize themselves—and have helped others see women—as literary heroes.

The change was slower to take hold on television. Detectives, male or female, were less popular on the small or big screen in the 1960s than they were in previous decades. Those crime fighters who did appear tended to be spies in the James Bond mode. Despite her physical similarity to the Bond girls and her high-tech gadgets, Honey West lasted only one season on television. A woman with her own detective business would not again appear on television for more than fifteen years.

Many of the female cops on television were disposable, replaceable, or dependent in some way, especially if they had a male partner. Emma Peel of *The Avengers*, Dee Dee McCall of *Hunter*, and Nancy Drew of *The Hardy Boys/Nancy Drew Mysteries* all left or were replaced before the series' end. Female detectives with male partners often could not even investigate alone. Nancy Drew works with the Hardy Boys, though the two book series never featured this kind of crossover, nor did Drew ever require assistance on the page. In the first season, the episodes alternated between the brothers and Drew, but eventually the number of Hardy Boys stories grew, and Drew disappears from the show without explanation. Dee Dee McCall of *Hunter* faced regular attacks in the course of the series and needed the reassurance of her male partner, Hunter. She leaves her police job (and the show) to get married. Marriage commonly explained the disappearance of female characters of any type on television, just as it ended the sleuthing careers of girl detectives in books. Sally McMillan of *McMillan & Wife* is an exception in that she dies, but then, as the title of the show says, she's already married to the male star of the show, Stuart McMillan, so the common storyline couldn't apply.[5]

The Mod Squad, which premiered in 1968, featured a relatively ineffectual flower child as female detective Julie Barnes. She's part of a trio of young criminals recruited by the police to become undercover operatives in exchange for dropping charges pending against them. Barnes had been arrested for vagrancy after running away from her prostitute mother in San Francisco. The first young undercover cops on TV, the three stars used their age, attitude, and style to get close to the criminals they investigated: drug dealers, radicals, and other members of the underworld. As the only woman of the group, Julie was usually left out of physical confrontations, and her male partners often had to rescue her from dangerous situations. The show was loosely based on the experiences of creator Bud Ruskin, who had worked with young undercover narcotics cops in the 1950s. *The Mod Squad* proved wildly popular among its target demographic—young people—and created a space for the counterculture on television, with its hippie cops in leading roles.[6]

Several shows about women cops debuted in 1974, but only one, *Police Woman*, survived the first season. Despite sharing a name with the 1940s radio show based on the life of New York homicide detective Mary Sullivan, the two series had little in common. Angie Dickinson portrayed Sergeant Suzanne "Pepper" Anderson, an undercover officer with the Criminal Conspiracy Unit of the Los Angeles Police Department. Sexy, blonde, and glamorous, Anderson posed as everything from a prostitute and a gangster's girlfriend to a prison inmate, reporter, and murder victim's sister to catch criminals. Dressed in miniskirts, stilettos, and low-cut tops, she's more bait for criminals than butt kicker. Her cover was also frequently broken and the real cops—white men—saved her. Wildly popular, *Police Woman* aired until 1978 and was the first hour-long drama on American television to feature a woman in a starring role.[7]

Another, more innovative detective appeared in a made-for-television movie and then in the short-lived 1974 television drama *Get Christie Love!*, which featured the first black woman hired by a large urban police department on television. The series was based on Dorothy Uhnak's crime thriller *The Ledger*, which in turn was based on Uhnak's own experiences as a policewoman, including fourteen years with the New York Transit Police and twelve as a detective. Uhnak's novel featured a white main character as the detective, but the television producers had other ideas. Teresa Graves starred as detective Christie Love, who went undercover to bring down a drug cartel. She did so with all the style common to the popular blaxploitation films of the early 1970s. She even had a catchphrase: "You're under arrest, Sugah!"[8]

Overlapping with the last years of *Police Woman*, *Charlie's Angels* provided a similar image of gorgeous women solving crimes in high heels but with a campier sensibility. Its stars—Kate Jackson, Jaclyn Smith, Farrah Fawcett—looked like traditional sex goddesses and even took orders from a man, a private investigator named Charlie, heard only in voiceover. But the Angels were radical in that they did not have Charlie's direct help and worked together to solve problems—the first instance of the female buddy formula, a twist on the male version that had become so popular on TV police shows. These women were highly competent in a traditionally masculine arena as they triumphed over evil men on their own.[9]

Perhaps the most capable female detective on television in the early 1970s—and feasibly one of the most competent ever—was a cartoon: Velma Dinkley of *Scooby-Doo*. While her friends stumble onto clues or make the occasional deduction, the final solution and explanation of the case is usually Dinkley's domain. She has a particularly Holmesian knack of deducing man-made causes for events that appeared supernatural or impossible—not unlike the Gothics of Ann Radcliffe from centuries earlier. Dinkley isn't perfect, though. Besides solving mysteries, her other job on the show seems to be losing her thick glasses. She gropes around for them on her hands and knees—invariably at the feet of the monster terrorizing the gang that week—a literal blindness that undercut her all-knowing sleuth status among a group that includes two men.[10]

Longer lasting than any of her younger, sexier (non-cartoon) peers was the innocuous middle-aged lady Jessica Fletcher of *Murder, She Wrote* (1984–1996). Fletcher, a mystery writer and widow, was the TV version of the mystery writer and widow sleuth popular since Amelia Butterworth. She lives in picturesque Cabot Cove, Maine, where she rides her bike and chats with neighbors, many of whom became regular characters. In nearly every episode, an innocent person is accused of a crime. Fletcher then remembers an important clue or piece of evidence and rushes off to confront the suspect in a deserted place. The suspect usually confesses but then attempts to flee or harm Fletcher, though without success. Justice prevails. Fletcher's reliable, polite, and respected, as one would expect with such a woman, but she still manages to surprise. She can't drive, but often rides her bike, and in the *Murder, She Wrote* books, coauthored by the fictional Fletcher and the very real Donald Bain, she earns a pilot's license. She's also far more mobile than the typical sleuth of a certain age. Traveling to visit friends and relatives, to teach, or to give book talks finds her solving cases around the world. Like most of the book-bound female sleuths, though, the widowed Fletcher has no romantic entanglements beyond a few extremely mild flirtations.[11]

Strong female investigators made it to the small screen in 1982 with *Cagney & Lacey* and *Remington Steele*. These were shows with main characters aimed at a female audience with far more in common with the investigators in the books of Sue Grafton and Sara Paretsky than their TV sisters Jessica Fletcher or Pepper Anderson. *Remington Steele* twisted expectations for a male-female detecting duo by making the woman the more serious investigator. The female protagonist, Laura Holt, decides to front her agency with an invented male figurehead so as to be taken seriously. In her first-season-opening voiceover, Holt explains that she "studied and apprenticed . . . but absolutely nobody broke down my door. A female private investigator seemed so . . . feminine. So I invented a superior—a decidedly *masculine* superior. Suddenly there were cases around the block. It was working like a charm." That is, until a mysterious con artist shows up, claiming he is Remington Steele, and won't leave. Fortunately, he and Holt get along. Gender bias became a recurring theme throughout the program, as the man who comes to impersonate the fictitious Remington Steele is treated with far more respect than Holt, a fact that never ceases to frustrate her.

Cagney & Lacey, the police procedural about two New York City female detectives, said to have been modeled on Helen Kidder and Peggy York, the first female homicide team in California, were smart rather than sexy and provided a realistic portrayal of women. Chris Cagney was single and ambitious but also dealt with personal challenges, including alcoholism. Mary Beth Lacey was a married, working mom who struggled to balance her home and work life. The two were good at their jobs, but they also argued and made mistakes. Most episodes dealt with the ongoing difficulties encountered by two women in a male-dominated profession. This went beyond the workplace to the cases themselves, in which Cagney and Lacey confronted violence, male criminals, and dangerous streets. These were all common elements of police fiction, but had a negative resonance on TV. The tough and aggressive female heroines proved jarring to the network, which canceled the show twice before a letter-writing campaign and an Emmy nomination led to its return. The series ran for seven seasons. Despite its popularity, strong female detectives on television declined for a time after *Cagney & Lacey*.[12]

Inspector Jane Tennison redefined the television crime genre for women when she broke into a disdainful band of male detectives in 1991 on the British serial *Prime Suspect*. The newly promoted head of the London homicide squad, Tennison lives for her job, mulling over case files late into the night, not unlike Catherine Pirkis's fictional investigator Loveday Brooke nearly a century earlier. The drama of Tennison's investigations matched the drama of her career as she struggled against the hostility and sexism of a male force that, in real life, had only four female detectives out of a total of five hundred at the time. Part of what made her so compelling is that she had achieved her high rank in an era when women could reach such a position, yet also one in which society viewed a woman who had won that status as strange and unpleasant. At one point in the series, Tennison cites a survey that attests that 90 percent of the public preferred male officers, results that likely had some basis in fact.[13]

Tennison's skill is not female intuition but in seeing and hearing evidence differently than her male colleagues. It's a skill that female detectives had deployed on the page for decades. Anna Katherine Green's spinster sleuth Amelia Butterworth and Inspector Gryce draw different conclusions about the murderer of Louisa Van Burnam from the same evidence in their first outing, *That Affair Next Door* (1897), but before Tennison, this difference had not been seen on screen. Tennison is relentless in her pursuit of criminals and in getting what she feels is her due, even though it has a bitter personal cost.[14]

By the 1990s, more complicated, not to mention more competent, women like Tennison did start to appear on television, particularly in police procedurals and legal thrillers like *Hill Street Blues* and the many *CSI* shows. Most work on teams, never alone like a female Colombo or Rebus, though the procedural drama *Rizzoli & Isles*, created by author Tess Gerritsen, features a female team, Boston detective Jane Rizzoli and medical examiner Maura Isles, busting some of the city's most notorious criminals. Like modern detective fiction, the female detective drama has almost become its own category.

In 1999, one of the longest-running and highest-rated shows on television, *Law & Order: SVU*, debuted. Charged with investigating sex crimes, the show features Detective Olivia Benson, played by Mariska Hargitay, as a sergeant and commanding officer with the New York City Police Department. She's tough but empathetic, working cases in which the victims are predominantly women. Benson is herself the child of rape and was raised by an alcoholic mother who emotionally and physically abused her. It's this personal history that helps Benson do her job so well, even though she tends to leave her personal baggage behind in helping to assuage the pain of others. She's partnered first with Elliot Stabler, who often countered her compassion for the victims with outrage toward the perpetrators. After Stabler leaves, Benson is paired with Nick Amaro, who has a difficult time at first dealing with the horrible crimes that come with the job. Benson's already complicated past becomes even more so in the course of the show after she's assaulted while undercover and then is kidnapped and tortured by a serial rapist in the course of another case. She narrowly avoids becoming a rape victim herself, but she continues to put herself in vulnerable and dangerous positions to fight for justice. Like the victims she works with, Benson wrestles with her identity after these assaults and even struggles to follow her own advice, confiding in one episode, "The hardest part is not beating myself up every day for getting into that situation."[15]

Besides these women, the girl sleuth, too, has seen a reboot and redefinition on television. Veronica Mars is a popular high school student in Neptune, California, who works part-time for her town sheriff-turned-private investigator father, Keith Mars. Her life starts to fall apart after the murder of her best friend, Lilly Kane, and an ensuing scandal that costs her father his job when he accuses Kane's father, a popular and wealthy businessman, of involvement in his daughter's death. Ostracized for her decision to stand by her father, Mars uses her detecting skills to clear her father's name and to conduct her own investigations. These events turn the once carefree Mars cynical and contemptuous, and though these feelings temper with time, Mars never loses her sharp-witted and often snarky edge, something Violet Strange and Nancy Drew never had. "It's all fun and games til one of you gets my foot up your ass," says Mars in an episode titled "M.A.D."[16] Most episodes featured Mars solving a new case while continuing to work on larger mysteries that spanned several episodes. The show lasted three seasons despite poor ratings, and Mars's story was continued in novels and a crowd-funded film after the show was canceled in 2007.[17]

Like their modern literary counterparts, female detectives on television have complicated lives, both past and present. The heroines of contemporary detective dramas are flawed and resist easy solutions. Before Veronica Mars's best friend is murdered, Veronica's mother abandons her family, and Mars herself is raped after imbibing a drink spiked with GHB, or Gamma hydroxybutyrate, the so-called date-rape drug. Deputy Chief Brenda Leigh Johnson of *The Closer* heads the Major Crimes Division of the Los Angeles Police Department. A CIA-trained interrogator, Johnson coaxes confessions out of suspected killers with a mix of charm, bluff, and determination. She's also an acerbic workaholic who struggles to win over her male squad and have a life outside her job. Stella Gibson, the senior police officer in *The Fall*, is beautiful, well dressed, and confident but also aloof and inscrutable. Like the original hard-boiled men, little is said about her background. She's at ease in her skin while presenting an image of womanhood that is neither maternal nor buddy-buddy. It's a deliberate choice on Gibson's part. "The media loves to divide women into virgins and vamps, angels or whores. Let's not encourage them," Gibson says to a colleague.[18] *Happy Valley*'s Sergeant Catherine Cawood is not just a police officer but a divorced grandmother with a sorrow-filled past.

In these shows, gender changes meaning. Although a female detective is less of an oddity now, in all of these programs, women's behavior is judged against that of her male colleagues: it is never invisible. If it were, there would no writers and websites proclaiming these women "bad asses" for doing their jobs. And there's something different about a female investigator examining the body of a sexually abused and murdered woman. Women still suffer sadistic violence in these stories, but there are now many heroic, determined fictional women, including those like Olivia Benson, who have suffered firsthand, who can help them.

Though television would have you think there is a woman homicide detective in every police department in America, only 15 percent of homicide detectives are women. Real women have fared far worse professionally than their fictional sisters. We're far more comfortable with powerful, competent policewomen in books and on television than in real life. That's not to suggest that these fictional women are more authentic and reflective of real women, only that there are more of them in fictional detection than in life. Television, in particular, has broken down barriers in public perceptions of women's capability in law enforcement, despite the stereotyped and sexist portrayal suffered by these female characters. Marketing surely explains some of this fictional gender equality, with efforts to appeal to a broad audience composed of women and men. Tough guys killing other tough guys in stories written by tough guys can't be the only story. But the way many of these fictional women are portrayed, as beautiful but icy women cut off from spouses and children and often even without friends, may make the field undesirable for real women, even apart from a macho work culture that can make women feel unwelcome.

Holly Pera was one of twenty women in the San Francisco Police Department when she joined the force in 1980.[19] She became the department's first female homicide detective, in 1998. Among her cases was that of Mei Leung, a nine-year-old found sexually assaulted, stabbed, and strangled in the basement of her family's home in the Tenderloin. Pera helped uncover DNA evidence that led to Mei Leung's killer, Richard Ramirez, better known as "The Night Stalker," responsible for thirteen murders. When Pera retired in 2012, the department had three hundred women on staff but still only two in homicide. "It is the most fascinating job, but it is also not anywhere near as glamorous as maybe she [the woman viewer] thinks it is from watching TV. It's just not; it is very tedious," said Pera, sounding much like New York detective Mary Sullivan more than seventy years earlier.

More than a century after women entered policing, women still have not become equal players in police departments. There are more policewomen in the United States now than ever before, but they face many of the same obstacles encountered by the matrons who first signed up for duty in the 1840s. Most of the strides women have made in policing have happened in large metropolitan areas. The biggest cities tend to have the most female officers, up to 18.1 percent of the officers in some cases, while some small forces have no women at all. In the 1980s, some researchers predicted that by the twenty-first century women would compose 50 percent of the police forces. At the time, there was a slight upsurge in the number of women, as more attention was given to recruiting female officers (it certainly helped that popular television programs like *Cagney & Lacey* and *Hill Street Blues* showed strong women holding their own with men). But that prediction never materialized.[20] Today, women make up approximately 13 percent of law enforcement and about 1 percent of all chief positions. There's no easy way to know how many of these officers are actually assigned detective work. The National Center for Women and Policing, which promotes increasing the number of women in policing, tracks the number of women in law enforcement but not their ranks and assignments. But given the small representation of women in law enforcement overall, it's presumably a small fraction of the total. These numbers reflect lingering inequality at a time when women make up nearly 48 percent of the labor force.[21]

Cultural prejudices about what a police officer should and does look like are still widely prevalent. "*You* are a police officer? You're so small!!" is the standard response when Commander Kristen Ziman tells people of her job in Aurora, Illinois.[22] Ziman, a past president of the National Association of Women Law Enforcement Executives, has a playful response: "I may be small but I can maim you in 17 different ways." But the stereotype rankles her. Over time, the image of a woman with a badge has been protested, ridiculed, deflected, and resisted outright but eventually, albeit reluctantly, accepted. Newspapers and magazines no longer run sensational front-page stories about policewomen. A press staple from the 1910s into the 1980s, these stories tended to make light of women's achievements, while glossing over the obstacles they faced along the way. The basics that male officers took for granted—the power to make arrests, patrol duty, squad cars, firearms, and even the uniform itself—were not given to female officers. Women had to fight for each one.

Brenda Tate joined the Pittsburgh police department in 1980, one of few women and even fewer African Americans on the force. "You get a lot of intimidation from supervisors and your peers," said Tate.[23] "Some people who are on the force say that you're here because the government says you're here, not because you deserve to be, so I had to work harder." Tate became a detective in the Dignitary Witness Security Unit/Intelligence in 1995, a special unit formed to halt gang killings in the city by protecting witnesses who have stepped forward to testify in homicide cases. She also provided protection to visiting dignitaries from presidents and British royalty to civil rights legend Rosa Parks. Like many real female detectives, but unlike many of those of fiction, she's married with five children.

In 1985, eighty years after Lola Baldwin was hired to protect women and girls at the Lewis and Clark Exposition in Portland, Penny Harrington became the nation's first female police chief in the same city, overseeing more than nine hundred officers.[24] It was a position she fought for, working her way through the ranks and filing sexual-discrimination complaints along the way. Harrington had entered the Portland police force in 1964 as part of the Women's Protective Division, where she worked primarily with women, children, and young boys. Portland's policewomen were paid less than men, despite having college degrees while most men had GEDs; policewomen did not wear uniforms or work in patrol cars, and they could not transfer out of the Women's Protective Division. Harrington filed twenty-two lawsuits against the department and succeeded in getting women hired as full officers. She became the first woman to transfer out of the Women's Protective Division, and the first woman to become a detective, sergeant, lieutenant, captain, precinct commander, and, finally, chief of police. The second female police chief was Elizabeth Watson, who served with the Houston Police Department from 1990 to 1992 and then with the Austin Police Department from 1992 to 1997.

The male monopoly on police work is supported by pervasive stereotypes about the nature of the job and the characteristics of the officers necessary to deal with it. The notion that police work is largely bullets and dangerous confrontations with criminals remains widespread, despite studies showing that approximately 90 percent of an officer's time is spent in noncriminal or service activities.[25] This image of the work appears inside the stationhouse, too, in an occupational culture that glamorizes violence and denigrates women. Police need to show bravery, but displaying any other emotion can lead to a lack of confidence about someone's ability to deal with the pressures of policing. "I could see that my coworkers were wondering if I could handle a fight, or a subject who was cussing me out calling me every name in the book, and if I could keep it together when I had a homicide," wrote Christin Rudell of the Indianapolis Metropolitan Police Department.[26] Research has shown that women who act assertively are isolated and harassed, while women who conform to more feminine roles are treated differently, though not necessarily equally. Studies of police departments have found as many as 63 percent to 68 percent of policewomen have experienced sexual harassment on the job, though few report it for fear of repercussions.[27] It should be noted that not all harassment on the job comes from men. Women also antagonize other women on the force. Some women learn to tolerate a degree of disempowerment to fit in and be rewarded. They conform because there are emotional, social, or financial benefits to be gained, but these compromises and accommodations likely dissuade many women from even considering the job. "The only way to achieve success," noted one female officer, "was to relinquish traditional female attributes and adopt traditional masculine attitudes."[28]

Sergeant Annette Darr, the first female supervisor in the Las Vegas homicide division, was one woman who did seek this path. She knew she wanted to work in homicide from a young age. The married mother of five became a homicide detective in 2012 after stints working patrol, elite intelligence, sexual assaults, and crisis negotiation. "One of the plusses of being a female homicide sergeant is that at the scenes, often, family members will gravitate to me for comfort," she said.[29] When Yadira and Karla Martinez were found slain in their home, in April 2012, Darr spearheaded a round-the-clock investigation that resulted in the arrest of Bryan Clay. Darr believes that her previous experience working with "the worst of the worst" helps her in cases like these. But unlike many fictional cases, the arrest is just the beginning of the story. "So much time goes into preparing for court, and we still have a family that is left broken," said Darr. "So the case will never be done, even when we go to trial, it continues."

Many women also work as private investigators. Approximately nine thousand of the sixty thousand private investigators in the United States are women, though exact numbers are hard to come by.[30] These private sleuths often coexist uncomfortably with police, not unlike the situation in novels and TV shows. Rebecca Jane formed her own detective agency in Manchester, England, after being unable to find a male detective willing to investigate her cheating husband. She took matters into her own hands, launching her own investigation, which ended in divorce from her wayward husband. Sensing a gap in the market for empathetic private detectives willing to take on cases like her own, Jane and a friend formed the Lady Detective Agency in 2009 to investigate unfaithful husbands, missing spouses, and child support fraud, among other domestic cases. It's an investigating docket not all that unlike that undertaken by Cora Strayer and her agents in Chicago at the turn of the twentieth century.[31]

Integration since the 1970s has been imposed on policing by legislation and litigation. But even with laws dictating fair hiring practices, policewomen continue to go to court to ensure equal access to positions and fair treatment on the job. In 2002, for instance, retired officer Catherine M. Volpe-Wasserman sued the New York City Police Department on charges of harassment and discrimination, alleging that she and other women in supervisory positions were passed up for promotion due to pregnancy.[32] Legislated equality was often subverted through lax recruitment efforts and physical fitness and agility tests with baseline scores that had no foundation in research. Even as recruitment and hiring practices have been standardized to leave less room for arbitrary decisions, candidates still tend to be judged on qualities associated with men, such as aggression, strength, and emotional detachment. The belief that women are more empathetic and better suited to certain tasks still holds sway in some departments (and in American culture), just as it did in the nineteenth century.[33] So, women often find themselves relegated to so-called "female jobs" in support positions or in jobs dealing with juveniles, women, and sex crimes. Areas where women are more likely to serve are often perceived as less important to law enforcement: "real police work" means crime fighting and physical force.[34]

The overwhelming evidence of women's equal capacity for all types of police work has done little to change perceptions or employment numbers.[35] Nor have the studies pointing to the advantages women bring to law enforcement. "If you can talk and rationalize with the most irrational person, you have a tool that's not in your gun belt or your car that's often your best tool," explained Pennsylvania patrolman Hallie Miller.[36] Research has shown that women officers provide an alternate point of contact for some victims of crimes who might otherwise not seek police assistance or protection. Just as male officers might think a male criminal will not respond to a female officer, some female criminals may not respond to a male officer. The evidence is also strong in showing a reduction in complaints of police misconduct and in the use of unnecessary force with more women officers. Perhaps Sandra Bland would never have ended up in a jail cell after being pulled over for a routine traffic stop in Texas in the summer of 2015 had the arresting officer been a woman.[37]

Women continue to make progress. In 2011, women outnumbered men in the new class of recruits to the Madison Police Department, eight to seven. The Wisconsin city was already ahead of national averages, though, with women composing more than 30 percent of the force. Many male officers, especially newer ones, are more accepting of female officers as well. The lives of real female homicide detectives have even made it onto television with a reality show on TLC called *Women of Homicide*, which follows detectives in Cincinnati and Atlanta. As depictions of women officers have long done, the personal lives of these women are a major part of the show, though now it's said to be done in the interest of "humanizing" policewomen, rather than "feminizing" them. No matter the word, the intent to show working women as "regular women" connected to family and friends remains the same.[38]

But women's place in policing and detection is not assured, no matter how it appears on television or in books, without consistent and targeted efforts to diversify the force.

In 1912, the United States' first official policewoman, Alice Wells, asserted that she was doing everything she could to further the cause of policewomen. But, she conceded, "all one woman can do is very little. She can but find the needs and point the way. Where she leaves off many women may begin and do much toward the betterment of social conditions."[39] Thousands of women have followed in the steps of Wells and those who came before her to find a place in law enforcement. It's a journey to "betterment" that women are still undertaking, within the pages of detective novels and in life.

ACKNOWLEDGMENTS

I AM GRATEFUL TO THE MANY LIBRARIES, HISTORICAL SOCIETIES, AND ONLINE collections that make book research while working infinitely more possible. As always, I am indebted to the Wisconsin Historical Society and the tremendous collections contained in the many libraries of the University of Wisconsin-Madison. Thank you, in particular, to Sarah Haggerty at the National Law Enforcement Museum for her assistance and archival sleuthing, and to Terri Garst at the Los Angeles Public Library.

Thanks to Janet Rosen for her support, and to my editor, Helene Atwan, for believing that something real existed in the midst of my scattershot enthusiasm for the topic. Thanks as well to Amanda Beiner for her assistance and for keeping me organized.

Special thanks to my husband for his patience, insight, and love, and to my mom for championing everything I do. Thanks also to my friends and coworkers, who live with my work nearly as much as I do.

My dad introduced me to detective movies and television shows as a child. That, along with his great love of history and reading, profoundly influenced me. I only wish he were still here for me to share these stories.

CHAPTER 1: DETECTING WOMEN

1. Dorothy Craigie, "Female Sherlock Holmes Tells How She Always 'Gets Her Man,'" *Evening Telegram* (NY), 21 May 1922.

2. Dorothy Craigie, "Grandmother Good Detective," *Plattsburgh (NY) Sentinel*, 19 May 1922.

3. Bryan Smith, "Alice Clement: The Detective Wore Pearls," *Chicago Magazine*, 10 February 2012, http://www.chicagomag.com/Chicago-Magazine/December-2003/The-Detective-Wore-Pearls/.

4. "Eloper Nemesis Outwitted by Own Daughter," *Chicago Daily Tribune*, 29 December 1918.

5. "Grool Censors Halt Garrity as Movie Hero: Film Starring Him and Mooney," *Chicago Daily Tribune*, 25 September 1920.

6. Ibid.

7. Ibid.

8. "Policewoman's Film Gets Some More Setbacks," *Chicago Daily Tribune*, 26 September 1920.

9. "Grool Censors Halt Garrity as Movie Hero."

10. Allan T. Duffin, *History in Blue: 160 Years of Women Police, Sheriffs, Detectives, and State Troopers* (New York: Kaplan, 2010), 46–47; Smith, "Alice Clement"; Craigie, "Grandmother Good Detective."

11. Catherine Louisa Pirkis, *The Experiences of Loveday Brooke, Lady Detective* (London: Hutchinson & Co., 1894), 7.

12. Ibid., 232–33.

13. Ibid.

14. Dale Townshend, "An Introduction to Ann Radcliffe," in *Discovering Literature: Romantics and Victorians*, British Library, http://www.bl.uk/romantics-and-victorians/articles/an-introduction-to-ann-radcliffe.

15. Ruth Facer, "Ann Radcliffe (1764–1823)," Chawton House, http://www.chawtonhouse.org/wp-content/uploads/2012/06/Ann-Radcliffe.pdf.

16. Ibid.; Townshend, "An Introduction to Ann Radcliffe."

17. Patrick Brantlinger, "What Is 'Sensational' About the 'Sensation Novel'?," *Nineteenth-Century Fiction* 37 (June 1982): 3, 5–6, 8.

18. Lucy Worsley, *The Art of the English Murder: From Jack the Ripper and Sherlock Holmes to Agatha Christie and Alfred Hitchcock* (New York: Pegasus, 2014), 179–86; Brantlinger, "What Is 'Sensational' About the 'Sensation Novel'?"

19. Margaret Oliphant, "Novels," *Blackwood's Edinburgh Magazine* 102 (September 1867), 263.

20. "The Popular Novels of the Year," *Fraser's Magazine* 68 (August 1863): 262.

21. Wilkie Collins, *The Woman in White* (orig. 1860; New York: Harper & Brothers, 1873), 48.

22. Anna M. Dzirkalis, "Investigating the Female Detective: Gender Paradoxes in Popular British Mystery Fiction, 1864–1930," PhD diss., Ohio University, 2007, 165; Brantlinger, "What Is 'Sensational' About the 'Sensation Novel'?"; Gene Smith, "The National Police Gazette," *American Heritage* 23 (October 1972), http://www.americanheritage.com/content/national-police-gazette; Anne-Marie Beller, *Mary Elizabeth Braddon: A Companion to the Mystery Fiction* (Jefferson, NC: McFarland, 2012), 2–9.

23. LeRoy Lad Panek, *Before Sherlock Holmes: How Magazines and Newspapers Invented the Detective Story* (Jefferson, NC: McFarland, 2011), 5, 35–37.

24. Robert Huish, *The Progress of Crime, or The Authentic Memoirs of Maria Manning* (London, 1849); ibid., 30.

25. Charles Dickens, "Letters to the Editors," *Times* (UK), 14 November 1849.

26. "Dying Speeches & Bloody Murders: Crime Broadsides Collected by the Harvard Law School Library," Harvard Law School Library, Historical and Special Collections, January 2013, http://broadsides.law.harvard.edu/home.php; Collins, *The Woman in White*, 147, 190–91.

27. Mansel quoted in Brantlinger, "What Is 'Sensational' About the 'Sensation Novel'?," 9–10.

28. Shawn Rosenheim, "The King of 'Secret Readers': Edgar Poe, Cryptography, and the Origins of the Detective Story," *ELH* (Summer 1989): 389; Robin Woods, "'His Appearance Is Against Him': The Emergence of the Detective," in *The Cunning Craft: Original Essays on Detective Fiction and Contemporary Literary Theory*, ed. Ronald G. Walker and June M. Frazer (Macomb: Western Illinois University Press, 1990), 16–17; Worsley, *The Art of the English Murder*, 2–3, 75–77, 118–19, 145.

29. Eric H. Monkkonen, "History of Urban Police," *Crime and Justice* 15 (1992): 548–49.

30. "Night Watch," *New York Gazette*, 21 February 1757.

31. John W. Draper, *Stratford to Dogberry: Studies in Shakespeare's Earlier Plays* (Pittsburgh: University of Pittsburgh Press, 1961), 273.

32. Samuel Walker, *A Critical History of Police Reform: The Emergence of Professionalism* (Lexington, MA: Lexington Books, 1977), 3.

33. Ibid., 3–5.

34. Monkkonen, "History of Urban Police," 549; "Sir Robert Peel 2nd Baronet," History: Past Prime Ministers, Gov.uk, https://www.gov.uk/government/history/past-prime-ministers/robert-peel-2nd-baronet.

35. Monkkonen, "History of Urban Police," 551; Ronald R. Thomas, *Detective Fiction and the Rise of Forensic Science* (Cambridge, UK: Cambridge University Press, 1999), 13; Walker, *A Critical History of Police Reform*, 5–6.

36. Carol Archbold, *Policing: A Text/Reader* (Thousand Oaks, CA: Sage Publications, 2012), 2–7; Walker, *A Critical History of Police Reform*, 11–12.

37. Eric H. Monkkonen, *Police in Urban America, 1860–1920* (Cambridge, UK: Cambridge University Press, 2004), 44–46.

38. Ibid., 45.

39. Walker, *A Critical History of Police Reform*, 13.

40. Monkkonen, "History of Urban Police," 547, 555–57; Alexandra Gillen, "Equality and Difference in the Evolution of Women's Police Role," PhD diss., University of Chicago, 2003, 7–8; Walker, *A Critical History of Police Reform*, 21.

41. Walker, *A Critical History of Police Reform*, 21.

42. Rosenheim, "The King of 'Secret Readers,'" 384; Rashmi Sahni, "Collins's 'Detective Business': *The Moonstone* as a Detective Novel," *The Victorian Web*, October 2007, http://www.victorianweb.org/authors/collins/sahni1.html.

CHAPTER 2: SLEUTHS IN SKIRTS

1. Allan Pinkerton, *The Expressman and the Detective* (Chicago: W. B. Keen, Cooke & Co., 1874), 94–95.

2. Ibid.

3. Lucile Torkelson, "Lady Pinkertons," *Milwaukee Sentinel*, 5 March 1969.

4. Ibid.; Frank Morn, "'The Eye That Never Sleeps': A History of the Pinkerton National Detective Agency* (Bloomington: Indiana University Press, 1982), 41–47; Daniel Stashower, *The Hour of Peril: The Secret Plot to Murder Lincoln Before the Civil War* (New York: St. Martin's Press, 2013), 55–57.

5. "Poe to Roberts," in *The Complete Works of Edgar Allan Poe: Letters of Poe and His Friends*, ed. James A. Harrison (New York: John D. Morris, 1902), 112.

6. Rosenheim, "The King of 'Secret Readers,'" 386–89; Daniel Stashower, *The Beautiful Cigar Girl: Mary Rogers, Edgar Allan Poe, and the Invention of Murder* (New York: Dutton, 2006), 118–19.

7. Panek, *Before Sherlock Holmes*, 42–43; Julian Symons, *Bloody Murder: The Classic Crime Fiction Reference*, 3rd ed. (London: Pan Books, 1992), 42–50.

8. Kathleen Gregory Klein, *The Woman Detective: Gender and Genre*, 2nd ed. (Urbana: University of Illinois Press, 1995), 7; Symons, *Bloody Murder*, 42–43.

9. Catherine Crowe, *Adventures of Susan Hopley; or, Circumstantial Evidence* (London: Saunders and Otley, 1841), 34, 37.

10. Ibid., 75.

11. Lucy Sussex, "The Detective Maidservant: Catherine Crowe's Susan Hopley," in *Silent Voices: Forgotten Novels by Victorian Women Writers*, ed. Brenda Ayres (Westport, CT: Praeger, 2003), 59–60.

12. Graham Storey et al., eds., *The Letters of Charles Dickens: 1853–1855* (Oxford, UK: Oxford University Press, 1993), 285–86.

13. Worsley, *The Art of the English Murder*, 212–14.

14. Morn, "The Eye That Never Sleeps," x, 12–13.

15. Ibid., 26, 30; Thomas Reppetto, *The Blue Parade*, vol. 2 of *American Police, a History: 1945–2012*, 2nd ed. (New York: Enigma Books, 2010), 256.

16. Pinkerton quoted in Stashower, *The Hour of Peril*, 56–57.

17. Katherine Ramsland, "Kate Warne: First Female Detective," *Forensic Examiner* 19 (Spring 2010), http://www.biomedsearch.com/article/Kate-Warne-first-female -detective/219374135.html.

18. Ibid.

19. Mrs. Greenhow (Rose O'Neal Greenhow), *My Imprisonment and the First Year of Abolition Rule at Washington* (London: Richard Bentley, 1863), 61–63.

20. Morn, *"The Eye That Never Sleeps,"* 41–47.

21. Ibid., 54–55.

22. Pamela Bedore, "Games, Doubles, and Gender in Detective Dime Novels," PhD diss., University of Rochester, 2005, 86–92.

23. Morn, *"The Eye That Never Sleeps,"* 41–44.

24. Pinkerton, *The Expressman and the Detective*, 261.

25. Morn, *"The Eye That Never Sleeps,"* 82.

26. Bedore, "Games, Doubles, and Gender in Detective Dime Novels," 93; Morn, *"The Eye That Never Sleeps,"* 80–84.

27. Kimberly J. Dilley, *Busybodies, Meddlers, and Snoops: The Female Hero in Contemporary Women's Mysteries* (Westport, CT: Greenwood, 1998), 52–53.

28. Anthea Trodd, "The Policeman and the Lady: Significant Encounters in Mid-Victorian Fiction," *Victorian Studies* 27 (Summer 1984): 436–37, 441, 444, 460.

29. Mary Towell Schroeder, "Reflections of a Female Eye: An Exploration of Metta Victor's Contribution to the Detective Genre," PhD diss., Saint Louis University, 1998, 38–39.

30. Catherine Ross Nickerson, "Women Writers Before 1960," in *The Cambridge Companion to American Crime Fiction*, ed. Catherine Ross Nickerson (Cambridge, UK: Cambridge University Press, 2010), 31–32.

31. Schroeder, "Reflections of a Female Eye," 21–23.

32. Ibid., 91.

33. "Metta Victor," American Women's Dime Novel Project, http://chnm.gmu .edu/dimenovels/the-authors/metta-victor.

34. "Mr. Furbush," by Harriet E. Prescott [Spofford], from *Harper's New Monthly Magazine*, April 1865, Westminster Detective Library, http://www2.mcdaniel .edu/WestminsterDetectiveLibrary/text%20files%20of%20stories/Mr.%20Furbush .html.

35. Kate Watson, *Women Writing Crime Fiction, 1860–1880: Fourteen American, British, and Australian Authors* (Jefferson, NC: McFarland, 2012), 79–84.

36. Louisa May Alcott, "V.V.: or, Plots and Counterplots," *The Flag of Our Union* (February 1865): 382.

37. Ibid.

38. Martha Saxton, *Louisa May: A Modern Biography* (New York: Farrar, Straus and Giroux, 1995), 272–74.

39. Patricia D. Maida, *The Mother of Detective Fiction: The Life & Works of Anna Katherine Green* (Bowling Green, OH: Bowling Green State University Popular Press, 1989), 22–23.

40. Michael Davitt Bell, *Culture, Genre, and Literary Vocation: Selected Essays on American Literature* (Chicago: University of Chicago Press, 2001), 141.

41. Anna Katharine Green, *The Leavenworth Case: A Lawyer's Story* (New York: A. L. Burt, 1906).

42. Maida, *The Mother of Detective Fiction*, 55.

43. Green, *The Leavenworth Case*, 5.

44. Ibid.; Sara Paretsky, ed., *Sisters on the Case: Twenty Years of Sisters in Crime* (New York: New American Library, 2007) ix.

45. Maida, *The Mother of Detective Fiction*, 54–55.

46. Ibid., 6–7; Martha Hailey DuBose and Margaret C. Thomas, *Women of Mystery: The Lives and Works of Notable Women Crime Novelists* (New York: Thomas Dunne Books, 2000), 6–7, 9–10.

47. Wilkie Collins, "Wilkie Collins on *The Leavenworth Case*," *Critic* 52 (28 January 1893), 152.

48. Watson, *Women Writing Crime Fiction*, 123.

49. Maida, *The Mother of Detective Fiction*, 77.

50. Quoted in Lucy Sussex, *Women Writers and Detectives in Nineteenth-Century Crime Fiction: The Mothers of the Mystery Genre* (New York: Palgrave, 2010), 176.

51. Patricia D. Maida, "Anna Katherine Green," *Legacy* 3 (Fall 1986): 53–54; Sussex, *Women Writers and Detectives in Nineteenth-Century Crime Fiction*, 165, 170–71, 176; Michael Mallory, "The Mother of American Mystery: Anna Katharine Green," *Mystery Scene* 94 (Spring 2006), http://www.mysteryscenemag.com/index.php?option =com_content&view=article&id=1867.

52. Schroeder, "Reflections of a Female Eye," 1, 10; Adrienne E. Gavin, "Feminist Crime Fiction and Female Sleuths," in *A Companion to Crime Fiction*, ed. Charles J. Rzepka and Lee Horsley (Malden, MA: Wiley-Blackwell, 2010), 258.

53. Dzirkalis, "Investigating the Female Detective," 20–27.

54. Gavin, "Feminist Crime Fiction and Female Sleuths," 258–59.

55. Andrew Forrester, *The Female Detective: The Original Lady Detective, 1864* (London: British Library, 2012), 240.

56. Klein, *The Woman Detective*, 17–19.

57. Forrester, *The Female Detective*, 1.

58. Ibid.

59. Dzirkalis, "Investigating the Female Detective," 110–11.

60. Forrester, *The Female Detective*, 3; Klein, *The Woman Detective*, 18–22.

61. W. Stephens Hayward, *The Revelations of a Lady Detective* (London: George Vickers, 1864), 3; Ellery Queen, *In the Queens' Parlor: And Other Leaves from the Editors' Notebook*, reprint (New York: Biblo and Tannen, 1969), 42–43.

62. Hayward, *The Revelations of a Lady Detective*, 4; Klein, *The Woman Detective*, 24–25.

63. Hayward, *The Revelations of a Lady Detective*.

64. Sussex, *Women Writers and Detectives in Nineteenth-Century Crime Fiction*, 72; ibid., 27, 71, 155.

65. Hayward, *The Revelations of a Lady Detective*, 27.

66. Ibid., 182, 188–89.

67. Klein, *The Woman Detective*, 27–28.

68. Panek, *Before Sherlock Holmes*, 155–57.

CHAPTER 3: SISTERHOOD BEHIND BARS

1. Susan Barney, "Police Matrons," in *Report of the International Council of Women*, ed. National Woman Suffrage Association (Washington, DC: Rufus Darby, 1888), 120–22.

2. Edward Ryder, *Elizabeth Fry: Life and Labors of the Eminent Philanthropist, Preacher, and Prison Reformer* (New York: E. Walker's Son, 1883), 9, 13–15, 27–30.

3. "Elizabeth Fry (1780–1845)," Quakers in Britain, https://www.quaker.org.uk /fry; "Elizabeth Fry: Helping Society's Outcasts and Poor," History's Heroes?, http:// historysheroes.e2bn.org/hero/108; Ryder, *Elizabeth Fry*, 120–35.

4. Susan Hammond Barney, "Care of the Criminal," in *Woman's Work in America*, ed. Annie Nathan Meyer (New York: Henry Holt and Co., 1891), 359.

5. "Elizabeth Fry," History's Heroes?

6. Estelle B. Freedman, *Their Sisters' Keepers: Women's Prison Reform in America, 1830–1930* (Ann Arbor: University of Michigan Press, 1981), 23–24.

7. Ibid., 8–9, 24–28.

8. Nicole Hahn Rafter, "Prisons for Women, 1790–1980," *Crime and Justice* 5 (1983): 144.

9. Freedman, *Their Sisters' Keepers*, 27–29.

10. Martha Vicinus, *Independent Women: Work and Community for Single Women, 1850–1920* (Chicago: University of Chicago Press, 1985), 4.

11. Rafter, "Prisons for Women," 137.

12. Freedman, *Their Sisters' Keepers*, 11–14.

13. Manon S. Parry, "Dorothea Dix," in *American Journal of Public Health* 96, no. 4 (April 2006): 624–25.

14. Estelle B. Freedman, "Their Sisters' Keepers: An Historical Perspective on Female Correctional Institutions in the United States: 1870–1900," *Feminist Studies* 2 (1974): 80.

15. Rafter, "Prisons for Women," 140.

16. Ibid., 139–40.

17. Georgiana Bruce Kirby, *Years of Experience: An Autobiographical Narrative* (orig. 1887; New York: AMS Press, 1971), 190–91.

18. E. W. Farnham, "Music in Prison," *New York Daily Tribune*, 22 April 1845.

19. Rafter, "Prisons for Women," 141.

20. Ibid.

21. "Female Prison at Sing Sing," *New York Daily Tribune*, 28 January 1847.

22. Rafter, "Prisons for Women," 141–42.

23. Freedman, *Their Sisters' Keepers*, 29.

24. Ibid., 28–29; Cynthia Owen, ed., *Imprisoned in America: Prison Communications, 1776 to Attica* (New York: Harper and Row, 1973), 82.

25. Freedman, "Their Sisters' Keepers," 81, 84.

26. C. M. Kirkland, *The Helping Hand* (New York: Scribner, 1853), 51.

27. Freedman, "Their Sisters' Keepers," 85–86.

28. Freedman, *Their Sisters' Keepers*, 40; Luella D'Amico, "'The Baby Became Horrible': The Traumatized Adolescent Mother in Elizabeth Stuart Phelps' 1870 Reform Novel, *Hedged In*," *Journal of the Motherhood Initiative for Research and Community Involvement* 5 (2014): 23–47.

29. Rafter, "Prisons for Women," 154–55; Freedman, "Their Sisters' Keepers," 84.

30. Dorothy Moses Schulz, *From Social Worker to Crimefighter: Women in United States Municipal Policing* (Westport, CT: Praeger, 1995), 10–11.

31. Ibid.

32. Sharon E. Wood, *The Freedom of the Streets: Work, Citizenship and Sexuality in a Gilded Age City* (Chapel Hill: University of North Carolina Press, 2005), 106.

33. Kerry Segrave, *Policewomen: A History* (Jefferson, NC: McFarland, 1995), 5–6; Schulz, *From Social Worker to Crimefighter*, 12–13.

34. Segrave, *Policewomen*, 7–8.

35. Ibid., 7; Schulz, *From Social Worker to Crimefighter*, 13.

36. Barney, "Care of the Criminal," 368.

37. Segrave, *Policewomen*, 8, 11.

38. Quoted in ibid., 14–15.

39. Quoted in Wood, *The Freedom of the Streets*, 121.

40. Raphael W. Marrow and Harriet I. Carter, *In Pursuit of Crime: The Police of Chicago, Chronicle of a Hundred Years, 1833–1933* (Sunbury, OH: Flats Publishing, 1996), 128–29.

41. "Mollie Mott's House, Alleged Thieves' Den," *Chicago Tribune*, 15 April 1900.

42. "Jury Acquits Mollie Mott," *Chicago Tribune*, 26 June 1904;

43. "Miss Quinn as Sleuth Leads Poolroom Raid: She's a Police Matron, Drafted for the Occasion," *New York Times*, 20 November 1904.

44. "Wholesale Raids on Fortune Tellers," *New York Times*, 26 November 1910.

45. "High School Girl a Female Raffles," *New York Times*, 18 June 1915.

46. Segrave, *Policewomen*, 10; Rafter, "Prisons for Women," 144.

47. Freedman, "Sisters' Keepers," 87.

48. Segrave, *Policewomen*, 11.

49. Ibid., 4–5.

50. Ibid., 10.

51. Schulz, *From Social Worker to Crimefighter*, 22–23.

CHAPTER 4: SPINSTER SLEUTH

1. Anna Katharine Green, *That Affair Next Door* (New York: A. L. Burt, 1897).

2. Maida, *The Mother of Detective Fiction*, 64.

3. Ibid., 65–66; Anna Katharine Green, *Lost Man's Lane: A Second Episode in the Life of Amelia Butterworth* (New York: G. P. Putnam's Sons, 1898).

4. Dashielle Horn, "An Early Loss of Bloom: Spinsters, Old Maids, and the Marriage Market in Persuasion," PhD diss., Lehigh University, 2012, 4; "Civil War Casualties," Civil War Trust, http://www.civilwar.org/education/civil-war-casualties.html.

5. Horn, "An Early Loss of Bloom," 4–6; Kathy Mezei, "Spinsters, Surveillance, and Speech: The Case of Miss Marple, Miss Mole, and Miss Jekyll," *Journal of Modern Literature* 30 (Winter 2007): 104.

6. Horn, "An Early Loss of Bloom," 6–8; Sarah Amyes Hanselman, "Spinster," in *Encyclopedia of Feminist Literary Theory*, ed. Elizabeth Kowaleski-Wallace (New York: Routledge, 1996), 544–46.

7. Klein, *The Woman Detective*, 125–26; Trisha Franzen, *Spinsters and Lesbians: Independent Womanhood in the United States* (New York: New York University Press, 1996), 6.

8. "Bachelor Girls Find Defender," *Washington Herald*, 26 July 1912.

9. "New York Girls Organize Club," part 1, *St. Louis Republic*, 22 June 1902; Helen Rowland, "Woman's Rights and Man's Privileges," *Washington Herald*, 1 March 1908.

10. "New York Girls Organize Club."

11. Elizabeth K. Stratton, "The Bachelor Girl Confesses," *New York Tribune*, 4 April 1909.

12. Franzen, *Spinsters and Lesbians*, 5.

13. Horn, "An Early Loss of Bloom," 4; Mezei, "Spinsters, Surveillance, and Speech," 104.

14. Mary Jane Jones, "The Spinster Detective," *Journal of Communication* 25 (June 1975): 110–11.

15. Ada Coe, "The Detective: A Myth for Our Time," PhD diss., University of California, Davis, 2000, 174; Green, *That Affair Next Door*, 23.

16. Jones, "The Spinster Detective," 110–11.

17. Green, *That Affair Next Door*, 24, 1.

18. Maroula Joannou, *"Ladies, Please Don't Smash These Windows": Women's Writing, Feminist Consciousness and Social Change, 1918–38* (Oxford, UK: Berg, 1995), 77–85; Mezei, "Spinsters, Surveillance, and Speech," 104.

19. Philippa Gates, *Detecting Women: Gender and the Hollywood Detective Film* (Albany: State University of New York Press, 2010), 27–29.

20. Maida, *The Mother of Detective Fiction*, 50–51.

21. Agatha Christie, *The Murder at the Vicarage* (orig. 1930; New York: William Morrow Paperbacks, 2011).

22. DuBose and Thomas, *Women of Mystery*, 152.

23. "Christie's Life," Agatha Christie official website, http://www.agathachristie.com /about-christie/christies-life/; Joan Acocella, "Queen of Crime," *New Yorker*, 26 August 2010, http://www.newyorker.com/magazine/2010/08/16/queen-of-crime.

24. Agatha Christie, *The Body in the Library* (orig. 1942; New York: William Morrow Paperbacks, reprint edition, 2011), 13.

25. Quoted in Ruth Margolis, "Agatha Christie: Four Heroines That Make Her an Unlikely Feminist Icon," BBC America, 3 September 2015, http://www.bbcamerica .com/anglophenia/2015/09/agatha-christie-four-heroines-that-make-her-an-unlikely -feminist-icon/.

26. Agatha Christie, *Easy to Kill* (orig. 1939; New York: Pocket Books, 1984), 19; Penelope J. Fritzer, "Women in the Detective Novels of Agatha Christie," PhD diss., Florida Atlantic University, 1979, 8–11.

27. Fritzer, "Women in the Detective Novels of Agatha Christie," 12.

28. Dorothy Sayers, *Strong Poison* (orig. 1930; New York: Harper and Row, 1987), 54.

29. Dorothy Sayers, *Unnatural Death* (orig. 1927; New York: Harper and Row, 1987), 28.

30. Sayers, *Strong Poison*, 54–55.

31. Sayers, *Unnatural Death*, 35.

32. Catherine McGehee Kenney, *The Remarkable Case of Dorothy L. Sayers* (Kent, OH: Kent State University Press, 1990), 130–33; Deborah Blum, "The Science of Mysteries: Instructions for a Deadly Dinner," *Speakeasy Science* (PLOS blog), 20 December 2011, http://blogs.plos.org/speakeasyscience/2011/12/20/the-science-of -mysteries-instructions-for-a-deadly-dinner/.

33. Green, *That Affair Next Door*, 71, 186, 399.

34. Klein, *The Woman Detective*, 139–43.

35. Michael Mallory, "Murder She Taught: The Puzzling Career of Hildegarde Withers," *Mystery Scene* 119 (Spring 2011), http://www.mysteryscenemag.com/blog-article/3224-murder-she-taught-the-puzzling-career-of-hildegarde-withers; J. Randolph Cox, "Miss Withers," in *Whodunit? A Who's Who in Crime & Mystery Writing*, ed. Rosemary Herbert (New York: Oxford University Press, 2003), 210; Stuart Palmer, *The Penguin Pool Murder* (orig. 1931; Lyons, CO: Rue Morgue, 2007), 17.

36. Torrey Chanslor, *Our First Murder* (New York: F. A. Stokes, 1940); Torrey Chanslor, *Our Second Murder: A Beagle Sisters Mystery* (New York: F. A. Stokes, 1941).

37. Klein, *The Woman Detective*, 138.

38. Green, *That Affair Next Door*, 396–97.

39. Mezei, "Spinsters, Surveillance, and Speech," 105–6.

CHAPTER 5: THE FIRST POLICEWOMEN

1. Wells quoted in Duffin, *History in Blue*, 30.

2. Gail Ryan, "Legendary Ladies of the LAPD," *100 Years of Women in Law Enforcement* (Tampa, FL: Faircount Media, September 2010), 26–27, http://issuu.com/faircountmedia/docs/lawpoa100.

3. Wells quoted in Bertha H. Smith, "The Policewoman," *Good Housekeeping*, March 1911, 296.

4. Schulz, *From Social Worker to Crimefighter*, 23–25.

5. Duffin, *History in Blue*, 30; ibid., 24; Ryan, "Legendary Ladies of the LAPD," 27.

6. Colleen Mastony, "Was Chicago Home to the Country's 1st Female Cop?," *Chicago Tribune*, 2 September 2010; Fran Spielman, "First Female Cop Hired in 1891, 22 Years Earlier Than Thought," *Chicago Sun Times*, 30 September 2010; Cathy Hayes, "First Ever Female Cop in U.S. Was an Irish Woman," *Irish Central*, 3 September 2010, http://www.irishcentral.com/news/first-ever-female-cop-in-us-was-an-irish-woman-102142114–237714101.html; Segrave, *Policewomen*, 11.

7. Mrs. Marie Owens, "Enforcement of the Child Labor Law," *Chicago Tribune*, 28 July 1901.

8. "The Only Woman Detective on the Chicago Police Force," *Chicago Tribune*, 28 October 1906.

9. Owens, "Enforcement of the Child Labor Law."

10. Segrave, *Policewomen*, 1–2; Janis Appier, *Policing Women: The Sexual Politics of Law Enforcement and the LAPD* (Philadelphia: Temple University Press, 1988), 1, 24; Wood, *The Freedom of the Streets*, 21, 28.

11. Schulz, *From Social Worker to Crimefighter*, 27.

12. Louise de Koven Bowen, "Women Police," *Survey* 30 (12 April 1913): 64.

13. Segrave, *Policewomen*, 25–26; Cecily Devereux, "White Slavery," in *Encyclopedia of Prostitution and Sex Work*, vol. 2, ed. Melissa Hope Ditmore (Westport, CT: Greenwood, 2006), 539–41.

14. Edwin W. Sims, "Why Girls Go Astray," *Juvenile Court Record* 10 (June 1909), 11.

15. Karen Abbott, *Sin in the Second City: Madams, Ministers, Playboys, and the Battle for America's Soul* (New York: Random House, 2007), 11, 86, 70–71; Appier, *Policing Women*, 22.

16. Egal Feldman, "Prostitution, the Alien Woman, and the Progressive Imagination, 1910–1915," *American Quarterly* 19 (Summer 1967): 192–94; Ernest A. Bell, ed., *Fighting the Traffic in Young Girls, or War on the White Slave Trade* (Chicago: Charles C. Thompson, 1909), 70–71; Marrow and Carter, *In Pursuit of Crime*, 56–57.

17. George Kibbe Turner, "The Daughters of the Poor," *McClure's Magazine* 34 (November 1909): 57–58.

18. Feldman, "Prostitution, the Alien Woman, and the Progressive Imagination," 198–99.

19. Elizabeth Carolyn Miller, "The New Woman Criminal: Crime Fiction, Gender, and British Culture at the Turn of the Century," PhD diss., University of Wisconsin, Madison, 2003, 35–37.

20. William Douglas Morrison, *Crime and Its Causes* (New York: Charles Scribner's Sons, 1902), 156.

21. Craigie, "Female Sherlock Holmes Tells How She Always Gets Her Man."

22. Smith, "The Policewoman," 297.

23. Gloria E. Myers, *A Municipal Mother: Portland's Lola Greene Baldwin, America's First Policewoman* (Corvallis: Oregon State University Press, 1995), 5, 9, 11–12.

24. Ibid., 20–21.

25. Gloria E. Myers, "Lola Greene Baldwin (1860–1957)," *The Oregon Encyclopedia*, http://www.oregonencyclopedia.org/articles/baldwin_lola_1860_1957_/#.

26. Lola Baldwin, "Our Policewomen," *Oregonian*, May 1953.

27. Duffin, *History in Blue*, 28–29; Schulz, *From Social Worker to Crimefighter*, 22.

28. Marrow and Carter, *In Pursuit of Crime*, 193, 371.

29. Chicago Vice Commission, *The Social Evil in Chicago: A Study of Existing Conditions* (Chicago: Gunthorp-Warren, 1911); "Women Sift Store Work," *Chicago Daily Tribune*, 6 March 1913.

30. US Immigration Commission, *Abstracts of Reports of the Immigration Commission*, II, 61st Congress 3rd Session (Washington, DC, 1911), 342–43.

31. "She Still Insists on Policewomen," *New York Times*, 31 March 1907.

32. "Call for Policewomen to Protect the Boys," *New York Times*, 7 March 1906.

33. Maud Darwin, "Policewomen: Their Work in America," *Nineteenth Century and After* 75 (June 1914): 1371.

34. Schulz, *From Social Worker to Crimefighter*, 25; Mary Jane Aldrich-Moodie, "Staking Out Their Domain: Women in the New York City Police Department, 1890–1935," PhD diss., University of North Carolina, Chapel Hill, 2002, v, 5.

35. Duffin, *History in Blue*, 21, 24; Segrave, *Policewomen*, 2.

36. "Famous Policewoman Urges Prevention of Crime," *New York Times*, 22 December 1912.

37. Schulz, *From Social Worker to Crime Fighter*, 24–25.

38. Segrave, *Policewomen*, 15.

39. "The First Municipal Woman Detective in the World," *New York Times*, 3 March 1912.

40. "Our Policewoman Won't Be Snubbed," *New York Times*, 15 December 1912.

41. "The First Municipal Woman Detective in the World."

42. Frank Parker Stockbridge, "A Woman Who Spends Over Forty Million Dollars Each Year and Some Others Who Hold Positions of Financial Power and Moral Responsibility in the Government of New York City," *American City* 6 (June 1912): 817.

43. Paul Reda, "Miss Cora M. Strayer's Private Detective Agency," http://paulreda.com/corastrayer/; "Is Chicago Detective Miss Cora Strayer in Secret Service Agency," *Goshen (IN) Daily Democrat*, 14 May 1904.

44. "Woman Directs a Detective Bureau," *Chicago Tribune*, August 1903.

45. "Female Detective Agency," *Alton (IL) Evening Telegraph*, 6 April 1906 [?].

46. Reda, "Miss Cora M. Strayer's Private Detective Agency."

47. Mark Hawthorne, *Fingerprints: Analysis and Understanding* (Boca Raton, FL: CRC Press, 2009), 8–11.

48. "How Chicago's Women Detectives Have Accomplished Feats That Have Baffled Men," *Chicago Daily Tribune*, 19 July 1908.

49. George Kennan, "The Fight for Reform in San Francisco," *McClure's Magazine* 29 (September 1907): 547–60.

50. "Woman Is Best Aid of Detective Burns," *Los Angeles Times*, 27 April 1907.

51. "How to Be a Sherlock Holmes: Pay $5 to the Detective Factory," *Chicago Daily Tribune*, 4 August 1907.

52. "Miss Fisher in Custody," *Chicago Daily Tribune*, 27 February 1896.

53. "Need for Police Women in City Work," *City Club Bulletin* (Chicago), 31 October 1912; Appier, *Policing Women*, 66–67.

54. Quoted in Appier, *Policing Women*, 66–67.

55. Edith Abbott, "Training for the Policewoman's Job," *Woman Citizen* (30 April 1926): 30.

56. Feldman, "Prostitution, the Alien Woman, and the Progressive Imagination," 199–200, 204–6.

CHAPTER 6: GIRL DETECTIVES

1. Anna Katherine Green, *The Golden Slipper, and Other Problems for Violet Strange*, Project Gutenberg, http://www.gutenberg.org/files/3071/3071-h/3071-h.htm.

2. Bobbie Ann Mason, *The Girl Sleuth* (Athens: University of Georgia Press, 1995), 10–15.

3. John Cornillon, "A Case for Violet Strange," in *Images of Women in Fiction: Feminist Perspectives*, ed. Susan Koppelman Cornillon (Bowling Green: Bowling Green University Popular Press, 1972), 208; Nancy Tillman Romalov, "Mobile and Modern Heroines: Early Twentieth-Century Girls' Automobile Series," in *Nancy Drew and Company: Culture, Gender, and Girls' Series*, ed. Sherrie Inness (Bowling Green: Bowling Green University Popular Press, 1997), 75–76.

4. Green, *The Golden Slipper*.

5. Green, *The Golden Slipper*, 14.

6. Ibid., 82.

7. Ibid., 213; Maida, *The Mother of Detective Fiction*, 73–77.

8. Sarah Grand, "The New Aspect of the Woman Question," *North American Review* 158 (March 1894).

9. "The New Woman," *Harper's Bazaar* 28 (27 July 1895): 594.

10. "Modern Women: The Extent to Which They Are Invading the Industrial World," *Los Angeles Times*, 7 July 1907; Melanie Rehak, *Girl Sleuth: Nancy Drew and the Women Who Created Her* (Boston: Houghton Mifflin Harcourt, 2005), 50.

11. Mary Eads, "The Modern Working Woman and Marriage," *Sewanee Review* 23 (October 1915): 409.

12. Joanne J. Meyerowitz, *Women Adrift: Independent Wage Earners in Chicago, 1880–1930* (Chicago: University of Chicago Press, 1988), 123–25.

13. Stanley quoted in Cynthia Eagle Russett, *Sexual Science: The Victorian Construction of Womanhood* (Cambridge, MA: Harvard University Press, 1989), 120.

14. Meyerowitz, *Women Adrift*, 123–25.

15. Myers, *A Municipal Mother*, 175–77.

16. Andrzej Diniejko, "The New Woman Fiction," *The Victorian Web*, 17 December 2011, www.victorianweb.org/gender/diniejko1.html.

17. Catherine Ross Nickerson, *The Web of Iniquity: Early Detective Fiction by American Women* (Durham, NC: Duke University Press, 1998), 97–98.

18. "Anna Katharine Green Replies," *New York Times*, 4 November 1917.

19. Sussex, *Women Writers and Detectives*, 173–74.

20. Nickerson, *The Web of Iniquity*, 62.

21. J. Randolph Cox, *The Dime Novel Companion: A Source Book* (Westport, CT: Greenwood, 2000), 77–78.

22. Garyn G. Roberts, Gary Hoppenstand, and Ray B. Browne, "Who Was That Androgynous, Angelic, Society Lady Female Detective?," in *Old Sleuth's Freaky Female Detectives (From the Dime Novels)*, ed. Roberts, Hoppenstand, and Browne (Bowling Green, OH: Bowling Green State University Popular Press, 1990), 5–7.

23. Klein, *The Woman Detective*, 96–97.

24. Pirkis, *The Experiences of Loveday Brooke*, 4.

25. Klein, *The Woman Detective*, 69–71; ibid.

26. Michael Sims, ed., *The Penguin Book of Victorian Women in Crime: Forgotten Cops and Private Eyes from the Time of Sherlock Holmes* (New York: Penguin, 2011), 103–5.

27. Reginald Wright Kauffman, *Miss Frances Baird, Detective: A Passage from Her Memoirs* (Boston: Colonial Press, 1906).

28. Mary Roberts Rinehart, *Miss Pinkerton: Adventures of a Nurse Detective* (orig. 1914; New York: Rinehart, 1959).

29. Rinehart, "The Buckled Bag," in ibid., 8.

30. Maida, *The Mother of Detective Fiction*, 52–54; Mary P. Freier, "The Decline of Hilda Adams," in *Women Times Three: Writers, Detectives, Readers*, ed. Kathleen Gregory Klein (Bowling Green, OH: Bowling Green State University Popular Press, 1995), 130–42.

31. Maida, *The Mother of Detective Fiction*, 52.

32. Mary Roberts Rinehart, *The Circular Staircase* (Indianapolis: Bobbs-Merrill, 1908).

33. Ibid., 217, 295; Nickerson, *The Web of Iniquity*, 119–20.

34. Terrie Farley Moran, "Mary Roberts Rinehart: The American Agatha Christie," *Criminal Element*, http://www.criminalelement.com/blogs/2014/03/mary-roberts-rinehart-the-american-agatha-christie-terrie-farley-moran.

35. Maureen T. Reddy, *Sisters in Crime: Feminism and the Crime Novel* (New York: Continuum, 1988), 22–23.

36. Worsley, *The Art of the English Murder*, 250–54; S. L. Clark, "Harriet Vane Goes to Oxford: *Gaudy Night* and the Academic Woman," *Sayers Review* 2 (August 1978): 22–43.

37. Joanna Scutts, "Second Glance: Dorothy Sayers and the Last Golden Age," *Open Letters Monthly*, August 2007, http://www.openlettersmonthly.com/second-glancedorothy-sayers/.

38. Klein, *The Woman Detective*, 143–45.

39. George R. Sims, *Dorcas Dene: Her Life and Adventures* (London: F. V. White and Co., 1897), 27.

40. Dzirkalis, "Investigating the Female Detective," 215–17, 242–44.

41. Ibid., 250–52.

42. Dennis Butts, "How Children's Literature Changed: What Happened in the 1840s?," *Lion and the Unicorn* 21, no. 2 (April 1997): 159–60.

43. Robert Baden-Powell, *Scouting for Boys: A Handbook for Instruction in Good Citizenship* (London: Horace Cox, 1908), 79–80.

44. Girl Scouts of the United States of America, *Scouting for Girls: The Official Handbook of the Girl Scouts* (New York: Girl Scouts, Inc., 1920), 42.

45. Michael G. Cornelius and Melanie E. Gregg, eds., *Nancy Drew and Her Sister Sleuths: Essays on the Fiction of Girl Detectives* (Jefferson, NC: McFarland, 2008), 3–5.

46. Anne H. Lundin, "Everygirl's Good Deeds: The Heroics of Nancy Drew," *Lion and the Unicorn* 27, no. 1 (January 2003): 126; 10.1353/uni.2003.0005.

47. Christopher Routledge, "Crime and Detective Literature for Young Readers," in Rzepka and Horsley, *A Companion to Crime Fiction*; also at http://chrisroutledge.co.uk/writing/crime-and-detective-literature-for-young-readers/.

48. Sally E. Parry, "The Case of the Neglected Girl Sleuth: Margaret Sutton's Judy Bolton," *Judy Bolton Society Newsletter*, http://www.judybolton.com/jbparry.html.

49. Judith Sears, "Trixie Belden the Girl-Next-Door Sleuth," *Mystery Scene* 83 (Winter 2004), http://www.mysteryscenemag.com/index.php?option=com_content&view=article&id=41:trixie-belden-the-girl-next-door-sleuth&catid=19:children andya&Itemid=124; Cornelius and Gregg, *Nancy Drew and Her Sister Sleuths*, 140–41.

50. Cornelius and Gregg, *Nancy Drew and Her Sister Sleuths*, 125–30, 137.

51. Quoted in Gates, *Detecting Women*, 115.

52. Ibid., 115–20.

53. Philippa Gates, "The Maritorious Melodrama: Film Noir with a Female Detective," *Journal of Film and Video* 61 (Fall 2009): 24–26.

54. Gates, *Detecting Women*, 64.

55. Duffin, *History in Blue*, 125; Jack French, "Lady Crimefighters," Old Time Radio Articles, 1998, http://www.otrsite.com/articles/artjf009.html.

CHAPTER 7: BREAKING THROUGH THE RANKS

1. Courtney Riley Cooper, "The Cases of Alice Clement: True Stories of the World's Greatest Woman Sleuth as Told by Herself to Courtney Riley Cooper," *Escanaba (MI) Morning Press*, 27 July 1913.

2. "Kidnaped by Her Father," *Chicago Daily Tribune*, 27 September 1902.

3. Marrow and Carter, *In Pursuit of Crime*, 117.

4. Segrave, *Policewomen*, 19–20; Schulz, *From Social Worker to Crimefighter*, 14.

5. Segrave, *Policewomen*, 20–21.

6. Marrow and Carter, *In Pursuit of Crime*, 397.

7. Segrave, *Policewomen*, 21.

8. Quoted in "Policewomen in Chicago," *Literary Digest* 47 (23 August 1913): 271.

9. "Policewomen Make Arrest," *New York Times*, 8 August 1913.

10. Segrave, *Policewomen*, 21–22.

11. "Dealer in Pretty Girls Caught by Policewoman," *Chicago Defender*, 3 September 1921.

12. "Greets Runaway Girl," *New York Times*, 27 November 1936.

13. "Will Clean Up Job 'Agencies,'" *Los Angeles Times*, 16 May 1923.

14. Ryan, "Legendary Ladies of the LAPD," 27.

15. Schulz, *From Social Worker to Crimefighter*, 52–53.

16. Courtney Q. Shah, "Against Their Own Weakness: Policing Sexuality and Women in San Antonio, Texas, During World War I," *Journal of the History of Sexuality* 19 (September 2010): 463–64.

17. Schulz, *From Social Worker to Crimefighter*, 32–35.

18. Andrew T. Darien, *Becoming New York's Finest: Race, Gender, and the Integration of the NYPD* (New York: Palgrave Macmillan, 2013), 47–49.

19. Ibid., 48.

20. Segrave, *Policewomen*, 53–55.

21. "Detective Ranks Opened to Women," *New York Times*, 24 October 1926; Mary Sullivan, *My Double Life: The Story of a New York Policewoman* (New York: Farrar & Rinehart, 1938), 11–12.

22. Sullivan, *My Double Life*, 34–35.

23. Ibid., 35.

24. Ibid., 46–47.

25. Ibid., 65–66.

26. "Mary A. Sullivan, Police Detective," *New York Times*, 12 September 1950.

27. Sullivan, *My Double Life*, 77.

28. Ibid., 92–104.

29. Ibid., 88–91.

30. Alice Stebbins Wells, "Policewomen," in *Proceedings of the National Conference of Charities and Correction*, 42nd Annual Session (1915), 411–12.

31. "Women Police Withdrawn," *New York Times*, 4 March 1914.

32. Segrave, *Policewomen*, 22–23.

33. "Policewomen to Wrestle," *New York Times*, 8 March 1914.

34. "Women Police of Detroit," *New York Times*, 13 March 1921.

35. Uthai V. Wilcox, "Interesting Westerners," *Sunset* 46 (June 1921): 47–48.

36. "Candidates," *IAP Bulletin* 25 (November 1926): 4.

37. Josephine Nelson, "On the Policewoman's Beat," *Independent Woman* 15 (May 1936): 138.

38. Segrave, *Policewomen*, 49–50.

39. Mina C. Van Winkle, "Report of the Woman's Bureau," in *Report of the Major and Superintendent of the Metropolitan Police, District of Columbia for 1919* (Washington, DC: Government Printing Office, 1919), 80.

40. Chloe Owings, *Women Police: A Study of the Development and Status of the Women Police Movement* (Hitchcock, NY: Bureau of Social Hygiene, 1925), 176–78.

41. Mina Van Winkle, "Policewomen—Their Duties and Opportunities," in *National Police Journal* (August 1921): 14.

42. Ibid.

43. Quoted in Owings, *Women Police*, xi.

44. Albert R. Roberts, "Police Social Workers: A History," *Social Work* 21 (July 1976): 295; Robert L. Snow, *Policewomen Who Made History: Breaking Through the Ranks* (Lanham, MD: Rowman and Littlefield, 2010), 50–51.

45. Snow, *Policewomen Who Made History*, 52.

46. Segrave, *Policewomen*, 50–51; "Mrs. Van Winkle Faces Suspension by Commissioner Oyster," *Washington Times*, 24 March 1922.

47. "A Policewoman on Trial," *Survey* (15 April 1922), 69–70; Appier, *Policing Women*, 35–36.

48. "Mrs. Van Winkle Acquitted of Insubordination Charge in Washington Police Department," *Social Hygiene Bulletin* 9 (May 1922): 3.

49. Gillen, "Equality and Difference in the Evolution of Women's Police Role," 72–73, 84–86.

50. Quoted in Clarice Feinman, *Women in the Criminal Justice System*, 3rd ed. (Westport, CT: Praeger, 1994), 97.

51. Quoted in Appier, *Policing Women*, 58.

52. Segrave, *Policewomen*, 55–56; Darien, *Becoming New York's Finest*, 48–49.

53. Mary E. Hamilton, *The Policewoman: Her Service and Ideals* (orig. 1924; New York: Arno Press, 1971), 18, 20, 58–61.

54. Segrave, *Policewomen*, 55–56.

55. Quoted in ibid., 56.

56. Schulz, *From Social Worker to Crimefighter*, 72–73; Aldrich-Moodie, "Staking Out Their Domain," 247–51, 254; Segrave, *Policewomen*, 57–59; Snow, *Policewomen Who Made History*, 74.

57. "Women Police of Detroit"; Appier, *Policing Women*, 60; Segrave, *Policewomen*, 27, 49.

58. Craigie, "Female Sherlock Holmes Tells How She Always 'Gets Her Man.'"

59. Duffin, *History in Blue*, 33–34.

60. "Department History," Police Department (Portsmouth, New Hampshire), http://www.cityofportsmouth.com/police/depart-history.htm.

61. Duffin, *History in Blue*, 48–49.

62. Valeria H. Parker, "A Policewoman's Life," *Woman Citizen* 9 (28 June 1924): 16.

63. Owings, *Women Police*, 103.

64. "Famous Policewoman Urges Prevention of Crime."

65. Schulz, *From Social Worker to Crimefighter*, 54–56.

66. Gillen, "Equality and Difference in the Evolution of Women's Police Role," 108–10.

67. Helen Bauer quoted in Wayne Phillips, "Detective Story, Female Department: Laurette Valente, Detective First Class," *New York Times Magazine*, 28 February 1960, 59.

CHAPTER 8: HARD-BOILED HEROES

1. Raymond Chandler, "The Simple Art of Murder," *Atlantic Monthly* 174 (December 1944): 59.

2. Erin A. Smith, *Hard-Boiled: Working-Class Readers and Pulp Magazines* (Philadelphia: Temple University Press, 2000), 20.

3. Ibid., 10, 20–22.

4. Sean McCann, "The Hard-Boiled Novel," in Nickerson, *The Cambridge Companion to American Crime Fiction*, 42–43.

5. Jennifer R. Weiss, "Clue, Code, Conjure: The Epistemology of American Detective Fiction, 1841–1914," PhD diss., City University of New York, 2014, 12–15.

6. Lewis D. Moore, *Cracking the Hard-Boiled Detective: A Critical History from the 1920s to the Present* (Jefferson, NC: McFarland, 2006), 20.

7. Carroll John Daly, *The Snarl of the Beast* (New York: E. J. Clode, 1927), 63.

8. McCann, "The Hard-Boiled Novel," 45–46.

9. Laura Ng, "Feminist Hard-Boiled Detective Fiction as Political Protest in the Tradition of Women Proletarian Writers of the 1930s," PhD diss., Louisiana State University, 2005, 13–15, 19.

10. Sue Grafton, *B Is for Burglar* (orig. 1985; Oxford, UK: Macmillan, 2007), 150.

11. Smith, *Hard-Boiled*, 21–23.

12. Carroll John Daly, "The False Burton Combs," in *A Century of Detection: Twenty Great Mystery Stories, 1841–1940*, ed. John Cullen Gruesser (Jefferson, NC: McFarland, 2010), 311.

13. Chandler, "The Simple Art of Murder," 18; Priscilla L. Walton, "Form and Forum: The Agency of Detectives and the Venue of the Short Story," *Narrative* 6 (May 1998): 125–26.

14. Smith, *Hard-Boiled*, 77–78; Chandler quoted in Leon Arden, "A Knock at the Backdoor of Art: The Entrance of Raymond Chandler," in *Art in Crime Writing: Essays on Detective Fiction*, ed. Bernard Benstock (New York: St. Martin's, 1983), 77.

15. Chandler, "The Simple Art of Murder," 56.

16. Paul Skenazy, *The New Wild West: The Urban Mysteries of Dashiell Hammett and Raymond Chandler* (Meridian, ID: J & D Printing, 1982), 7–8; David I. Grossvogel, "Death Deferred: The Long Life, Splendid Afterlife and Mysterious Workings of Agatha Christie," in Benstock, *Art in Crime Writing*, 5.

17. Christie, *The Murder at the Vicarage*.

18. Chandler, "The Simple Art of Murder," 56–57.

19. Worsley, *The Art of the English Murder*, 257–66.

20. Mitzi Burnsdale, *Gumshoes: A Dictionary of Fictional Detectives* (Westport, CT: Greenwood, 2006), 8–9.

21. Coe, "The Detective," 1–2.

22. Smith, *Hard-Boiled*, 39–42.

23. John G. Cawelti, *Adventure, Mystery, and Romance: Formula Stories as Art and Popular Culture* (Chicago: University of Chicago Press, 1976), 146–51.

24. McCann, "The Hard-Boiled Novel," 43–44.

25. Reddy, *Sisters in Crime*, 95, 102.

26. Agatha Christie, *The Thirteen Problems* (orig. 1932; New York: Berkley, 1985), 4–5.

27. Raymond Chandler, *The Big Sleep* (orig. 1939; New York: Vintage, 1988), 8.

28. Dzirkalis, "Investigating the Female Detective," 307–8.

29. Quoted in LeRoy Panek, *An Introduction to the Detective Story* (Bowling Green, OH: Bowling Green State University Popular Press, 1987), 164.

30. Chandler, *The Big Sleep*, 157.

31. George Grella, "The Hard-Boiled Detective Novel," in *Detective Fiction: A Collection of Critical Essays*, ed. Robin W. Winks (Englewood Cliffs, NJ: Prentice Hall, 1980), 109–10; Reddy, *Sisters in Crime*, 102–3.

32. Peter Brooker and Andrew Thacker, eds., *The Oxford Critical and Cultural History of Modernist Magazines, Vol. II: North America: 1894–1960* (Oxford, UK: Oxford University Press, 2012), 207, 211.

33. Smith, *Hard-Boiled*, 29.

34. David M. Earle, *Re-Covering Modernism: Pulps, Paperbacks, and the Prejudice of the Form* (Burlington, VT: Ashgate, 2009), 79–80.

35. Erle Stanley Gardner (as A. A. Fair), *Bedrooms Have Windows* (orig. 1949; New York: Avon Books, reprint, 1990), 11.

36. Erle Stanley Gardner (as A. A. Fair), *You Can Die Laughing* (orig. 1957; New York: Pocket Books, 1961), 3.

37. Earl F. Bargainnier, ed., *Comic Crime* (Bowling Green, OH: Popular Press, 1987), 129–30.

38. Gale Gallagher (Will Oursler and Margaret Scott), *Chord in Crimson* (New York: Collier, 1962), 137.

39. Klein, *The Woman Detective*, 126–31.

40. Ibid., 129–30; Reddy, *Sisters in Crime*, 94–95.

41. Raymond Chandler, *Farewell, My Lovely* (orig. 1940; New York: Vintage, 1988), 143.

42. Chandler, *The Big Sleep*, 1.

43. "Candy Matson, Old Time Radio Show," Candy Matson Online, http://www.candymatson.com/index.html; "Candy Matson, YUKON 2-8209," Internet Archive, https://archive.org/details/OTRR_Candy_Matson_Singles.

44. Eddy Von Mueller, "The Police Procedural in Literature and on Television," in Nickerson, *The Cambridge Companion to American Crime Fiction*, 97–98.

45. Jennie Melville, *Come Home and Be Killed* (London: Michael Joseph, 1962).

46. Jennie Melville, *Burning Is a Substitute for Loving* (New York: London House and Maxwell, 1964), 19.

47. Jennie Melville, *Footsteps in the Blood* (New York: St. Martin's Press, 1993), 83.

48. Jennie Melville, *A Death in the Family* (New York: St. Martin's Press, 1994), 145.

49. Laura Wagner, "Private Eyeful," Classic Images (15 October 2008), http://www.classicimages.com/people/article_6cc5ca05–5735–53e2-aac8–644fbcc8a6ec.html; Klein, *The Woman Detective*, 132–34; Lee Server, *Encyclopedia of Pulp Fiction Writers* (New York: Facts on File, 2002), 94–95.

50. Klein, *The Woman Detective*, 132–34.

51. Quoted in Laura Wagner, *Anne Francis: The Life and Career* (Jefferson, NC: McFarland, 2011), 72.

52. Ibid.

53. Wagner, "Private Eyeful"; Server, *Encyclopedia of Pulp Fiction Writers*, 94–95.

54. Klein, *The Woman Detective*, 132–34; Server, *Encyclopedia of Pulp Fiction Writers*, 94–95.

55. Coe, "The Detective," 194; Ng, "Feminist Hard-Boiled Detective Fiction," 49–50.

56. P. D. James, *An Unsuitable Job for a Woman* (London: Sphere, 1972).

57. Klein, *The Woman Detective*, 153–58; Maroula Joannou, *Contemporary Women's Writing: From* The Golden Notebook *to* The Color Purple (Manchester, UK: Manchester University Press, 2000), 139–40.

58. Gray was portrayed on television by two actresses: Pippa Guard, in the 1982 TV adaptation of *An Unsuitable Job for a Woman*, and Helen Baxendale, in a series

called *An Unsuitable Job for a Woman*, which comprised four feature-length dramas and ran from 1997 to 2001. DuBose and Thomas, *Women of Mystery*, 361.

59. Kimberly J. Dilley, "Not Just Sam Spade in a Skirt: Women Redefine the Heroic and Ordinary," PhD diss., University of California, San Diego, 1995, 116, 118; Walton, "Form and Forum," 129.

60. Marcia Muller, "What Sharon McCone Learned from Judy Bolton," in *Deadly Women: The Woman Mystery Reader's Indispensable Companion*, ed. Jan Grape, Dean James, and Ellen Nehr (New York: Carroll and Graf, 1998), 67–69.

61. Dilley, "Not Just Sam Spade," 118–19.

62. Sue Grafton, *A Is for Alibi* (orig. 1982; New York: St. Martin's Paperbacks, 2005), 2.

63. Leonard Cassuto, *Hard-Boiled Sentimentality: The Secret History of American Crime Stories* (New York: Columbia University Press, 2009), 190–91; LeRoy Lad Panek, *New Hard-Boiled Writers, 1970s–1990s* (Bowling Green, OH: Bowling Green University Popular Press, 2000), 78–79.

64. Gavin, "Feminist Crime Fiction and Female Sleuths," 264–65.

65. Dilley, "Not Just Sam Spade," 117, 166–67.

66. Ibid., 122–23.

67. Gavin, "Feminist Crime Fiction and Female Sleuths," 265; Dilley, "Not Just Sam Spade," 128–29.

68. Dulcy Brainard, "Marcia Muller: 'The Time Was Ripe,'" *Publishers Weekly* 241, no. 32 (August 8, 1994): 361.

69. Winter S. Elliott, "Changing the World, One Detective at a Time: The Feminist Ethos of Marcia Muller and Sharon McCone," in *Marcia Muller and the Female Private Eye: Essays on the Novels That Defined a Subgenre*, ed. Alexander N. Howe and Christine A. Jackson (Jefferson, NC: McFarland, 2008), 15–18.

70. Dilley, "Not Just Sam Spade," 125–26.

71. Ibid., 133.

72. DuBose and Thomas, *Women of Mystery*, 393–95.

73. Weiss, "Clue, Code, Conjure," 154.

74. Hugh C. Weir, *Miss Madelyn Mack, Detective* (Boston: Colonial Press, 1914), 68.

75. DuBose and Thomas, *Women of Mystery*, 393–98; Dilley, *Busybodies, Meddlers, and Snoops*, 86–87.

76. Catherine Garcia, "Questions for Linda Fairstein," *Entertainment Weekly*, 19 March 2010, http://www.ew.com/article/2010/03/19/questions-for-linda-fairstein; Guy Savage, "An Interview with Linda Fairstein," MostlyFiction.com, http://mostlyfiction.com/authorqa/fairstein.html, accessed November 9, 2015.

77. Carol Gilligan, *In a Different Voice* (Cambridge, MA: Harvard University Press, 1982), 21, 160; Dilley, "Not Just Sam Spade," 219–20, 223–26.

78. Dilley, "Not Just Sam Spade," 227–28.

79. Ng, "Feminist Hard-Boiled Detective Fiction," 47, 55–59.

80. Sue Grafton, *H Is for Homicide* (New York: St. Martin's Paperbacks, 1991), 40.

81. Sue Grafton, *G Is for Gumshoe* (orig. 1990; New York: St. Martin's Paperbacks, 2007).

82. Dilley, *Busybodies, Meddlers, and Snoops*, 63–64, 71, 73–74; Dilley, "Not Just Sam Spade," 167–68.

83. Linda J. Waite, *U.S. Women at Work* (Santa Monica, CA: Rand, 1981), 1.

84. Frances A. DellaCava and Madeline H. Engel, *Sleuths in Skirts: Analysis and Bibliography of Serialized Female Sleuths* (New York: Routledge, 2002), 4–5.

85. Dilley, *Busybodies, Meddlers, and Snoops*, 116–20, 124–28.

86. Ibid., 99, 110–11, 138.

87. Ibid.

88. Moira Davison Reynolds, *Women Authors of Detective Series: Twenty-One American and British Writers, 1900–2000* (Jefferson, NC: McFarland, 2001), 105–9.

89. Michael Tapper, *Swedish Cops: From Sjöwall and Wahlöö to Stieg Larsson* (Chicago: Intellect/University of Chicago Press, 2014), 249–52; Robin S. Rosenberg, "Salander as Superhero," *Psychology Today* blog, 9 December 2011, https://www.psychologytoday.com/blog/the-superheroes/201112/salander-superhero; Stieg Larsson, *The Girl with the Dragon Tattoo* (New York: Vintage Crime/Black Lizard, 2008).

90. David W. Madden, "Anne Riordan: Raymond Chandler's Forgotten Heroine," in *The Detective in American Fiction, Film, and Television*, ed. Jerome Delamater and Ruth Prigozy (Westport, CT: Greenwood, 1998), 5–8.

CHAPTER 9: FROM MOTHERS TO CRIME FIGHTERS

1. "New Policewomen Warned on Obesity," *New York Times*, 10 March 1939.

2. Diana Rice, "Policewomen Perform Varied Tasks," *New York Times*, 19 June 1932.

3. Schulz, *From Social Worker to Crimefighter*, 177.

4. Gillen, "Equality and Difference in the Evolution of Women's Police Role," 113–14.

5. Eleanore L. Hutzel, *The Policewoman's Handbook* (New York: Columbia University Press, 1933), 2–6.

6. Ibid., 58.

7. Ibid., 21.

8. Darien, *Becoming New York's Finest*, 56–57.

9. Schulz, *From Social Worker to Crimefighter*, 103–4; Gillen, "Equality and Difference in the Evolution of Women's Police Role," 136–37.

10. "Police Test Open to Women of New Type; Ability for Detective Work Is Stressed," *New York Times*, 18 March 1938.

11. "Has Girl Detective Staff," *New York Times*, 14 March 1921.

12. Appier, *Policing Women*, 50–52.

13. Von Mueller, "The Police Procedural in Literature and on Television," 100–101.

14. Appier, *Policing Women*, 50–53.

15. George W. Wickersham, *National Commission on Law Observance and Enforcement: Report* (Washington, DC: Government Printing Office, 1931).

16. Appier, *Policing Women*, 103–5.

17. Schulz, *From Social Worker to Crimefighter*, 54–56.

18. Ibid., 178–82.

19. Ibid., 240–41.

20. Imra Buwalda, "The Policewoman—Yesterday, Today and Tomorrow," *Journal of Social Hygiene* 31 (May 1945): 291.

21. Schulz, *From Social Worker to Crimefighter*, 201.

22. Ibid., 201.

23. Ibid., 222–23.

24. Ibid., 211.

25. "Woman Detective Draws Pistol in Fifth Ave., Seizes Racketeer After a Chase in Crowd," *New York Times*, 21 December 1938; James Lardner and Thomas Reppetto, *NYPD: A City and Its Police* (New York: Henry Holt, 2000), 223–24; "Mary Shanley on Duty," *New York Times*, 30 April 1941; "Dead-Shot Mary to Quit the Force," *New York Times*, 13 September 1957.

26. Laura J. Miller, "Frances Glessner Lee," *Harvard Magazine* (September–October 2005), http://harvardmagazine.com/2005/09/frances-glessner-lee-html.

27. Jimmy Stamp, "How a Chicago Heiress Trained Homicide Detectives with an Unusual Tool: Dollhouses," *Smithsonian* (6 March 2014), http://www.smithsonianmag.com/arts-culture/murder-miniature-nutshell-studies-unexplained-death-180949943/.

28. Nigel Richardson, "Nutshell Studies: The Extraordinary Miniature Crime Scenes US Police Use to Train Detectives," *Telegraph* (UK), 30 January 2015, http://www.telegraph.co.uk/news/uknews/crime/11370223/Nutshell-Studies-the-extraordinary-miniature-crime-scenes-US-police-use-to-train-detectives.html.

29. Schulz, *From Social Worker to Crimefighter*, 102–4.

30. Karl Detzer, "Detroit's Lady Cops," *American Mercury* (March 1942): 345–49, 351; Schulz, *From Social Worker to Crimefighter*, 247.

31. Schulz, *From Social Worker to Crimefighter*, 248–49.

32. Lois Lundell Higgins and Edward A. Fitzpatrick, *Criminology and Crime Prevention* (Milwaukee: Bruce Publishing, 1958), 408–9.

33. Carol M. Williams, *The Organization and Practices of Police Women's Divisions in the United States* (Detroit: National Training School of Public Service, 1946), 1, 4–7, 13, 14, 16; Schulz, *From Social Worker to Crimefighter*, 257.

34. Imra Buwalda, "The Policewoman," *Police Journal* (February 1946): 6–7.

35. Darien, *Becoming New York's Finest*, 55.

36. Detzer, "Detroit's Lady Cops," 345–46.

37. Rolland McCombs, "Lady Constable: 'Sis' Dickerson Polices a Tough Texas County," *Life*, 17 September 1945, 19–20.

38. Quoted in Schulz, *From Social Worker to Crimefighter*, 247.

39. *Techniques of Law Enforcement in the Use of Policewomen with Special Reference to Social Protection* (Washington, DC: Federal Security Agency, Office of Community War Services, 1945), 31.

40. Ibid., 57.

41. Ibid., 57–60, 62; Gillen, "Equality and Difference in the Evolution of Women's Police Role," 117–20.

42. Gillen, "Equality and Difference in the Evolution of Women's Police Role," 124–25.

43. Sullivan, *My Double Life*, 287.

44. "The History of Women in the NYPD," Policewomen's Endowment Association, http://www.nypdpea.com/History.html, accessed November 9, 2015.

45. "Woman Detective Scorns Theatrics: Hotel Detective," *New York Times*, 8 June 1950.

46. Will Chasan, "New York's Finest (Female Div.)," *New York Times Magazine*, 20 November 1955, 26.

47. Gillen, "Equality and Difference in the Evolution of Women's Police Role," 123–24; Darien, *Becoming New York's Finest*, 62–64.

48. Schulz, *From Social Worker to Crimefighter*, 79–86, 88–93.

49. August Vollmer, "Policing as a Career for Young Women," *Education for Victory* 2 (1 October 1943): 11.

50. O. W. Wilson, *Police Administration*, McGraw-Hill Series on Political Science (orig. 1943; New York: McGraw-Hill, 1950), 217, 124–27.

51. Walter Arm, *The Policeman: An Inside Look at His Role in a Modern Society* (New York: E. P. Dutton, 1969), 73.

52. C. J. Flammang, *Police Juvenile Enforcement* (Springfield, IL: Charles C. Thomas, 1972), 199.

53. Ronald Sullivan, "Police Show Off 8 Burly Decoys," *New York Times*, 25 August 1962.

54. "Woman Detective Known as Shoplifters' Nemesis," *Chicago Daily Tribune*, 1 May 1938.

55. Phillips, "Detective Story, Female Department."

56. Bruce Smith, ed., *Chicago Police Problems: Report of the Citizens' Police Committee, Chicago Police Survey* (Chicago: University of Chicago Press, 1931), 175–76, 186.

57. City of Chicago, *Police Department: Annual Report, Year Ending December 31, 1948* (Chicago, 1949), 5; Schulz, *From Social Worker to Crimefighter*, 293.

58. "The Police Are Amazed at Life of Mrs. Reilly," *Chicago Tribune*, 3 October 1941.

59. Gillen, "Equality and Difference in the Evolution of Women's Police Role," 130–31.

60. Evabel Tenny, "Women's Work in Law Enforcement," *Journal of Criminal Law, Criminology and Police Science* (August 1953): 241–45.

61. Segrave, *Policewomen*, 97.

62. Gillen, "Equality and Difference in the Evolution of Women's Police Role," 134; Darien, *Becoming New York's Finest*, 64.

63. Schulz, *From Social Worker to Crimefighter*, 280–83; Darien, *Becoming New York's Finest*, 66–67.

64. Schulz, *From Social Worker to Crimefighter*, 285–86.

65. Ibid.

66. Marie Cirile, *Detective Marie Cirile: Memoirs of a Police Officer* (Doubleday: New York, 1975), 10, 11, 13.

67. Theresa Melchionne, "Where Policewomen Are Better Than Men," *American City* 75 (April 1960): 161.

68. Arthur Niederhoffer, *Behind the Shield: The Police in Urban Society* (Garden City, NY: Doubleday, 1967), 21.

69. "Are You as Smart as a Cop?" *This Week* (22 January 1966), 7.

70. Edmund A. Bosch, "The Spiritual Attitude of the Police Officer," *Spring 3100* (March 1956): 15.

71. Schulz, *From Social Worker to Crimefighter*, 127–28.

72. Duffin, *History in Blue*, 109–10.

73. Felicia Shpritzer, "A Case for the Promotion of Policewomen in the City of New York," *Journal of Criminal Law and Criminology* 50 (November–December 1959–1960): 416.

74. Lois Lundell Higgins, "Women in Law Enforcement: A Special Survey on Policewomen Throughout the United States," *Law and Order* (April 1958): 22–24; Schulz, *From Social Worker to Crimefighter*, 308.

75. Gillen, "Equality and Difference in the Evolution of Women's Police Role," 139.

76. Schulz, *From Social Worker to Crimefighter*, 335–36, 340–42; "History of Women in the NYPD," Policewomen's Endowment Association.

77. Shpritzer v. Lang, Appellate Division of the Supreme Court of the State of New York, 27 November 1962, http://www.leagle.com/decision/196230217AD2d285 _1227.xml/MATTER%20OF%20SHPRITZER%20v.%20LANG.

78. Segrave, *Policewomen*, 97; Richard Goldstein, "Gertrude Schimmel, First Female New York Police Chief, Dies at 96," obituary, *New York Times*, 12 May 2015.

79. Shpritzer, "A Case for the Promotion of Policewomen," 418.

80. Segrave, *Policewomen*, 98.

81. Alice Mulcahey Fleming, *New on the Beat: Woman Power in the Police Force* (New York: Coward, McCann & Geoghegan, 1975), 33–34, 196.

82. Segrave, *Policewomen*, 112–13.

83. Wells v. Civil Service Commission, Supreme Court of Pennsylvania, 6 January 1967, http://law.justia.com/cases/pennsylvania/supreme-court/1967/423-pa-602 -0.html

84. President's Commission on Law Enforcement and Administration of Justice, *Task Force Report: The Police* (Washington, DC: Government Printing Office, 1967), 125.

85. Sandra Wells and Betty Sowers Alt, *Police Women: Life with the Badge* (Westport, CT: Praeger, 2005), 11; Segrave, *Policewomen*, 98.

86. Segrave, *Policewomen*, 114–15; Gillen, "Equality and Difference in the Evolution of Women's Police Role," 164–65.

87. Snow, *Policewomen Who Made History*, 5.

88. Segrave, *Policewomen*, 99; Duffin, *History in Blue*, 140–43.

89. Frank Zahour, "Woman Detective Candidate Scores High in Competition," *Chicago Tribune*, 25 November 1971.

90. Lynette Miller, "City's 1st Gal Detective Gives Just the Facts," *Chicago Tribune*, 21 June 1973.

91. Schulz, *From Social Worker to Crimefighter*, 360; "IACP Memorandum on Uniforms," *A Symposium About Women in Politics* (9 April 1974), 56–58.

92. Darien, *Becoming New York's Finest*, 597.

93. Jane Leek, "A Policewoman's Lot—It's Improving," *Los Angeles Times*, 5 November 1972.

94. Segrave, *Policewomen*, 109; Schulz, *From Social Worker to Crimefighter*, 123.

95. Catherine Milton and Police Foundation, *Women in Policing: A Manual* (Washington, DC: Police Foundation, 1974), 41.

96. Leek, "A Policewoman's Lot."

97. Segrave, *Policewomen*, 112–13.

98. Quoted in Susan Ehrlich Martin, *Breaking and Entering: Policewomen on Patrol* (Berkeley: University of California Press, 1980), 92.

99. Anthony Vastola, "Women in Policing: An Alternative Ideology," *Police Chief* (January 1977): 64.

100. Quoted in Martin, *Breaking and Entering*, 91.

101. Ibid., 91–93.

102. "Women Police Rookies Display Prowess in Tests Ranging from Jiu-Jitsu to Boxing," *New York Times*, 28 July 1948.

103. Patrick A. Burns, "122 Pass Physical for Policewoman: The Weaker Sex Is Misnomer for Fair Sex at Police Physical Trials," *New York Times*, 17 August 1956.

104. Peter Bloch, *Policewomen on Patrol: Final Report* (Washington, DC: Police Foundation, 1974), 1–2, 7, 10–11, 47–48.

105. Segrave, *Policewomen*, 118–20.

106. Quoted in ibid., 107.

107. Ibid., 130, 112–13.

108. Jack Houston, "Wanted: Women for Police Work . . ." *Chicago Tribune*, 4 August 1974.

109. Pranay Gupte, "Women Officers Tested on Patrol," *New York Times*, 12 August 1973.

110. Schulz, *From Social Worker to Crimefighter*, 135–36.

111. Robert Hanley, "All-Women Class of Troopers Starting," *New York Times*, 10 February 1980.

112. Jan Lonsdale, "Homicide Team Believed a First in State: Two Women Detectives Win Commendations in L.A.," *Los Angeles Times*, 6 July 1980.

113. Julie D'Acci, "Defining Women: The Case of Cagney & Lacey," in *Private Screenings: Television and the Female Consumer*, ed. Lynn Spiegel and Denise Mann (Minneapolis: University of Minnesota Press, 1992), 180–83.

114. Howard Rosenberg, "Cagney & (Uh) Lacey: A Question of a Pink Slip," Calendar, *Los Angeles Times*, 23 June 1982.

115. Schulz, *From Social Worker to Crimefighter*, 333.

116. Ibid., 31.

117. Duffin, *History in Blue*, 54.

118. Connie Fletcher, *Breaking and Entering: Women Cops Break the Code of Silence to Tell Their Stories from the Inside* (New York: Pocket Books, 1995), 60.

119. Cynthia G. Sulton and Roi D. Townsey, *A Progress Report on Women in Policing* (Washington, DC: Police Foundation, 1981), 63–100.

120. Gillen, "Equality and Difference in the Evolution of Women's Police Role," 202–10.

121. Fletcher, *Breaking and Entering*, 5.

122. Carl Coates, "Sheriff's Promotes 1st Woman to Chief," *Los Angeles Sentinel*, 1 March 1995.

123. "Top New Orleans Detective Had to Overcome Being Black and a Woman," *Columbus (GA) Times*, 20 April 1993.

124. Akilah S. Nosakhere, "Beverly Harvard," in *Encyclopedia of African American History: Vol. 1, 1896 to the Present: From the Age of Segregation to the Twenty-First Century*, ed. Paul Finkelman (New York: Oxford University Press, 2009), 384–85; Pamela Noel, "Women with Clout in City Government," *Ebony*, October 1984, 88–90.

125. Nicole Decure, "In Search of Our Sisters' Mean Streets: The Politics of Sex, Race, and Class in Black Women's Crime Fiction," in *Diversity and Detective Fiction*, ed. Kathleen Gregory Klein (Bowling Green, OH: Bowling Green State University Popular Press, 1999), 158, 159.

126. Snow, *Policewomen Who Made History*, 115–17.

127. Schulz, *From Social Worker to Crimefighter*, 136, 137–38.

128. Lilian Wyles, *A Woman at Scotland Yard: Reflections on the Struggles and Achievements of Thirty Years in the Metropolitan Police* (London: Faber and Faber, 1952), 73.

CHAPTER 10: WOMEN DETECTIVES TODAY

1. Phryne Fisher, http://phrynefisher.com/, accessed November 9, 2015.

2. Linda Holmes, "Essie Davis: On Playing a Sexually Liberated 'Superhero' Without Apology," Monkey See, National Public Radio, 31 March 2014, http://www.npr.org/sections/monkeysee/2014/03/31/297126077/essie-davis-on-playing-a-sexually-liberated-superhero-without-apology.

3. Dilley, *Busybodies, Meddlers, and Snoops*, 146–47.

4. Barbara Fister, "Monitoring Project 2013," Sisters in Crime, January 9, 2014, http://sistersincrime.site-ym.com/?page=126.

5. Lisa Dresner, *The Female Investigator in Literature, Film, and Popular Culture* (Jefferson, NC: McFarland, 2006), 67–68.

6. D. K. Holm, "Mod Squad," in *American Countercultures: An Encyclopedia of Nonconformists, Alternative Lifestyles, and Radical Ideas in U.S. History*, vol. 2, G–Q, ed. Gina Misiroglu (New York: Routledge, 2015), 491–92.

7. Frank DeCaro, "Angie Dickinson Wasn't So Tough in 'Police Woman,' but She Sure Looked Good," *New York Times*, 16 April 2006.

8. "Will the Real Teresa Graves Please Stand Up,?" *Ebony*, 30 December 1974, 65–70; Roland Laird, "The Mammy Image: What's Christie Love Got to Do with It?," *Pop Matters*, 18 June 2012, http://www.popmatters.com/column/158665-whats-christie-love-got-to-do-with-it/.

9. Linda Mizejewski, *Hardboiled & High Heeled: The Woman Detective in Popular Culture* (New York: Routledge, 2004), 66–69; Susan J. Douglas, *Where the Girls Are: Growing Up Female with the Mass Media* (New York: Times Books, 1994), 210.

10. Hal Erickson, *Television Cartoon Shows: An Illustrated Encyclopedia, 1949–1993* (Jefferson, NC: McFarland, 1995), 437.

11. Leslie Gilbert Elman, "Being Jessica Fletcher: Donald Bain's Interview, She Wrote," *Criminal Element*, 13 June 2011, http://www.criminalelement.com/blogs/2011/06/being-jessica-fletcher-donald-bains-interview-she-wrote; Donald Bain, *Murder, He Wrote: A Successful Writer's Life* (West Lafayette, IN: NotaBell, 2002), 225.

12. Horace Newcomb, "Cagney and Lacey," Museum of Broadcast Communication, http://www.museum.tv/eotv/cagneyandla.htm, accessed November 9, 2015.

13. Mike Hale, "A Complete Look at a Complex Character," *New York Times*, 3 September 2010.

14. Lauren Thompson, "From Miss Marple to The Fall—the Rise and Rise of Women Detectives," *Telegraph*, 13 November 2014, http://www.telegraph.co.uk/culture/tvandradio/11212815/From-Miss-Marple-to-The-Fall-the-rise-and-rise-of-women-detectives.html.

15. "Wonderland Story," *Law & Order: SVU*, season 15, episode 5, 16 October 2013, NBC.

16. "M.A.D.," *Veronica Mars*, season 1, episode 20, 26 April 2005, UPN.

17. "Veronica Mars," The Thrilling Detective Web Site, http://www.thrillingdetective.com/eyes/veronica_mars.html, November 9, 2015.

18. "Insolence & Wine," *The Fall*, season 1, episode 3, 27 May 2013, BBC/Netflix.

19. Ama Daetz, "Inside Look at Female San Francisco Police Homicide Detective," ABC News 7, 3 May 2015, http://abc7news.com/news/inside-look-at-female-sfpd-homicide-detective/694749/.

20. Wells and Alt, *Police Women*, 16–21.

21. US Department of Justice, *Crime Data Brief: Women in Law Enforcement, 1987–2008* (Washington, DC: US Department of Justice, 2010).

22. Kristen Ziman, "Stereotypes Does Cops Disservice," *Commander Kristen Ziman*, 8 November 2010, http://www.kristenziman.com/2010/11/stereotypes-does-cops-disservice.html.

23. Genea Webb, "Brenda Tate: She Has Seen It All," *New Pittsburgh Courier*, 28 April 2001.

24. Duffin, *History in Blue*, 230–31.

25. Esther J. Koenig, "An Overview of Attitudes Toward Women in Law Enforcement," *Public Administration Review* 38 (May–June 1978): 270.

26. Christin Rudell, "Not Afraid to Be a Woman," *Women in Law Enforcement Blog*, 14 February 2014, http://www.policemag.com/blog/women-in-law-enforcement/story/2014/02/not-afraid-to-be-a-woman.aspx.

27. Angela A. Swan, "The Influence of Gender Identity on Job Satisfaction in Female Police Officers," PhD diss., Capella University, 2014, 102–3.

28. Pearl Jacobs, "Women in Police Work: A Study in Role Conflict," PhD diss., Fordham University, 1976, 47.

29. George Knapp, "I-Team: First Woman Homicide Sgt. Helps Crack Martinez Case," *8 News Now*, 29 June 2012, http://www.8newsnow.com/story/18920882/first-woman-homicide-sgt-helps-crack-martinez-case.

30. "How Many Women Are Private Investigators?," *PI Magazine*, http://www.pimagazine.com/women-private-investigators/.

31. Martha De Lacey, "Modern-Day Miss Marple Rebecca Jane Runs the Lady Detective Agency," *Daily Mail* (UK), 28 January 2013, http://www.dailymail.co.uk/femail/article-2269671/Modern-day-Miss-Marple-Rebecca-Jane-runs-The-Lady-Detective-Agency-Manchester-set-breaking-America.html.

32. Al Baker, "Retired Police Commander Sues, Charging Harassment," *New York Times*, 24 March 2002.

33. Snow, *Policewomen Who Made History*, 68–69.

34. Marilyn Corsianos, *Policing and Gendered Justice: Examining the Possibilities* (Toronto: University of Toronto Press, 2009), 100–102.

35. T. Prenzler and G. Sinclair, "The Status of Women Police Officers: An International Review," *International Journal of Law, Crime and Justice* (2013): 13.

36. Barbara Miller, "Female Police Officers Are Rare but Sought After for Unique Skills," *PennLive*, 8 December 2012, http://www.pennlive.com/midstate/index.ssf/2012/12/female_police_officers.html.

37. Prenzler and Sinclair, "The Status of Women Police Officers," 2–3.

38. Philip E. Carlan and Elizabeth C. McMullan, "Contemporary Snapshot of Policewomen Attitudes," *Women and Criminal Justice* 19, no. 1 (January–March 2009): 60–79.

39. "Famous Policewoman Urges Prevention of Crime."